Aspects of Britain's Railway History

An Anthology Edited by
David Jenkinson

TRANSPORT

PUBLISHERS

This fine close-up study of former GWR 4-6-0 No.6018 *King Henry VI* was taken by Driver Peter Rawson on a visit to Old Oak Common shed on 3rd July 1957. Peter's experiences as a 'driver with a camera' are recounted elsewhere in this book.

BEDSIDE BackTrack

ASPECTS OF
BRITAIN'S RAILWAY HISTORY

An Anthology Edited by David Jenkinson

There is nothing in this picture to reveal that it was taken on 14th August 1948 some 7½ months after the nationalisation of Britain's railways. The engine is Stanier 'Jubilee' Class 4-6-0 No.5696 *Arethusa* (in full 1946 LMS livery) and the train (mostly LMS standard stock with a former LNWR corridor third at the head) is the down 5.32pm St Pancras to Nottingham express, climbing the 1 in 176 gradient between Radlett and Sandridge on the Midland main line of the old LMS. This view typifies the changeover from private to public ownership, a subject explored in more detail by the same photographer later in this work. (Eric Bruton)

TRANSPORT

PUBLISHERS

INTRODUCTION

In the relatively few years since they first appeared, BACKTRACK and MODELLERS' BACKTRACK have attracted a considerable volume of excellent material over and above that which could be fitted into the six issues per year of each title and I have often been asked why they are not produced monthly.

The answer is quite simple: firstly, the time demands of monthly frequency for each of two magazines would not allow me to give to either of them the level of care and attention justified by the scholarship of our authors, even were the material available. But more important, although there is much more material than a bi-monthly publication can absorb, to publish twice as many magazines per year would run a real risk of 'padding', simply to fill the pages. During the time I have been editing the magazines, I have become acutely aware that readers would soon see through *that* subterfuge! Thus was the idea of this anthology born.

There is, of course, nothing new about this type of approach; it is often, for example, produced in the form of magazine annuals and/or supplements. But it seemed to me that the quality of material at my disposal was such that if it could not be fitted into the magazine proper, then the only appropriate solution was to give it the distinction of appearing in a proper casebound book form as, I hope, a definitive addition to the 'Railway Bookshelf'.

It should therefore not be assumed that *Bedside Backtrack* will become an annual publication. It has been designed as a 'stand alone' permanent companion to the magazines themselves and for this reason is not cover-dated. Whether or not it will found a subsequent dynasty will depend entirely upon your reaction as a reader and on the output and goodwill of our many fine authors.

Meantime, there being no need in this work to find page space for letters, reviews and other similar items, I have been able to include a few examples of the sort of feature which it is sometimes difficult to fit into the magazines themselves. For example, I sometimes receive articles which are too long to print in one issue but not quite long enough to split into two parts; several such appear in this work, John Horton's delightful model and prototype account of Stanier's LMS Turbomotive and the masterly Anthony Bower/Charles Long feature on early Pullmans springing immediately to mind in this context. Secondly, such is the appetite expressed by our readers for a 'good read' in the parent magazines, that it leaves few opportunities for extended black and white picture features of genuinely archival and historical interest. This too I have attempted to rectify, along with trying to ensure that the subject variety and balance which has come to be expected of us is fully represented. I have also included an offering from my own pen, exercising an editorial prerogative which I rarely have the opportunity to do in BACKTRACK itself!

I would therefore like to think that this book not only offers a pleasant and authentic dip into the broad spectrum of real railway history but also, and let us not be ashamed of it, more than a bit of nostalgia in its most genuine form. And I must not conclude these preliminaries before expressing my continued and sincere thanks to all those writers and photographers, be they included in this work or not, who continue to send me the most wonderfully eclectic mixture of superb material which any editor of historical inclination could ever wish to receive. I thank them for all their efforts, I have learned much by reading the end-product of their researches and I hope that readers will do likewise.

DAVID JENKINSON
Penryn, Cornwall
November 1993

© David Jenkinson,
Atlantic Transport Publishers and
contributors as credited.

Published by
Atlantic Transport Publishers,
Trevithick House, West End, Penryn,
Cornwall, TR10 8HE.
All rights reserved.

ISBN 0 906899 58 3

No part of this publication may be reproduced, stored in a retrieval system, transmitted in any form by any means electronic or mechanical or photocopied or recorded by any other information or retrieval system without prior permission in writing from the publishers.

Layout and Design by
Barnabus Design & Print, Truro,
Cornwall.

Typesetting by Ian D. Luckett
(Typesetting), St. Austell, Cornwall

Printed by
The Amadeus Press Ltd,
Huddersfield, West Yorkshire

British Cataloguing in Publication Data:
A catalogue record for this book is held by
the British Library

Note: Unless otherwise annotated, all photographs appearing in this work should be assumed to be from the publisher's own collection. It is regretted that it is not possible to make copies of any pictures in this book available to readers.

CONTENTS

4-4-0T *North Walsham,* **the first example to enter service with the Yarmouth and North Norfolk Railway in 1878 and without running number. This was one of the 'small' 4-4-0Ts (see text) and became E&MR No.32, later E&MR/M&GN No.41.**

Kings Lynn **was one of the last three Hudswell Clark 4-4-0Ts of the largest variant (see text) and delivered to the Lynn and Fakenham Railway in this form in 1881. Note the different style of nameplate compared with** *North Walsham* **but again the lack of running number. It became M&GN No.20, later 20A.**

M&GNR LC

By David Jenkinson

The celebrated historian E. L. Ahrons once described the early M&GNR locomotive fleet as "The quaintest assortment that ever adorned a railway of this length". By way of celebrating the centenary of the formation of this long vanished but still widely studied and much lamented system, a recently acquired set of early photographs of some of these old engines forms the basis for offering a taster of the sort of complexities whose full story would require a book!

A later view of No.20 in M&GN colours, now fitted with a numberplate but no longer named. Note the removal of the original cylinder covers, the MR style of safety valves and the replacement chimney.

COMOTIVES
A CENTURY AGO

Historical Background

The M&GNR came into existence under that name as recently as 1st July 1893 and only by understanding the history of the system can one appreciate how such a varied mix of motive power came to be in existence when the new Joint Committee was incorporated. This final 'coming together' marked the conclusion of a complex story of independent lines, some of which had previously amalgamated with each other; but not all of them owned their own locomotives.

The M&GN on its formation was a self-contained system, with headquarters at Kings Lynn, whose directorate was drawn from the two companies whose names were incorporated in its title. Many matters were shared but each company had sole responsibility in one specific area. The Locomotive Department was in charge of the MR while the GNR supervised the Engineering Department, including signalling and permanent way. The locomotive headquarters and works were both situated at Melton Constable and for many years were in charge of William Marriott who, while nominally answerable to Derby, enjoyed much local autonomy — which was just as well, given the nature of his fleet.

At the grouping, the M&GN formed part of a through route from many of the East Coast resorts and fishing ports of Norfolk to the Midlands and North — and to a less extent to London. It consisted of 183¼ miles of railway (including dock sidings) of which no less than 109 were single track, the remainder double. In addition, the two sections of the Norfolk and Suffolk Joint Railways (between Gorleston North Jct and Lowestoft and between Runton East Jct and Antingham Road Jct via Mundesley-on-Sea), 22¼ miles in all, including 11 miles of double track, were promoted and worked in partnership with the Great Eastern from the early part of the twentieth century. There were various running powers over the GNR and GER at some of the more important centres like Peterborough, Spalding, Kings Lynn and Lowestoft and certain periodical workings over the MR line from Little Bytham to Saxby. This line was opened broadly coincidentally with the formation of the M&GN to give more direct access to the Midlands.

So far so good and the appended map should clarify the geography. At the time of the incorporation of the Joint Line, by far the largest single part of the system was under the supervision of the Eastern and Midlands Railway which totalled 173 miles. But this concern had only been in existence from January 1883 (incorporated in 1882) when it became the successor to a series of smaller lines. These were of two quite different kinds in terms of locomotive history. To the east of Kings Lynn (usually referred to as the eastern section of the M&GN´, was a group of small lines, each of which had owned its own locomotives; while to the west of Kings Lynn in July 1883 (the phrase 'lines west of Lynn' was almost a mandatory part of the local railway vocabulary at the time), the E&MR also took over responsibility for a further pair of smaller railways which did *not* own their own locomotives.

The lines West of Lynn had always been worked by locomotives of MR or GNR ownership and this remained the situation after they were added to the E&MR in 1883. In consequence, when the M&GN was formed ten years later, the locomotive situation already had a dual personality. West of Lynn, MR and GNR lineaments prevailed while the eastern section was 'home' to the miscellaneous assortment of engines which had been acquired over the years by the several companies which combined to form part of the E&MR in 1883 and to which were added a few more in that company's brief ten-year life. It is some of these engines (and one of their lineal descendants) which form the subject of this account and the history of the pre-1883 lines explains how and why the 'inherited' locomotive situation took the form it did; for the 39 examples which constituted the E&MR fleet were the only locomotives actually owned by the M&GN at the time of its formation in 1893.

Engines Inherited by the E&MR in 1883

The locomotive history of the M&GN proper begins with the E&MR engines. But as already stated, the E&MR was itself only ten years old when the M&GN was formed and the first group of pictures covers some of those types which came into the fold when the E&MR was formed in 1883. All told, there were 26 examples of which 22 were left by the time the M&GN was formed and although not all are featured here, it may be helpful to get them into perspective by summarising the whole fleet at the time of handover. Two pre-1883 companies were involved (Yarmouth and North Norfolk and Lynn and Fakenham Railways), but as can be seen from the table, each of these contributed locomotives from two earlier sources.

Of this fascinating list, it is proposed to look at two of the longer-lived and more celebrated examples.

The 4-4-0Ts

This distinctive group of engines, over the years, came to symbolise much of what was distinctive about the M&GN. They were not 100% identical in all respects and both of the pre-1883 railways acquired them, the three Y&NNR examples actually representing 75% of the *new* locomotive acquisitions of that particular company. The type was introduced almost simultaneously in 1878 on the L&FR as well, but the Y&NNR could claim 'primus inter pares' in that its own first example *North Walsham* had the lower works number (Hudswell, Clark and Rogers No.208 of 1878). When delivered to the Y&NNR it arrived at Yarmouth dockside and was pulled through the streets to the Beach station. It seems probable that it was ordered for the GY&SLR before the latter was absorbed into the Y&NNR and entered service without carrying a running number. According to Alan Wells, to whom I am indebted for much of the information included in this account, it seems likely that this was true of all the 4-4-0Ts, whether Y&NNR or L&FR.

Within the 4-4-0T group there were three

SUMMARY TABLE: E&MR LOCOMOTIVES HANDED OVER TO THE M&GN IN 1893			
YARMOUTH AND NORTH NORFOLK RAILWAY			
From Great Yarmouth and Stalham Light Railway			
M&GN No.	**Type/Name**	**Builder/Date**	**Remarks**
7	0-6-0ST *Ida*	Black Hawthorn 1877	Sold 1894
15	0-6-0ST *Ormesby*	Fox Walker 1876	Sold 1990
16	0-6-0ST *Stalham*	Fox Walker 1876	To M&GN No.16A
Supplied direct to Y&NNR			
M&GN No.	**Type/Name**	**Builder/Date**	**Remarks**
17	0-6-0ST *Aylsham*	Black Hawthorn 1881	To M&GN No.17A
19	4-4-0T *Great Yarmouth*	Hudswell Clark 1881	
40	4-4-0T *Martham*	Hudswell Clark 1879	Ex-E&MR No.31
41	4-4-0T *North Walsham*	Hudswell Clark 1878	Ex-E&MR No.32
LYNN AND FAKENHAM RAILWAY			
Supplied direct to L&FR			
M&GN No.	**Type/Name**	**Builder/Date**	**Remarks**
4	0-4-0ST *Alpha*	Hudswell Clark 1878	To M&GN No.4A
5	0-4-0ST *Vici*	Hudswell Clark 1880	To M&GN No.5A
6	0-6-0ST *Holt/Chairman*	Black Hawthorn 1881	Sold 1894
8	4-4-0T *Hillington*	Hudswell Clark 1878	
9	4-4-0T *Fakenham*	Hudswell Clark 1879	To M&GN No.9A
10	4-4-0T *Norwich*	Hudswell Clark 1880	
20	4-4-0T *Kings Lynn*	Hudswell Clark 1881	To M&GN No.20A
From Cornwall Minerals Railway			
M&GN No.	**Type/Name**	**Builder/Date**	**Remarks**
1	0-6-0 *Melton Constable*	Sharp Stewart 1874	To M&GN No.1A
2	0-6-0 *Reepham*	Sharp Stewart 1874	To M&GN No.2A
3	2-4-0 (ex-0-6-0 *Blakeney*)	Sharp Stewart 1874	To M&GN No.3A
11	0-6-0	Sharp Stewart 1874	To M&GN No.11A
12	0-6-0	Sharp Stewart 1874	To M&GN No.12A
13	2-4-0 (ex-0-6-0)	Sharp Stewart 1874	To M&GN No.13A
14	2-4-0 (ex-0-6-0)	Sharp Stewart 1874	To M&GN No.14A
18	2-4-0 (ex-0-6-0)	Sharp Stewart 1874	To M&GN No.18A

sub-types defined by original size. The smallest were *North Walsham* (Y&NNR) and *Hillington* (L&FR) followed by *Martham* (Y&NNR) and *Fakenham* (L&FR) with enlarged cylinders and heating surface. The final variant with larger fuel and water capacity was represented by *Norwich* and *Kings Lynn* (L&FR) and by *Great Yarmouth* (Y&NNR).

In 1894, the first two were rebuilt and received new boilers with slightly increased dimensions — barrel length 8ft 10in, boiler diameter 3ft 9in, 190 tubes of 1⅝in diameter, grate area 11.3 sq ft and a total heating surface of 821.7 sq ft. When built, the engines had been fitted with Ramsbottom safety valves but this was to be replaced by a lock-up valve housed in a polished brass cover with two Salter spring balanced valves on the dome, the original dome cover being retained.

Former Cornwall Minerals Railway Locomotives

These engines were acquired by the L&FR but their story began in 1874 when they were built by Sharp Stewart & Co. to a design by F. B. Trevithick for the Cornwall Minerals Railway. Originally, eighteen of these engines had been built as 0-6-0Ts with high sided tanks surmounted by a coal space. Their lack of any form of conventional bunkers was because they were designed to work in pairs, coupled footplate to footplate — a sort of quasi-articulation one supposes!

In 1877, three of them (CMR Nos.15-17) were returned to the makers, it is believed in discharge of some sort of debt, while a further nine (CMR Nos.1-9) were taken over by the GWR and in due course (1883-

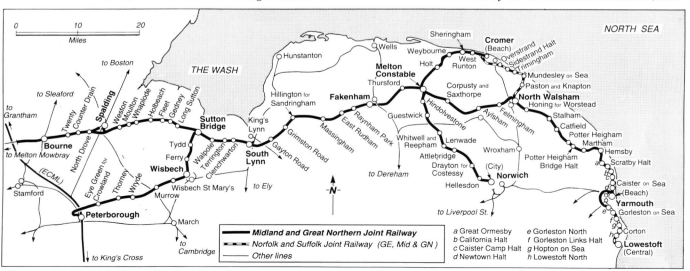

This picture shows 4-4-0T No.40 (formerly *Martham*), one of the two 'medium sized' engines (see text) in a sort of intermediate condition just before the formation of the M&GNR, its first number (31) having been allocated to a new Beyer Peacock 4-4-0 in 1886. It is still largely as built but the original flat cylinder covers and nameplate have been replaced. It is in E&MR livery and the new number is just visible on the original print on the front buffer plank behind the driver's right hand.

No.40 again in M&GN colours, now with replacement boiler fittings, sundry other detail changes compared with the previous view and a new number-plate where the works plate was originally fitted. A new 'Derby' style works plate has been fixed to the outside rear of the front frame.

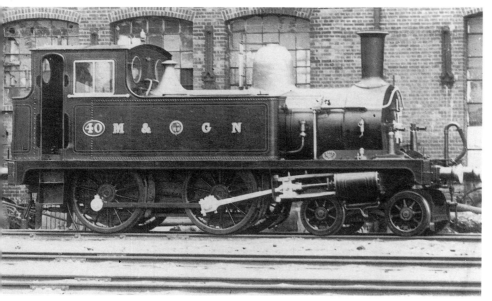

system (in reverse order to their original CMR numbers) and they were named *Melton Constable*, *Reepham* and *Blakeney* respectively. In 1883 they were fitted with tenders (below).

These three engines were joined on the L&FR in March 1881 by five of the six remaining CMR engines which had also been set aside four years earlier and which were eventually disposed of to Sharps for similar conversion. On arrival on the L&FR, they retained their original CMR numbers (11-14, 18) and had tenders from the outset. Some half of the total were converted to 2-4-0 arrangement — see table. Purely for the record, the last of the final CMR engines (CMR No.10) went to the Colne Valley and Halstead Railway (where it bore the name *Haverhill*) and from thence to South Hetton Colliery where it survived until 1948.

The full history of these engines is quite involved and has been covered in a book by Alan Wells and published by the M&GN Circle. Regularly referred to as the 'Cornwall Minerals' engines, a brief description will not be out of order. In many respects, in spite of their 'Trevithick' origin, they were fairly typical mid-Victorian 'Sharpies' and not too dissimilar (save for their outside cylinders) from broadly contemporary examples on, for example, the Cambrian and Furness Railways. The new tenders were definitely 'Sharp Stewart' in design and tended to reinforce this 'look'.

The outside cylinders of 16¼in x 20in drove coupled wheels of 3ft 6in diameter on a wheelbase of 11ft; leading to driving 5ft, driving to trailing 6ft. Handbrakes were fitted to engines and tenders and the engines were fitted originally with wooden brakeblocks, later replaced by iron, acting on the leading and trailing wheels only. Like the 4-4-0Ts already described, in their early days, sand was only available for forward running but later changes saw the addition of sandboxes beneath the cab for use when running in reverse. Cylinders had no drain cocks but the steam chest was so equipped. Giffard type injectors were located on top of the side tanks, control being exercised by enginemen putting their arms through the forward spectacle plate. New chimneys of the built up type fairly soon replaced the originals.

Neither as 0-6-0s or 2-4-0s were the engines really popular and no tears were shed when they were finally withdrawn. Six went between 1897-9 which was no great lifespan for an engine built in 1874. In theory, six of them (Nos.1A, 2A, 3A, 11A, 12A, 14A) were officially to have been rebuilt as 0-6-0 shunting tanks but all were, in fact, eventually scrapped as they stood. No.12A was the only one to last into

4) rebuilt as conventional saddle tanks with rear bunkers (GWR Nos.1392-1400). Meanwhile, Sharps had given the three 'returnees' more substantial cabs with proper back plates and sold them in 1880 to the L&FR. They became Nos.1-3 on that

This view, seemingly taken for some special reason at an unspecified location, shows one of four former Cornwall Mineral engines rebuilt to 2-4-0 form. The engine is in E&MR livery but is not positively identified. The cabside number looks as if may have a flat topped '3' and if so, Nos.3 or 13 are the contenders.

Two similar views of E&MR 0-6-0 No.11, one of the four Cornwall Mineral engines which retained 0-6-0 configuration and one of the five examples converted to tender form by Sharp Stewart before being delivered to the Lynn and Fakenham in 1881 — see text. Only those engines remaining as 0-6-0s kept the original high sided tanks. Note too the short-lived painted numerals.

the Twentieth Century being latterly at Yarmouth in connection with building the new Yarmouth to Lowestoft line of the Norfolk and Suffolk Joint system. It was withdrawn in 1902.

The inherited engines of the E&MR in 1883 were an interesting if not always wholly successful collection but they undoubtedly gave character to the system if only because their visual lines were quite different from anything which the MR or the GNR added after 1893. This was further emphasised by the modest additions made to the E&MR fleet during 1883-93 and it is to these which I now turn.

Engines acquired by/built for the E&MR 1883-93

On formation of the E&MR in 1883, the railway was not too lavishly endowed with locomotives, even allowing for the fact that the MR and GNR continued to work the lines of the network 'west of Lynn'. It is therefore no surprise that in the brief ten year existence of the E&MR, it added no fewer than seventeen further engines to its lists. In 1893, when the M&GN was

formed, these 'extras' formed some 44% of the total E&MR fleet in numerical terms but probably constituted a far higher percentage in terms of the work done; for all but two of them were acquired new — the subsequently very celebrated and characteristic Beyer Peacock 4-4-0s.

The need for more power had clearly been obvious even before the formation of the E&MR. The first order for the Beyers was actually placed by the Lynn and Fakenham and the first of them just managed to enter service as L&FR engines before the 1883 amalgamations, but since the full class of Beyer Peacock 4-4-0s was essentially put in service as E&MR engines it is appropriate to deal with them here. Firstly, however, it is important to consider yet another 'maverick' group — a pair of locomotives acquired by purchase from a somewhat unlikely source — the Lancaster and Carlisle section of the old LNWR.

Ex-London & North Western Railway 2-4-0s

There can be little doubt that it was the shortage of main line motive power which

prompted the E&MR to purchase two second hand engines (presumably as a stop-gap until more of the Beyer Peacock 4-4-0s were in service) in 1883. The reason why the particular examples (or type) were chosen does not seem to have been recorded — or at least I have seen no reasons put forward in print.

Age does not seem to have been a consideration, for unlike the 'Cornwall Minerals' engines (above), they were both near-veterans of 26 years old when purchased. But they were to a well proven and reliable design and this may have been important in the circumstances. They were 2-4-0s of the celebrated 'Crewe' type with massive double frames at the front end, fully integrated with the outside cylinders and smokebox wrapper. This idea, conceived principally to eliminate the curse of broken crank axles on inside cylinder engines in earlier days, is often wrongly attributed to Alexander Allan; but it was more properly the brainchild of William Barber Buddicom and Francis Trevithick who pioneered its use on the Grand Junction Railway and later exported it to many other parts, including France, where such engines were

always known as 'Les Buddicoms'.

They were numbered 42 and 43 in sequence after the 4-4-0Ts and both are featured here, one in E&MR livery.

The Beyer Peacock 4-4-0s

Of all the many and varied locomotives associated with the old M&GN, the Beyer Peacock 4-4-0s can lay soundest claim to have symbolised the difference of the system compared with its neighbours — including its two parent companies for that matter, if for no other reason than that they were neither MR nor GNR in lineaments. Even though the M&GN designs of the latter companies were never quite like those of the owning company they had a strong family resemblance; but no matter how many later changes were made, the Beyers were quintessentially M&GN in character. A full description of these engines, along with drawings and illustrations, was given in MODELLERS' BACK-TRACK Volume 1 No.6, so to repeat it all here is unnecessary; but a brief resumé will not be out of place in context.

In 1882, the Lynn and Fakenham Railway received four outside cylinder 4-4-0s

The other ex-LNWR 2-4-0 became No.43 and is seen here in its E&MR colours. The 'A' suffix suggests that the picture was taken in early M&GN days before the locomotive was repainted.

from Beyer Peacock & Co. (Nos.21-4, works Nos.2105-8 of 1881) which cost £3000 each. They represented a tremendous step forward in terms of motive power and were quite sophisticated in contemporary locomotive terms. Though designed by the builders and carrying many of the characteristic Beyer Peacock 'trademarks' — including the distinctive concentric works plate on the outer edge of the leading coupled wheel splasher — they bore more than a slight resemblance to some of the contemporary William Adams designs for the London and South Western Railway, than which there can be no higher praise.

Smaller than contemporary Adams 4-4-0s, they nevertheless shared the well balanced and classical looks of the LSWR

product. Their front-end symmetry with a vertical line precisely bisecting chimney, cylinders and leading bogie was surely no accident, any more than was the descending height of the chimney, dome and cab roof from front to rear. Truly a classic looking design, their performance in no way betrayed their lineaments until in far more recent times, increasing train weights started to tax their absolute power and they began to be moved onto lighter services.

When built, they had 17in x 24in cylinders (massive by older L&FR standards), bogie wheels of 3ft 0in diameter and 6ft 0in coupled wheels whose wheelbase of only 8ft 2in prevented the later fitting of the Midland Class B boiler. Bogie wheelbase was 6ft 6in and between bogie and leading driving wheel, 6ft 9in. The boiler, pressed to 140 psi, was 10ft 3½in long and 4ft 1in mean diameter and had 204 tubes of 1¾in outside diameter. This gave a heating surface of 988sq ft which, added to the 95sq ft of the firebox, gave a quantum leap by previous standards.

Several series, differing in detail, were eventually put into service and they exhibited many changes down the years. This survey includes examples of some of them

Beyer Peacock 4-4-0 No.25, the first of the second series, at Yarmouth soon after the formation of the M&GN. The engine is in original condition and almost identical to the first series, save for the much taller dome.

This relatively well known view shows the first of the 'third series' of Beyer Peacock 4-4-0s, No.29 in immaculate E&MR livery shorty after delivery in 1886. This was the first to have a compensating beam between the driving wheels behind the brake rigging. In spite of the success of this feature on some other railways (eg the Adams 4-4-0s of the LSWR), it is reported that no significant difference was observed on the M&GN lines.

4-4-0 No.30, also from the third series, showing an early version of M&GN insignia on the tender side. The livery is obviously very new and the picture may well date from the year of formation of the M&GN — 1893.

in their original form. For the record, the full list was as follows:

The 'Melton' 0-6-0 Tanks

Melton Constable works was a very versatile place, given its size, undertaking rebuilding and other activities which contributed much to the nature of the line.

M&GN Nos.	Date Built	Remarks
21-24	1881	Built for L&FR
25-28	1883	Generally as 21-24 but with taller domes
29-31	1886	As 25-28 but also with compensating beams between driving wheels
32-35	1888	As 29-31

N.B. Further details of subsequent changes will be found in MBT Vol.1 No.6

One of the most enterprising results of this situation was that from time to time the M&GN actually constructed its own locomotives. This was rare indeed for a small concern but Melton Constable was to do so twice during the period of MR supervision. The rate of output was not exactly at the Derby or Doncaster rate but the engines concerned gave very good service over a long period of time. Two designs were produced of which the neat 0-6-0Ts, the final subject of this survey, were the more numerous. Nine were built from 1897 to 1905, approximately one per year.

The reason for the random numbering was because the engines were built as replacements of nine engines whose numbers they then took. These were six of the Cornwall Mineral Engines (Nos. 1A, 2A, 3A, 11A, 12A, 14A), one Black Hawthorn tank (No.17A) and the two remaining Fox Walker tanks (Nos.15, 16) and it would seem that the original intention was to rebuild the ex-CMR engines (above). Not

The first of the 'Melton' 0-6-0Ts, M&GN No.1A at about the turn of the century. The broadside view clearly shows the stylistic 'marriage' between Derby (above the footplate, rear of the smokebox) and the earlier E&MR configuration elsewhere.

'Fourth Series' 4-4-0 No.33 in service on a short train of mainly GNR style vehicles at an unknown location. Although the signal is 'off', the poses of the staff suggest that the train was standing still at the time!

all the replaced engines were withdrawn, of course, being either sold out of service or retained for internal works use.

When they appeared, the 'Melton' tanks, as they were called, displayed an interesting fusion of Derby practice and what might be termed the 'M&GN style' in the form inherited from the E&MR and its various predecessors. Outside cylinders typified the E&MR but boiler mountings were pure Midland; tank and cab detail had a 'Johnson' feel to it but the chimneys were pure Melton Constable. In fact, they rather gave the appearance of an outside cylindered version of the Class 1 Johnson shunting tanks of the parent system but with

distinct local overtones.

Amongst their detail fittings may be noted their above-axle springs and below-tank injectors; while the steam brake was applied by a vertical handwheel in cab, rather like that of the 4-4-0Ts. Rod operated sandboxes (located at the front and rear below the running plate) were placed so as to allow either direction sanding.

The 'Melton' tanks represented the last stylistic linkages with the original constituents of the M&GN and although the line was to acquire many more engines over the years, to a large extent Derby (and to a lesser degree, Doncaster) was now to reign supreme.

BRITANNIAS
ON THE
EAST COAST ROUTE

By Tom Burns

On a railway with a host of world famous trains, there are bound to be services that are overlooked and somewhat forgotten. The ECML in general and its southernmost portion in particular boasted numerous trains that were noteworthy. First and foremost amongst these was surely the 'Flying Scotsman', though the pre-war streamliners ran the non-stop a close second. Nationalisation saw such trains as 'The Elizabethan' and 'The Talisman', not forgetting the various Pullmans. The King's Cross suburban services had their famous (or perhaps that should be infamous) Quad-Arts, then there were the 'Beer Trains' on the Cambridge line. The ECML could even claim to have the country's most famous freight service, No.266 down, the King's Cross-Niddrie goods.

So with such an array of famous trains, it is not surprising that there were trains that, on other railways, might constitute a major service, but on the ECML, were just another express. Certainly, the Cleethorpes trains fell into this category. Prior to the arrival of the Britannias, these trains were in the hands of Immingham (40B) Class B1s. Crewed by 40B men to Boston, then Boston men on to London, it is probably

This contribution is typical of the sort of secondary research stimulated by the magazines. Some years ago, we printed a colour picture of a Britannia on the East Coast Route, not their most common stamping ground, and invited readers to offer further information, some of which came by way of routine letters to the editor. This contribution, too good for the latter role yet not quite full feature length, admirably fits the anthology format of this book.

true to say that these turns were amongst the hardest in the country for a mixed traffic 4-6-0.

With modernisation proceeding apace on the Eastern Region, many Pacifics began to fall redundant. But since the

No.70041 *Sir John Moore* **reverses out of King's Cross on 7th September 1961. The engine is somewhat grubby but the smokebox has been embellished.** (R. F. Orpwood)

Peterborough-Spalding line was weight restriction RA8 and the LNER Pacifics, together with the V2s were RA9, there was no chance of their regular use on these trains. But on the former GE lines, diesels had displaced many of their Standard Pacifics from top class work and so the motive power authorities began to think of ways in which they might be put to more gainful employment. Soon the railway press been to speculate on the possibility of a transfer of Britannias to Immingham. And then, late in 1960, it was announced that Britannias would be transferred to Immingham for use on the Cleethorpes-London trains. Also to be included amongst their duties were the Whitland fish trains and cross-country trains to Birmingham. Whilst the 7MTs certainly worked the fish trains, I have yet to find any evidence of their being employed on the Birmingham trains.

Prior to this transfer, Britannias were a rare sight on GN metals. No.70000 herself had, of course, been in charge of the funeral train of King George VI on the 11th February 1952 but this mostly covered GE metals. Doncaster had assumed at least some responsibility for Britannia overhauls during the late 1950s and the sight of

Standard Pacifics either working out their time before overhaul or running in thereafter made them a slightly more common sight. Nos.70003/37/41 were all noted at work during the Summer of 1958. Towards the end of 1960, No.70054 must have made many an ECML spotter happy when it made an appearance, while September

No.70040 *Clive of India* **on arrival at King's Cross with the 6.52am ex-Grimsby on 16th November 1961. Once again the smokebox is embellished.** (R. F. Orpwood)

No.70036 *Boadicea* **awaits departure from King's Cross with an evening Grimsby working on 31st August 1962. Modelmakers might like to note the slight detailed front-end differences compared with the previous view: height of head-lamps above running plate, slight change in configuration of the 'platform' below the smokebox door, lack of smokebox embellishment &c.** (R. F. Orpwood)

No.70038 *Robin Hood,* **also on a Grimsby departure in August 1962, shows a few more front end variations when compared carefully with the previous views: lamp position as 70036, front platform as 70040.** (I. D. Loveday)

This earlier view of *Boadicea* **shows a somewhat cleaner locomotive getting into its stride at Harringay West in April 1962.** (I. D. Loveday)

1961 saw No.70000 herself employed on a fitted freight.

Perhaps someone at headquarters had a tidy mind and decided to transfer a block of engines to Immingham; that may have been the case, but by transferring a block of locomotives the old trick of getting rid of all the lame ducks was avoided. Whatever the reason, Nos.70035-41 were duly nominated as the transferees. There appears to be some doubt as to which engines were re-allocated first, but by early 1961

Nos.70039/40 were at work on one of the London turns and its return working.

No.70040 took part in speed and load trials during this period. Loaded to 12 coaches, a 79 minute booking was achieved between London and Peterborough. The outcome of these tests was quite dramatic: in the up direction the former 6.45am departure was retimed to 6.54am, reaching King's Cross at 10.33am, as opposed to the 10.48am arrival of the previous timing. The second departure retained its 8.43am slot,

but was now booked to arrive in London at 12.35pm rather than the previous 12.55pm arrival. In the down direction, the former 4.10pm was advanced to 4.12pm, but was now due at Cleethorpes at 7.57pm, thereby gaining some fifteen minutes over the previous booking. The second departure now left five minutes later at 6.50pm, but was due at its destination no less than 21 minutes earlier at 10.23pm. Most of the improvements took place on the leg of the journey to and from London and Peterborough and the contemporary *Trains Illustrated* voiced its disappointment at what it considered to be slack timings on the East Lincs. Line.

In their early days at Immingham, when not al the engines had been transferred, Britannia reliability was not all it might have been. On one occasion, when only three locomotives were on 40B's books, one had blown elements and another was laid up with a cracked bogie frame. It is interesting to note here that when the Clacton interval service was re-cast to take advantage of some of the Britannias displaced from the Norwich line, 4-6-0 power was hard pressed to keep time for a non-available Pacific. This proved to be the case on the Cleethorpes trains and replacement B1s often lost a lot of time on the run up or down the ECML. But as *Trains Illustrated* observed, thanks to the leisurely timings across the East Lincs. Line, down trains were sometimes able to gain enough time to actually turn a late arrival at Peterborough into an early arrival at Cleethorpes.

It would be interesting to hear the impressions of the Immingham and Boston men who handled the Britannias. It is known that, at least initially, crews from both sheds expressed a preference for B1s. Both the B1s and the Britannias had a reputation for less than perfect riding; but the extra capacity and good steaming qualities of the Britannias are also widely known and this would have surely made them popular with at least some crews. Immingham B1s and 9Fs were often to be

The once familiar complex of trackwork at Belle Isle has now mostly gone, but is well seen here as *Sir John Moore* **tackles the climb out of King's Cross with a Grimsby working on an unknown date in 1961.** (I. D. Loveday)

seen with their smokebox fittings picked out in silver paint and in due course this treatment was accorded to the Britannias. However, while the B1s in particular were usually kept in good external condition, the Britannias were often scruffy. This may be a reflection of staffing problems of course, but I find it strange that the smaller engines were often turned out in better condition. If a member of an Immingham or Boston crew of those time reads this article, it would be interesting to hear their comments.

No.70037 *Hereward the Wake* **makes a fine sight as it climbs past Belle Isle; sadly, most of the fascinating detail in the railway environment seen here has long gone.** (I. D. Loveday)

Britannia activity on the ECML increased during this time because the 11.25am Newcastle-Colchester through train became a March 7MT turn to and from York. While GE based engines were to be seen more frequently on the ECML, freight turns began to play an increasing important role in the Immingham engine's lives. Outside of their use on the fish trains already mentioned, the late summer of 1961 saw them at work on coal trains from Mansfield, while towards the end of that year No.70035 unusually worked through to the LTSR with a block nitrate train. These trains were more commonly associated with 9Fs.

But these freight trains heralded the end of the Britannias' short spell of use on the Cleethorpes trains. By November 1962, the

Boadicea **again, this time drifting down the hill at Belle Isle in April 1962, passes under the same bridge as is seen framing No.70037 in the previous view with Brush Type 2 (now Class 31) No.D5614 in the right foreground, probably on empty stock duty.** (I. D. Loveday)

Out on the main line: No.70000 *Britannia* **herself heads a down Class C fitted freight, believed to be in the Red Hall area.** (I. D. Loveday)

Eastern Region had enough diesels to turn these services over to the new power and regular sightings of 7MTs on the GN ceased. Immingham kept its Pacifics however, continuing to find employment for them on freight traffic.

But the Britannias did continue to appear spasmodically on the GN almost until the very end of regular steam working. On the 23rd January 1963 No.70036 took the second London departure from Cleethorpes, by then re-timed to 8.32am. The 6th April 1963 saw No.70038 at the head of an up extra. Just over a month later, on both the 9th and 11th May, No.70037 found itself pressed into use on the 8.32am diagram, returning with last evening departure from London, leaving at 6.50pm. Cup Final Day, 25th May saw No.70038 come up to town with a train from Cleethorpes, while No.70039 headed a special from Gainsborough. Six days later a remarkable event occurred when Saltley (21D) based No.70028, formerly allocated to the WR, was booked to haul a Peterborough-King's Cross train. It returned that evening on the 7.24pm departure. Possibly the last sighting of a 7MT on the southern end of ECML took place just before the end of GN steam when No.70037 worked the 8.32am/6.50pm turn, on 5th June.

So ended a brief but interesting period in GN motive power. On today's transformed ECML the Cleethorpes trains are once again worked by cascaded power — this time HSTs, displaced by electrification. How times change ...

In conclusion, I would like to thank my good friend and fellow Gresley Society member Dick Orpwood, who provided much useful information and encouragement plus some of the photographs.

A Glasgow and South Western Railway 4-6-0 in its prime: three year old Manson 4-6-0 No.385 glistens at Carlisle Citadel Station in 1906. (L&GRP Collection, NRM)

PRIVATE LOCOMOTIVE BUILDING AND THE INDIAN CONNECTION

The author of this article is the Librarian of the National Railway Museum and has made something of a special study of the comparisons between the 'domestic' British locomotive and its close relations built by private British industry for service overseas — or in some cases vice versa! In this lavishly illustrated feature he takes a look at some of the more significant of these linkages.

A lthough the British steam locomotive has been documented in considerable detail, one factor has been greatly overlooked, the contribution by the private British locomotive industry as regards

By PHILIP ATKINS

design. Prior to say, 1890, this influence ws considerable, particularly concerning the Manchester-based builders Sharp, Stewart & Co., and Beyer, Peacock & Co. Although business rivals, these were not unconnected in that Charles Beyer had been Chief Draughtsman at Sharp's prior to founding his own enterprise and his elegant styling became almost unconsciously enshrined in

Great Indian Peninsula Railway 4-6-0 No.231 ordered from Sharp Stewart & Co., pictured in photographic grey livery new upon arrival in India. (NRM Collection)

the locomotives of several disparate British as well as overseas railways. After about 1870 the larger British railways and some smaller ones became increasingly self sufficient as to both the construction and design of their locomotives, only resorting to the contractors when their 'house' capcity was insufficient to meet their requirements. Happily for the private builders the steady decline in domestic demand coincided with the rapid development of railways overseas, particularly in areas of British imperial and financial influence, notable India, Southern Africa, and South America.

As a result the private builders had considerable experience in designing and building large locomotives, e.g. 4-6-0s and 0-8-0s, long before these began to make

their first appearance in Britain around the turn of the century. It has ben suggested that the Indian State Railway Class L, introduced in 1880, was the forerunner of the first British 4-6-0, the Highland Railway 'Big Goods' of 1894.[1,2] However, a more plausible prototype was the dimensionally very similar Thow New South Wales Government Railways Class P6, first built by Beyer Peacock & Co. in 1892. This is a view which is strongly held in Australia, where of the 191 strong P6 class which was built until 1911, the last example remained in service until 1971, giving a remarkable operational span of all but 80 years.[3]

The home railways collectively made particularly heavy demands on the private industry during the 1898-1901 period, thereby compromising its ability to service also overseas markets, especially India. This actually resulted in American builders supplying engines both to India and the UK, which became a cause of considerable recrimination. After 1901 domestic demand on the contractors once again fell to a low level, but over the next 25 years or so the latter were sometimes call upon to *design* as well as to build locomotives for the British main line railways to a greater extent than has hitherto been recognised. Curiously this particularly involved the 4-6-0 wheel arrangement and initially was *not* unconnected with such engines being built for the 5ft 6in gauge in India.

In India itself the most progressive railway was the Bengal Nagpur, which in December 1901 placed orders for twelve

The handsome and celebrated GCR Class 8 'Fish' engines of 1902 (LNER Class B5) were Robinson's first 4-6-0 design and formed the basis from which other types were developed. No.186 was the penultimate member of the second (1904) series of these engines, built by Beyer Peacock in 1904. (NRM Collection)

large-wheeled passenger 4-6-0s of entirely new design with Sharp, Stewart & Co., which in 1887 had removed from Manchester to Glasgow. A few weeks earlier the Glasgow & South Western Railway had outlined in diagram form (regrettably now lost) a large boilered version of its experimental four-cylinder 4-4-0 No.11, and an alternative outside-cylinder 4-6-0 .[4] In April 1902 the G&SWR placed an order for ten such 4-6-0s with Sharp, Stewart providing a detailed specification but requiring a full set of drawings in addition to the engines. A comparison of the respective general arrangement drawings of the BNR and G&SWR 4-6-0s show many remarkable similarities which without any doubt indicate a common hand. It would be intriguing to discover precisely who masterminded these designs. Doubtless involved would have been the Sharp, Stewart & Co. Managing Director, J. F. Robinson, a man

East Indian Railway Class P 4-6-0 No.1328, built by Vulcan Foundry in 1908 and showing unmistakable similarities to the GCR Class 8. (NRM Collection)

of immense experience (who was not related to J. G. Robinson) who died in 1918.

The resemblance did not go entirely unnoticed at the time albeit in a somewhat confused manner. Thus *The Locomotive Magazine* for March 7th 1903 recorded that:

"The Bengal Nagpur Railway Company, probably the most progressive railway in British India, has recently received from Messrs. Sharp Stewart & Co. some passenger locomotives having six coupled drivers and a leading bogie. As will be seen from the illustration, these engines, 12 in number bear some resemblance to those delivered by the same firm to the Great Central Railway illustrated in our issue for January 3rd last."

In fact the GCR engines, of which more anon, were built by another Glasgow builder, Neilson, Reid & Co. which as from April 1st would amalgamate with Sharp Stewart & Co. and the other remaining Glasgow locomotive builder Dübs & Co., to form the mighty North British Locomotive Company in response to the perceived American threat.

The confusion, however, did not end there. Despite the illustration, which clearly showed *inside* steam chests, the article remarked that " ... the motion is Stephenson link, the valves being placed *on top* of the cylinders and worked by rocking shafts". This was an unusual feature of the

GCR Class 8C 4-6-0 No.196 (LNER Class B1, later B18), built by Beyer Peacock early in 1904 was the second of only two experimental engines which paved the way for the better known 'Imminghams' of 1906. Further details and drawings of these engines were published in Volume 2 of MODELLERS' BACKTRACK. (NRM Collection)

G&SWR engines, then still under construction (and possibly viewed thus by the anonymous correspondent), the first of which was completed by the newly constituted NBL in May 1903. The Glasgow & South Western Railway 4-6-0s with their outside cylinders, Belpaire fireboxes, and notably un-Scottish appearance were quite unlike any other locomotives which James Manson produced for that railway. In 1911 NBL designed and built two superheated versions for the G&SWR, with Schmidt superheaters and 10 inch diameter piston valves, which in themselves remarkably anticipated in appearance later rebuilds of the early GIP 4-6-0s in India.

In late 1901 the Great Central Railway under its new locomotive chief J. G. Robinson drew up specifications for interchangeable 4-6-0 and 0-8-0 engines with outside cylinders, which dimensionally seem to have derived from the corresponding Class S and T engines on the North Eastern Railway, introduced during 1899-1900. Contracts for the detail design and construction of pilot batches of both GC classes were placed with Neilson, Reid & Co. The 4-6-0s became known as the 'Fish' engines, because they were primarily employed on express fish trains from Grimsby. Interestingly between 1905 and 1914 NBL, Vulcan Foundry and Robert Stephenson & Co. built about 100 remarkably similar engines for the East Indian Railway.[5]

In early 1093, the Great Central put out enquiries for two pairs of interchangeable 4-4-2 and 4-6-0 passenger engines. The outline 4-6-0 sketch produced for tendering purposes by Neilson, Reid & Co., was executed by a draughtsman named Finlayson[6] but in the event the contract went just across the tracks from Gorton Works to

The GCR Class 8B 'Jersey Lily' 4-4-2s (LNER Class C4) were introduced in 1903, parallel with the Class 8C 4-6-0s (see previous view) for comparative purposes. In the event, many more 4-4-2s were actually built. This is No.1092 of the main 1905 North British batch at Neasden in 1905, probably when new. (NRM Collection)

Beyer Peacock & Co at Gorton Foundry. There is little doubt that BP were the *real* designers of the elegant Robinson 'Atlantics' and also for that matter of the later huge Wath three-cylinder 0-8-4 shunting tanks in 1907. This observation is confirmed by the paucity of relevant entries in the Gorton Works drawing registers;[7] the *detailed* design of the larger Robinson

engines at Gorton only appears to have commenced there c.1910 with his classic 2-8-0 and 4-6-2T.

The GCR initially preferred the 4-4-2 to the 4-6-0 for express passenger work, and the former inspired the North British Railway 'Atlantics', which not only reproduced exactly the same wheel spacing but also the 'joggled' main frame behind the cylinders. Contrary to popular belief these magnificent engines were designed by the NBR and not by NBL who actually built them. In 1907 NBL built forty 4-4-2s for the Great Indian Peninsula Railway which, their stovepipe chimneys apart, would not have looked out of place at either Neasden

Great Indian Peninsula Railway 4-4-2 No.924 *Lansdowne*, built by the NB Loco Co. in 1907. A lighter 4-4-2 for the East Indian railway even more resembled the Robinson GCR 'Atlantics'. (NRM Collection)

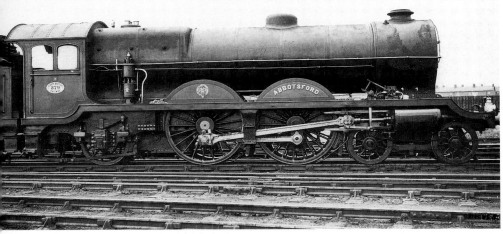

North British Railway 4-4-2 No.897 *Abbotsford* **(LNER Class C11), designed by Reid and built by the NB Loco Co. in 1906. The picture is undated.**

or St. Margaret's. Looking somewhere between the GC and NB 4-4-2s, which would respectively become extinct in 1950 and 1939, the GIPR engines in rebuilt form were still at work well into the 1960s in India, where one is now preserved.

As in Britain, so too in India, the 4-6-0 soon came to be preferred to the 4-4-2 to work the prestigious 'Indian Mail' trains. By 1907, 4-6-0s deriving from the initial BNR engines had been built for several Indian railways, and some were now begin-

ning to appear with outside Walschaerts valve gear in association with slide valves above the cylinders. By 1913 the superheater had also arrived and piston valves in association with Walschaerts gear has become standard.

It was just at this point in time that Robert Urie succeeded the formidable Dugald Drummond as locomotive superintendent on the London & South Western Railway, and recruited from industry a fellow Scot, Thomas Finlayson, as his chief

draughtsman. Latterly an estimator with NBL Finlayson had commenced his career with Neilsons and the significance of his arrival at Eastleigh seems to have been greatly underrated. Nigel Gresley on the GNR had already just begun to produce 2-6-0 and 2-8-0 locomotives with outside-cylinders and Walschaerts valve gear at a time when inside-cylinders still predominated. This was but one indication that the 'golden age' of abundant coal and cheap labour had already begun to slip away *before* August 1914. The former features also characterised all Urie's locomotive designs, although he had long been associated with Drummond.

This radical change must surely have been due to Finlayson and his recent experience in the private locomotive industry. Basic Urie 4-6-0s, improved by R. E. L. Maunsell with long-travel valve gear after 1922, continued to be built until 1936, and can still be examined in the form of the sole surviving Class N15, SR No.777 *Sir Lamiel* in the National Collection, and several privately preserved smaller-wheeled Class S15 engines of both the Urie and Maunsell varieties, all of which also incorporate the 'joggled' frame arrangement referred to earlier. The first Urie 4-6-0s utilised round-topped boiler shells authorised by his predecessor for some four-cylinder 0-8-0s which were never built, and Urie never subsequently resorted to the Belpaire firebox. Indeed the Belpaire firebox was also essentially alien to Scottish domestic prac-

Great Indian Peninsula Class D/4 'Mail' 4-6-0 No.405 built by Vulcan Foundry in 1912. This engine was superheated with piston valves, whereas an immediately preceding batch (Class D/3), although fitted with Walschaerts valve gear, was non-superheated with slide valves. (NRM Collection)

R. W. Urie's LSWR Class H15 mixed traffic 4-6-0 No.486, built at Eastleigh Works late in 1913.

tice before 1923, and its incorporation in the G&SWR 4-6-0s, NBR 4-4-2s and later Highland Railway 4-6-0s pointed to external influences in every case.

The Highland 'River' class 4-6-0 of 1915 was almost certainly another domestic offshoot of the 'Indian Mail' 4-6-0. A tentative contract sketch for these engines had been produced in August 1913 by the North British Locomotive Co., which seemingly overlooked the weight of water in the boiler, about six tons, when estimating the total weight.[8,9] Unusually the working drawings for the 'Rivers' were not made by NBL but by the NBR at Cowlairs, which worked in some Reid 4-4-2 details including the 'joggled' frame. The 4-6-0s were built by Hawthorn Leslie & Co. in Newcastle-upon-Tyne, who were in no way held to blame for the excess weight due to the earlier oversight, and who, following the HR's refusal to accept the new engines, unsuccessfully endeavoured to sell the engines to railways in France before the Highland sold the six engines direct to the Caledonian. Over the next six years Hawthorn Leslie supplied eighteen new locomotives to the Highland, two 4-4-0s, and sixteen 4-6-0s, of which the *doyen* were the eight much-loved 'Clans' built 1919-1921, which were scaled down versions of the 'Rivers'. All eighteen displayed a strong family resemblance and they were all entirely designed, as well as built, on the banks of the River Tyne by a team of remarkably young draughtsmen.[10] One of these was Fred Mills who later departed for Australia whence he ultimately became responsible for the notorious Australian Standard Garratt during World War Two.

It was normal practice where possible for private locomotive builders to incorporate the features of a design which they had already built if this would keep down costs and speed up delivery especially if this avoided the need for fabricating new patterns and flanging blocks. Thus when designing the HR 4-4-0, its boiler was closely based on that of the Taff Valve Class A 0-6-2T which Hawthorn Leslie had recently designed in detail and built (1914), but with the addition of a superheater. Similarly the boilers of the five majestic 4-6-4Ts of the Furness Railway (1920) were modified from the original specification to be based on those of the Great Central 2-8-0s, of which Kitson & Co. had recently built a considerable number, but this time with the superheater (not requested) omitted.

The Furness specification actually stated

Taff Vale Railway Class A 0-6-0T No.120, the final engine of a pilot batch of six designed in detail by Hawthorn Leslie in 1914. Eventually, 58 examples of this type were built by four different makers up to 1921. (NRM Collection)

Highland Railway 4-4-0 No.73 *Snaigow*, built by Hawthorn Leslie in 1916. The boilers of these engines were directly developed from those of the TVR Class A 0-6-2T and overall, the design set the standard for the later 'Clan' Class 4-6-0s. Remarkably, *Snaigow* and its one sister engine *Durn* were the only British 4-4-0s ever built with two outside cylinders and Walschaerts valve gear. (NRM Collection)

Caledonian Railway 4-6-0 No.941, completed in 1916 by Hawthorn Leslie & Co. to drawings prepared by the North British Railway for the Highland Railway. The latter company was unable to accept the design and sold the engines to the Caledonian. They were popularly known as 'Rivers' — a reference to the original naming theme which the Highland had intended to apply to them. (NRM Collection)

Highland Railway 'Clan' Class 4-6-0 No.49 *Clan Campbell,* **built by Hawthorn Leslie in 1919 as a scaled down version of the 'Rivers' (see previous view) and seen at Perth on 9th June 1924.** (R. D. Stephen Collection — NRM)

that the builder's own designs would be considered and it is known that NBL offered a modified Pickersgill 4-6-2T, which it had recently built to Caledonian drawings. The smaller builders also on occasion produced designs for the lesser railways. Thus the Yorkshire Engine Company in Sheffield was entirely responsible for the four *puissant* superheated inside-cylinder 0-6-4Ts for the Metropolitan Railway in 1915/16, and probably designed the large Class A 0-8-0s for the Hull & Barnsley Railway in 1907.

Reliant on contractors for the supply of its locomotives, it is now by no means clear to what extent the H&BR actually designed them. In 1910 Kitson & Co. supplied five elegant domeless 4-4-0s with very distinctive deep framing under the smokebox (rather like the later Furness 4-6-4Ts), a feature also found in three remarkably dimensionally similar 4-4-0s (with domed Belpaire boilers) built by Nasmyth Wilson & Co. the following year for the Eastern Bengal State Railway.[11] A diagram for a *Belpaire* 4-4-0 is said to have existed in the H&B drawing office at Springhead Works; was there any connection?

Following the 'grouping' of 1923 it might resonably have been expected that the newly formed 'Big Four' with their multiplicity of workshops and design facilities would have little need to resort to the private builders. But no; very soon three of them, the Southern, the LMS and the LNER would place urgent orders with the North British Locomotive Company with its three works, to build express passenger 4-6-0s in a matter of months. The Southern engines were improved Urie N15 4-6-0s, appropriately built by a Scottish builder to Scottish designs and by 1925 known as the 'King Arthur' class. In December 1926, the LMS ordered 50 three-cylinder 4-6-0s with delivery to commence in six months, having produced a preliminary outline diagram. The working drawings were produced by NBL incorporating standard LMS

details where possible, but the builder did *not* regard the 'Royal Scot' design as its own.

Just over a year later, in February 1928, the LNER also ordered ten three-cylinder 4-6-0s, to stringent weight limits for service on the ex-Great-Eastern main line with quick delivery (not in the event fulfilled). Although to incorporate LNER standard features, this was quite definitely *designed* by NBL: "we to draw out", according to the order book. Ultimately 73 Class B17 'Sandringham' 4-6-0s were built, but no repeat order came the way of NBL

Also during the mid-1920s Beyer Peacock & Co. employed its expertise to build 2-8-0+0-8-2 and 2-6-0+0-6-2 Beyer Garratts for the LNER and LMS respectively. In the interests of standardisation the LMS interfered, with the result that their engines, which would have been better as 2-6-2+2-6-2s, were not nearly as satisfactory as they might have been. They also greatly exceeded their specified weight and maximum axleload, the latter coming to no less than 21 tons as against 18½ tons.

Beyer Peacock unsuccessfully proposed more promising Garratt designs for service in Britain until as late as 1949, i.e. at the beginning of the British Railways era, including some for the Southern and the GWR, but particularly for the LMS. In August 1934 the Vulcan Foundry delivered the first Stanier Class 5 4-6-0 to the LMS, several months before the first Crewe-built example, and it is understood that it made some contribution to the design of these engines, particularly as regards the main frames. Vulcan's own particular speciality was the supply of locomotives to India, to which it had supplied the very first in 1851. For many years prior to his death in 1946 the Chief Draughtsman at Vulcan was Charles Finlayson, a cousin of Thomas. It is interesting to note that as late as 1946-1950, Vulcan built over 100 'Mail' 4-6-0s of the improved 'HPS' design for the sub-continent, some features of which could be directly traced back to the original BNR engines of 1903, several of which were then still running in rebuilt form.

BIBLIOGRAPHY

1. *The Chappar Rift, and the notable development of locomotive power on the light-rail Sind-Pishin route to Quetta,* by P. S. A. Berridge, Railway Magazine, February 1935, pp. 99-103.
2. *Loco Profile 17, Jones Goods & Indian L,* by Brian Reed, Profile Publications 1971.
3. *A Compendium of New South Wales Steam Locomotives,* By A. Grunbach, Australian Railway Historical Society, NSW Division, 1989, pp. 115-117.
4. *Kilmarnock Drawing Register, 1872-1923,* at National Railway Museum, York.
5. *Locomotive Magazine* June 15th 1906, p. 93.
6. *Neilson, Reid & Co/North British Loco, Co. Project Sketch Register c.1900-1924,* original at Mitchell Library, Glasgow, xerox copy at National Railway Museum, York.
7. *Gorton Drawing Registers 1859-1922,* at National Railway Museum, York.
8. *More light on the Highland 'Rivers' — the mystery solved?* by C. P. Atkins, Railway World, February 1978, pp. 75-78.
9. *The Highland Railway 'Rivers' — who or what was really to blame?* by C. P. Atkins, Railway World June 1985, pp. 300-302.
10. *R. & W. Hawthorn Leslie & Co. drawing register Vol. 3. January 1911-August 1928* at National Railway Museum, York.
11. *Locomotive Magazine* January 15th 1912, p. 27.

Note: 4-6-0s by H. D. Bowtell will be found in the *Journal of the Stephenson Locomotive Society* for October 1955.

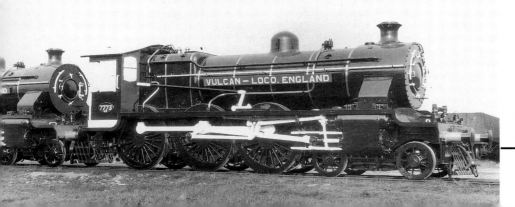

The pioneer LNER Class B17 4-6-0 No.2800 *Sandringham* **was built by the NB Loco Co. in 1928. This constituted the last design of main line steam locomotive to be designed by a private builder for a British railway. The tender was an ex-Great Eastern Railway standard design.** (NRM Collection)

And finally, one of the ultimate batch of Indian Mail 4-6-0s, newly completed by Vulcan Foundry, awaits despatch overseas from Birkenhead Docks on 14th May 1950. Many of its essential characteristics can be directly related to the original BNR 4-6-0s ordered almost 50 years earlier. (T. J. Edgington)

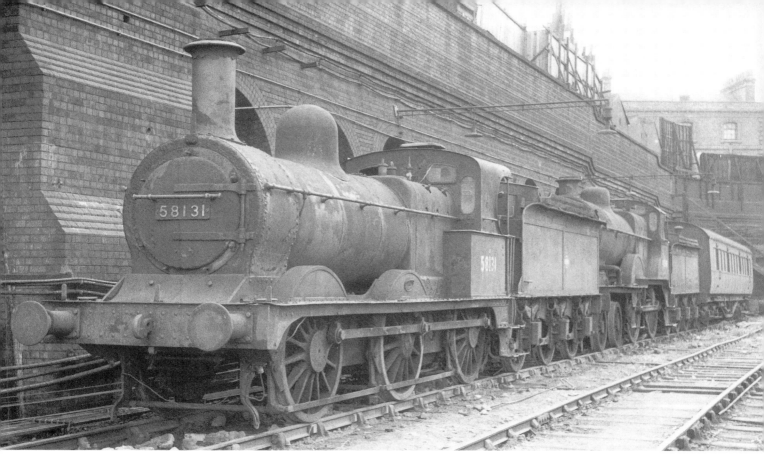

The Tottenham and Hampstead Line in the 1950s

Johnson 2F 0-6-0 No.58131 in store in the open at Kentish Town motive power depot, probably on 18th March 1961. In earlier years, this locomotive was used on light freight and permanent way maintenance trains over the Tottenham and Hampstead line. Behind is an ex-Midland 2P 4-4-0, one of which once, in emergency, powered a peak hour Kentish Town-Barking suburban train.

The ramifications of London and its railways are an endless source of interest to the historian, for it was in London where the majority of our independent railway companies met and exchanged traffic. Many 'joint' links were forged between all manner of companies whenever collaboration seemed likely to gain a better result than the more customary outright competition and in this account, **Ian Thompson** *recalls the final years of steam workings on one of the more important of these links on the north side of the Thames.*

(All photographs by the author)

In the 1950s, the Tottenham and Hampstead line was one of the major arteries for cross-London freight traffic between, to the west or south, the yards at Feltham, Hither Green, Willesden Brent, &c and, to the east, those at Ferme Park, Temple Mills and Tilbury Docks. Trains bound for the latter group from origin points north of London on the Midland main line also used the artery. In addition there was local freight traffic. The line had an intensive steam-powered suburban ser-

vice, was regularly traversed by boat trains running between St Pancras and Tilbury, was frequented by special trains carrying troops from one side of the country to

another, by excursions organized for special events at Harringay Stadium and weekend specials from stations on the Midland main line to Southend. It also handled cross-London parcels traffic and interregional transfers of locomotives.

As a result of these diverse traffics, the line was regularly visited by locomotives built by or for the following railway companies: Midland, LMS, Great Eastern, Great Northern, LNER, London and South Western, London Brighton and South Coast, South Eastern and Chatham, Southern and British Railways. On occasions, locomotives from other companies, such as the Great Western and Great Central, also passed through. The North London Railway and the lines through the tunnels of inner London have received deserved attention in the specialised press, but the Tottenham and Hampstead line

Feltham based Q1 0-6-0 No.33027 heads a cross-London freight train from Feltham to Temple Mills under the Holloway Road bridge, on 17th April 1961.

Cricklewood depot's ex-Midland Railway 4F 0-6-0 No.43935, in a dubious mechanical condition, heads away from Upper Holloway station on Whit Monday 1961, with an excursion train bound for Southend, probably originating at St Albans or Luton.

remains comparatively unknown, a situation which the next few pages try and do something to correct. Some thirty-five years ago, it was one of the most interesting railway lines in the country.

The line and its history

The Tottenham and Hampstead was envisioned as a cross London link between the Great Eastern Railway's Liverpool Street to Cambridge line, at Tottenham, and Gospel Oak, on the Hampstead Junction Railway. The Midland Railway and the Great Eastern Railway each contributed a third of the capital. It was opened from Tottenham to Highgate Road, on the Midland main line on 21st July 1868, but was not extended to Gospel Oak until First World War freight traffic demanded it. The connection was removed after that war, and not restored until the next one. Possibly the Midland Railway was not too keen on installing the link at Gospel Oak, since traffic from the Tottenham and Hampstead to the Midlands or north west of the country could go by its own tracks or those of the London and North Western (LNW). By there not being a link at Gospel Oak, use of the LNW alternative was effectively deterred.

On 4th August 1890, the Tottenham and Forest Gate Railway Company was formed and the line was opened four years later. By through running, this gave trains from the Midland Railway access to the London, Tilbury and Southend tracks at East Ham and Barking. They started running in 1894 and formed the backbone of the Tottenham and Hampstead's passenger service from that moment on. The physical link between the Midland and the London, Tilbury and Southend became an institutional one in 1912, when the former took over the latter.

The Midland and the Great Eastern took over the Tottenham and Hampstead in 1902. In the 1950s, the administration of line was split between the Eastern and London Midland Regions of British Railways, the frontier point being between the stations of Crouch Hill (which had dark blue station signs) and Upper Holloway (whose were red). The Midland Region's Kentish Town depot provided the line staple motive power, whilst the passenger service appeared in the Eastern Region timetable.

The Tottenham and Hampstead and the Tottenham and Forest Gate railways can be considered as one. Effectively, including the North London line from Gospel Oak to Willesden, the line forms an integral part of an east-west cross link — see the map. The Tottenham and Hampstead itself is twin tracked throughout, and has never been electrified. The distance from Kentish Town to Barking is 12.42 miles. The regular 1950s suburban passenger service called at the following intermediate stations: Upper Holloway (1.49 miles), Crouch Hill (2.48 miles), Harringay Park (3.23 miles), South Tottenham (4.47 miles), Black Horse Road (6.03 miles), Walthamstow (6.77 miles), Leyton Midland Road (7.77 miles), Leytonstone High Road (8.51 miles), Wanstead Park (9.75 miles) and Woodgrange Park (10.5 miles). There were a few closed stations, which had fallen victims of the electric tram, mainly on the Tottenham and Hampstead proper, for instance Junction Road, west of Upper Holloway, and Hornsey Road, which was sited between Upper Holloway and Crouch Hill. Both still had their platforms in place in the 1950s.

Freight traffic

In the days of steam and massive movements of coal and general freight by rail, getting wagons from one side of London to another constituted quite a problem. The Tottenham and Hampstead helped solve it.

The main origin and destination points for freight traffic routed via the Tottenham and Hampstead line are listed in Table 1. However, not all trains between every possible origin and destination point pairs were routed via the line. For many flows, for instance, that between the Great Eastern line and points in south London, the Tottenham and Hampstead route was just one routing option amongst several, and was a decidedly second best alternative for some of them, being used only because of congestion on more direct routes. For instance, for traffic between Ferme Park and the SEC and LBSC divisions of the Southern Region, the route via Victoria Park, Highbury and Islington, the North London line to Willesden and thence along the West London line through Kensington was a viable alternative.

More direct for traffic between Temple Mills or Ferme Park and the South Eastern and Chatham or London, Brighton and South Coast divisions was a route by way of the London Transport's East London line to New Cross or New Cross Gate, but this not only involved threading freight trains between surface stock Underground trains but also assigning the trains to diminutive J68 or J69 0-6-0Ts fitted with both condensing gear and trip cock gear to London Transport's specifications. On top of this,

TABLE 1	
ORIGIN AND DESTINATION ZONES FOR FREIGHT TRAFFIC ROUTES VIA THE TOTTENHAM AND HAMPSTEAD LINE	
Zones to the east	**Zones to the west**
E1. Great Eastern line, especially Temple Mills freight yard.	**W1.** Midland main line, Kettering, etc.
E2. Great Northern line, especially Ferme Park freight yard.	**W2.** The Midland line freight yards in the Brent/Cricklewood area.
E3. London, Tilbury and Southend line, especially, such as Tilbury docks and Ford plant at Dagenham.	**W3.** Willesden freight yard (LNW).
	W4. Acton freight yard (GW).
E4. Local freight yards on the T & H route, e.g. Harringay coal depot.	**W5.** Feltham freight yard (LSW).
	W6. Norwood Junction (LBSC).
	W7. Hither Green (SEC).
	W8. Local freight yards on the T & H route, such as that between Upper Holloway and Junction Road. Includes also Somers Town freight depot (Saint Pancras.)

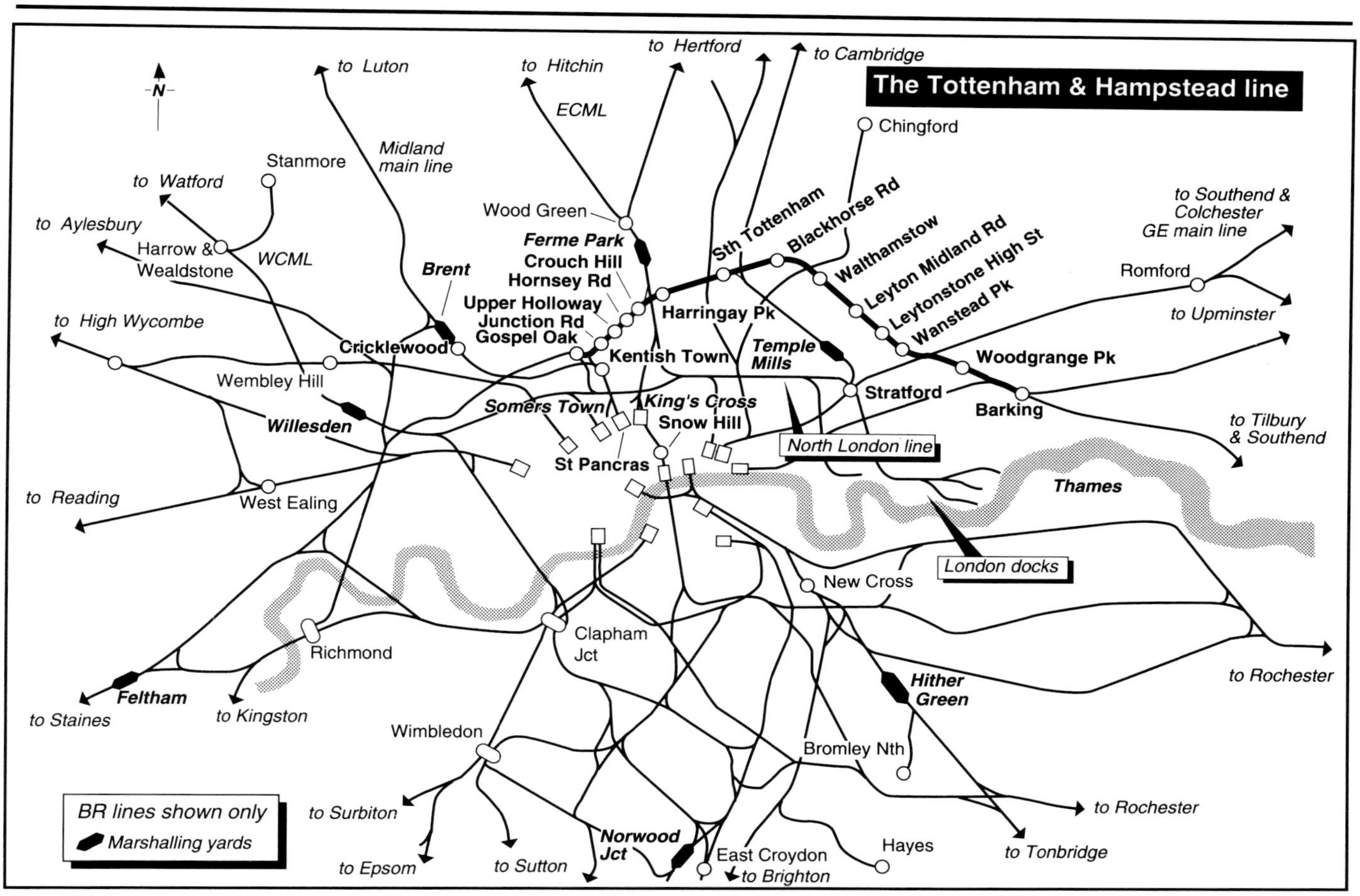
The Tottenham & Hampstead line
N
to Luton
to Hitchin
to Hertford
to Cambridge
ECML
Chingford
Midland main line
Stanmore
to Watford
to Aylesbury
Harrow & Wealdstone
WCML
Wood Green
Ferme Park
Crouch Hill
Hornsey Rd
Upper Holloway
Junction Rd
Gospel Oak
Brent
Sth Tottenham
Blackhorse Rd
Walthamstow
Leyton Midland Rd
Leytonstone High St
Wanstead Pk
to Southend & Colchester
GE main line
Romford
to Upminster
to High Wycombe
Cricklewood
Harringay Pk
Kentish Town
Temple Mills
Woodgrange Pk
Wembley Hill
Willesden
Somers Town
King's Cross
Snow Hill
Stratford
Barking
to Tilbury & Southend
North London line
St Pancras
to Reading
West Ealing
Thames
London docks
New Cross
Clapham Jct
Richmond
to Rochester
Hither Green
Feltham
to Staines
to Kingston
Wimbledon
Bromley Nth
to Rochester
BR lines shown only
Marshalling yards
to Surbiton
to Epsom
to Sutton
Norwood Jct
East Croydon
to Brighton
Hayes
to Tonbridge

trains had to be reversed near to the Great Eastern division's heavily used Liverpool Street station.

Similar problems were presented by routing trains via King's Cross Metropolitan Line station through Snow Hill and on to Hither Green. Freight trains routed via Snow Hill had to be banked up the 1 : 39 gradient to Ludgate Hill, right in the middle of London. A J52 saddle tank from Hornsey depot was kept waiting at Farringdon for this purpose, being replaced by a standard 350hp diesel shunter as from around 1957. No.13332 was often the engine involved.

Compared with the nightmare of weaving steam hauled freight trains through the tunnels of central London, also used by London Transport's metro trains, the problems beset by the Tottenham and Hampstead or the North London lines must have appeared positively benign in their nature. Even so, steam powered, unbraked, loose coupled freight trains were not the ideal track sharing partners for frequent suburban services. Passing loops were notable for their scarcity. The North London line westwards from Gospel Oak, which was fed by the Tottenham and Hampstead, was twin tracked and over it ran an electrically powered suburban service; the line included some quite steep gradients.

The Tottenham and Hampstead was also twin tracked, but carried a steam powered suburban service. Intermediate junctions, such as with the Great Northern main line at Harringay and the Great Eastern at Tottenham, complicated the problem of train scheduling.

The degree of congestion on shorter routes varied from time to time, and this caused changes in routing patterns. For instance, during the early and middle

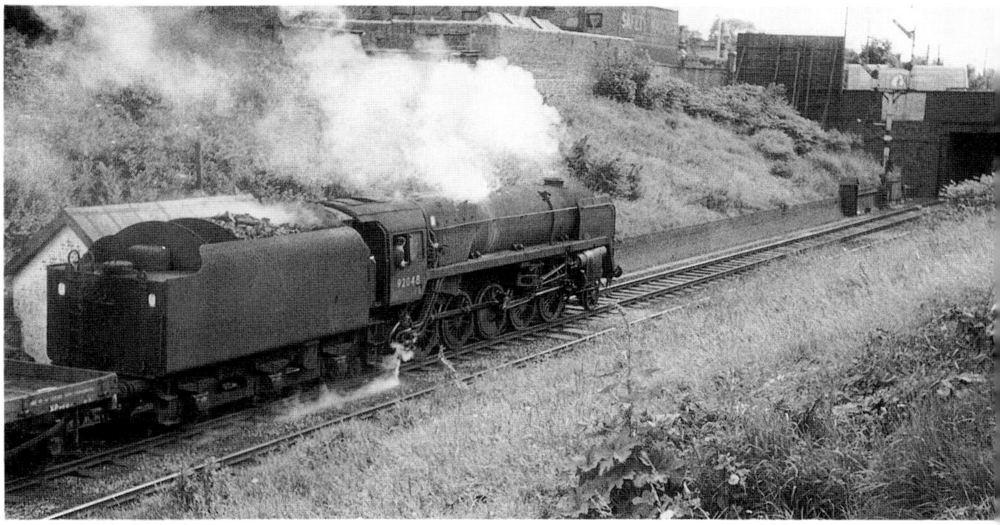

9F 2-10-0 No.92048 heads a freight bound for the Midland main line into Upper Holloway station in mid-July 1961.

Fowler 3F 0-6-0T No.47442 speeds a freight bound for Brent sidings westward towards Upper Holloway station in mid-July 1961.

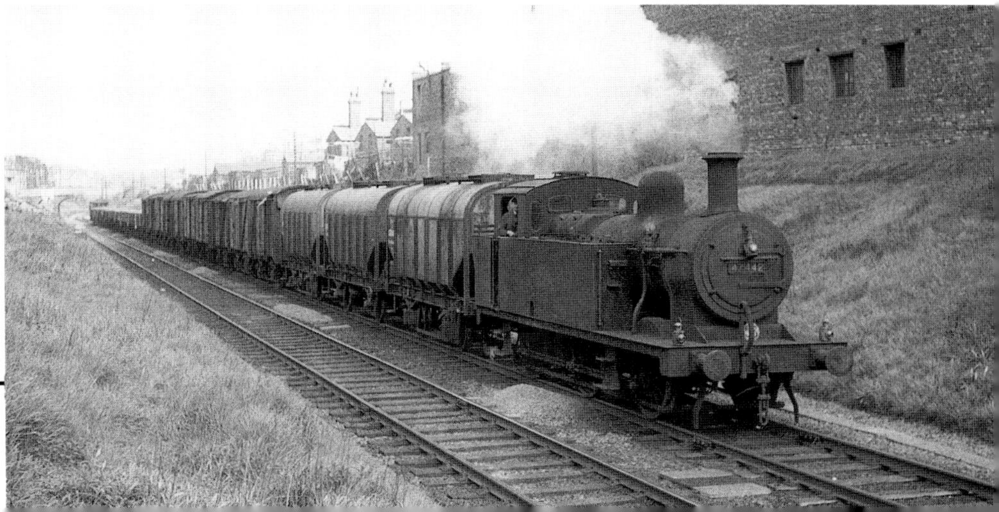

Condensing gear fitted Johnson 3F 0-6-0T No.47204 under light repair at Kentish Town m.p.d. The date is March 1960, but almost everything visible is pure Midland Railway.

A Fowler 3MT 2-6-2T, No.40029, waits opposite Kentish Town m.p.d. with the empty stock of a Moorgate-St Albans commuter train, which it will work after taking the stock into town. This was in the Spring of 1961 when trouble with some of the D50XX diesels required a partial return to steam.

Tottenham and Hampstead.

Once on the latter, they carried on past the active stations at Crouch Hill and Upper Holloway and the disactivated ones at Hornsey Road, Junction Road (where there was a British Road Services terminal) and Highgate Road and then onto the Junction Road Junction-Gospel Oak spur to reach the North London line. The link to the latter line was also reinstated during the Second World War, in this case on 11th March 1940. Both it and the Ferme Park link were restored so that the Tottenham and Hampstead line could relieve even more congested lines, such as the Highbury and Islington route, the physical capacity of which were being strained by wartime traffic demands.

Freight from Tilbury Docks or the Ford Motor Company plant at Dagenham joined the Tottenham and Hampstead at Barking. Trains from the Great Eastern division yard at Temple Mills in East London joined it via the Tottenham South Junction, to the east of the Tottenham and Hampstead's South Tottenham station. Trains from Brent or points to the north on the Midland main line gained access to the Tottenham and Hampstead via a spur between Kentish Town and Finchley Road. Trains from Somers Town joined the Tottenham and Hampstead via a spur which skirted the north-western fringes of the Kentish Town locomotive depot roundhouses.

Coal featured strongly in the freight flows, especially those from Ferme Park and Brent. Cement, automotive industry parts, imported fruit (especially bananas), oil (from Tilbury) and general merchandise made up most of the rest. There was also a regular midday freight from the Great Eastern section which included a significant number of oil tank wagons, which must, presumably, have originated in an East Anglian port, and which seemed not to have been remarshalled at Temple Mills, judging by the B1, B12 or K3 locomotive which normally hauled it.

There was also a significant traffic in parcels and suchlike items. In the early morning, often around daybreak, an ex-Great Eastern F5 2-4-2T or J68 or J69 0-6-T was used to pass through Upper Holloway on what may have been newspaper or mail trains. Most other exclusive mail trains were hauled by Kentish Town or Cricklewood locomotives, and were probably plying between Somers Town and the

1950s, judging by the daily appearances of ex-London, Brighton and South Coast type C2X 0-6-0s through Upper Holloway, Norwood Junction-Temple Mills freight was being routed via the Tottenham and Hampstead. Later, the C2Xs disappeared from the line, probably because their trains were routed through Highbury and Islington, although they might have been withdrawn in favour of sending freight bound for the London, Brighton and South Coast section first to Feltham behind an ex London and South Western type 700 0-6-0 or a Bulleid Q1, and thence to Norwood Junction by another train. Nevertheless, in 1953, 36 westbound freight were routed through Upper Holloway, many of them interdivisional workings.

Although the situation was not static, the following traffic was partially or wholly routed via Upper Holloway in the mid and late 1950s, using the codes of Table 1: E1 to/from W2, W3, W4, W5, W6 and W8; E2 to/from W2, W3, W4, W5 and W8; E3 to/from W1, W2, W3, W4 and W8, and E4 to/from W1, W2 and W8.

Space does not permit the description of all legs of all the freight trains involved. However, freights from the Great Northern line travelled as follows. All were formed at the Ferme Park yard, which was located to the south of Hornsey motive power depot, and was the arrival point for loaded coal and other freight trains routed southwards along the Great Northern main line. Coal

was a major component of cross-London freight traffic originating in Ferme Park. Being situated on the up side of the Great Northern main line, freights booked via the Tottenham and Hampstead had to start out towards King's Cross and then back up across the overbridge to get to the down side of the line. Then they set off once more in a southerly direction on a spur, reinstated during the Second World War, on 8th January 1940 to be precise, to the

Stored Fowler 3MT 2-6-2T No.40053 and still active 4F 0-6-0 No.44259 are hemmed in by a visiting B1 4-6-0 and a local Black Five in one of the now roofless Kentish Town roundhouses. No.40053 was a Willesden locomotive in the late fifties, until being transferred to Kentish Town when displaced from Euston empty stock workings. It was used on Kentish Town-Barking trains in the week before the DMU takeover. On the left is a B1 4-6-0 which had worked in from Canklow on freight.

The Barking-Kentish Town local services were taken over by DMUs as from January 1960, but a very few through trains from Southend remained steam-hauled for some time afterwards. In the spring of that year, Fairburn 2-6-4T No.42237 hauls the up train into Upper Holloway.

BR Standard 2-6-4T No.80099 runs into Southend Central station on a LTS line train on 30th October 1961.

Great Eastern or London, Tilbury and Southend sections.

Passenger traffic

The main passenger traffic was the cross London suburban service between Kentish Town and Barking. A few trains started from or were bound to St Pancras, at the western end of the route, or East Ham, at the other end. More than thirty suburban trains each way were routed through Upper Holloway each day in the mid 1950s. In the summer, a few trains started from or terminated at Cricklewood. Some through trains to Southend were operated, especially on weekends and in summer. Most trains stopped at all stations, but some of the through services skipped some of them. A summer Sunday through train from St Albans stopped only at Harringay Park, South Tottenham, Leyton Midland Road and Woodgrange Park, South Tottenham, Leyton Midland Road and Woodgrange Park, and then not at all until Benfleet.

On the weekends and Public Holidays, additional excursion trains often ran, mainly from Midland main line stations, such as St Albans or Luton. Passenger boat sailings and arrivals to/from Tilbury were serviced by through special passenger trains from St Pancras. These were normally run for the *Orient Line* or *Swedish and Lloyd*.

These were the only scheduled passenger trains. However, hardly a week passed by without special passenger trains putting in appearances. Troop trains were frequent visitors, as were specials scheduled to bring spectators to shows put on at Harringay Stadium. For instance, Billy Graham's Evangelical meetings could be guaranteed to suck in special excursions drawn by

unrebuilt Bulleid Light Pacifics from the Southern Region. Soccer games played at Wembley Stadium also drew special traffic through the line from the Great Eastern and London, Tilbury and Southern Sections. The Football Association Cup Final never generated a special train, but Schoolboy International games invariably did.

Interdivisional stock transfers

The Tottenham and Hampstead route was favoured for switching locomotives between Regions, or between different lines within the Eastern Region. When the Eastern Region transferred A3 Pacifics or V2 2-6-2s between the Great Northern and Great Central lines, it did so via the Tottenham and Hampstead. The line was obviously allowed to handle RA9 locomotives.* Evidence is lacking, but when Clan Pacific No.72009 *Clan Stewart* was tried out on the Great Eastern section in 1958, it probably went by way of the Tottenham and Hampstead, as would have done A5 4-6-2T No.69814, when *en route* to and from being tried out on King's Cross empty stock workings early in 1960. A number of Thompson L1 2-6-4Ts passed through westbound in the summer of 1960, presumably whilst being transferred from the Great Eastern section, which was well on the way to being completely dieselised or electrified, to the Great Central section.

Whenever Ian Allan or anybody else chartered a special from a London station with motive power from another Region, a to and fro routing via the Tottenham and Hampstead line was often involved. On one occasion, on 21st April 1960 to be precise,

this involved ex-Great Western 4-4-0 No.3440 *City of Truro*, the only definite sighting of an ex-Great Western locomotive on the line. Great Western locomotives were not assigned to cross-London workings to avoid possible loading gauge problems, especially width-wise with engines with two outside cylinders. A Western Region-based BR Class 5 4-6-0 No.73001 passed through light on 30th July 1959, but this would have caused no loading gauge worries.

City of Truro was by far from being the only thoroughbred locomotive to grace the tracks of the Tottenham and Hampstead line. Others included ex-Midland Railway Compound 4-4-0 No.1000, Gresley A3 Pacific No.60103 *Flying Scotsman* and A4 Pacific No.60022 *Mallard*. At least three 100mph+ steam locomotives have therefore passed through such lowly stations as Upper Holloway and Crouch Hill.

Freight train motive power

Staple motive power for freights from the Great Northern line was the Ivatt/Gresley J6 0-6-0, from Hornsey depot. Regular performers included Nos.64196, 64223 and 64233. Hornsey depot was not adverse to despatching a New England based WD 2-8-0, with nothing to do between arriving with a coal train from the north and being sent back there, across London with freight. When the depot was tight for motive power, a tank locomotive would be assigned, normally a J52 0-6-0ST or N1 0-6-02T in the early and middle 1950s, and later a J50 0-6-0T.

From the Great Eastern, there was more variety. Staple power was J17, J19 and J20 0-6-0s of original Great Eastern parentage, and later LNER type J39 locomotives of the same wheel arrangement. Stratford's BR Standard 2-6-0s were also regular visitors, as were WD 2-8-0s, ex-LNER K3 2-6-0s and B1 4-6-0s and ex-Great Eastern B12/3 4-6-0s. This wasn't all. The solitary K5 rebuilt from the K3 2-6-0s was seen more than once. J68 or J69 0-6-0Ts and N7 0-6-2Ts also appeared.

Slowly at first, Stratford-based diesel locomotives made appearances from the end of 1958. Again, as in the case with steam, there was considerable variety, the most frequent performers during 1959 and 1960 being Brush A1A+A1A of the D55XX series (later Type 31), North British Bo-Bos of the D61XX series (Type 21), Thomson-Houston Bo-Bos numbered in the D82XX series (Type 15), North British Bo-Bos numbered from D8400 to D8409 (Type 16) and BR Sulzer Bo-Bos numbered D5020 and upwards (Type 24). In spite of the early dieselisation of the Great Eastern section, J19 0-6-0s continued to be used on Stratford depots Tottenham and Hampstead line freight turns until July 1962, and possibly for a month or two more. The J19s outlasted the earlier Great Eastern J17s, the later J20s and even much more modern LNER and BR types.

Freights powered by the Southern Region were 'horsed' according to the particular section concerned. Those from the London, Brighton and South Coast section

* RA (Route Availability) was a former LNER system which indicated which locomotives (by axle weight) could traverse which routes — the higher the number, the more critical the axle loading. RA9 was the most restrictive category and thus any line given this grading was deemed capable of 'passing' any former LNER locomotive type — Ed.)

were hauled by C2X 0-6-0s, until trains from this division disappeared from the Tottenham and Hampstead in the mid-1950s. From the SEC section, type C 0-6-0s appeared, especially around 1957; later Q1s from Bricklayers' Arms motive power depot took over. Type W 2-6-4Ts also had regular freight turns over the line. Three-cylindered 2-6-0 No.31892 took over a Q1 turn for a few weeks in the summer of 1959 and two-cylindered type N or U 2-6-0s often appeared from different Southern Region divisions. From the London and South Western section, type 700 0-6-0s were steadily supplanted by Q1s towards the end of the 1950s, but continued to appear until 1960. Feltham depot was their home base.

The Q1s gave all the impressions of being the Southern Region's best freight power. They were fast, powerful and, when the driver put his mind to it, could show phenomenal powers of acceleration. Britain would have got a better deal were the steel and effort which went into producing around 935 War Department 2-8-0s to have been used instead to make 1320 Q1s!

Through freight from the Midland, during the mid 1950s, was usually powered by 3F and 4F 0-6-0s, Crab 2-6-0s, Black Five 4-6-0s and 8F 2-8-0s. As the years rolled on, the older and least powerful locomotives tended to pass away, and 9F 2-10-0s put in ever more frequent appearances. Local freight from Brent and Somers Town was often powered by 3F and 4F 0-6-0s, or by one or other of Kentish Town's small allocation of Johnson ex-Midland Railway 2F 0-6-0s, No.58131 of which was active until around 1959. Tank engines also put in everyday appearances on local freight turns, Johnson and Fowler 'Jinties' being very common, right up to 1962.

English Electric Bo-Bos of the D80XX series (Type 20), from Devons Road depot, first appeared in mid-1958, running light and seemingly on crew training exercises. The first recorded freight turn by these

Large-boilered Stanier 3MT 2-6-2T No.40203 is on pilot duty at St Pancras station in March 1961.

locomotives occurred on 22nd November 1959, when D8005 and D8015 worked over the line. Willesden-based examples appeared soon after. Cricklewood-based BR Sulzer Bo-Bos in the D50XX series (Type 24) and Metropolitan-Vickers Co-Bos numbered upwards from D5700 (Type 28) both started to appear, spasmodically, from the summer of 1960. Steam power predominated however, until July 1962, when BCW Bo-Bos numbered from D5380 upwards, recently delivered new to Cricklewood depot, started to take over Fowler 4F turns. Rapid dieselisation then set in.

Suburban train motive power

The dieselisation of freight traffic was relatively gradual. But the suburban service was almost completely dieselised in one fell sweep on 11th January 1960. Until then, staple motive power was Kentish Town-based 2-6-2Ts and 2-6-4Ts. The former were mainly used, the larger locomotives being preferred for Midland main line suburban turns. Kentish Town housed 12 or 13 of the Fowler variety of 2-6-2T during the mid and late 1950s, together with a few less of the Stanier version — see Table 2. The two types were used indiscriminately, normally on three carriage off-peak and five car peak period trains. These were mainly made up of standard LMS stock, although in the middle of the decade there were still some ex-Midland Railway carriages in use, and BR stock became more common as the years rolled on. The Fowler 2-6-2Ts carried with them a bad reputation for being overweight, having undersized boilers and inadequate valve arrangements, but they seemed to perform well enough as long as the load was not too heavy. All the Kentish Town allocation was

condensing gear fitted, since they also worked trains through the tunnels from Moorgate onto the Midland main line.

In 1956 or 1957, two of Kentish Town's Stanier 2-6-2Ts were rebuilt with the larger boiler fitted to a few locomotives of this class. One of these, No.40142, was never recognised as having been fitted with the larger boiler, at least not by Ian Allan's renowned registers of British Railway's locomotives, but I can guarantee that it was. These two engines, No.40167 being the other one, were happier with the six-carriage peak trains than were the unrebuilt Stanier locomotives or those of the Fowler type. At the end of the decade, another large boiler rebuild, No.40203, was drafted in.

During the last few months before the dieselisation of suburban services, Kentish Town depot played host to non-condensing Fowler 2-6-2Ts declared redundant elsewhere. This was done to make up for locomotives from the home team which had to be laid off because of skimped maintenance prior to the introduction of the diesel units. Nos.40019, 40020, 40053 and 40064, all from Willesden, where they had been out of work since 2-6-4Ts had taken over the empty carriage stock workings to and from Euston station, put in appearances on local services in the last two months of normal steam working. From further afield came No.40012, late of Heaton Mersey depot in Manchester.

Kentish Town's Fowler and Fairburn 4MT 2-6-4Ts were also regular performers, and were preferred for the six car peak period trains. From 1953 to 1956, Kentish Town was home to some new BR Standard 4MT 2-6-4Ts, but then, as part of a drive to reduce the number of different types at each depot, they were transferred away, being replaced by some of the Stanier two-cylinder variety. However, this did not alleviate the spare parts problem at Kentish Town, which had not housed that type before. They rarely ventured onto the

Local train bound for Kentish Town, made up of a four-car Derby-built, Rolls-Royce motored diesel multiple unit, approaching Upper Holloway station in mid-July, 1961.

Tottenham and Hampstead line. For a few days in the summer of 1959, the last built Ivatt 2-6-2T No.41329 worked some trains; it was based at Bedford and had probably been under repair at Cricklewood.

Very occasionally, a rostered locomotive broke down, and a replacement suburban tank could not be found; then Johnson 3F 0-6-0Ts could be seen handling up to six loaded carriages on peak hour services. The

TABLE 2

<u>ALLOCATIONS BY CLASS TO KENTISH TOWN MOTIVE POWER DEPOT IN MID AND LATE 1950S</u>

Type of locomotive	Number of locomotives allocated at:			
	End/54	Feb/56	Oct/57	Apr/59
Fowler 3MT 2-6-2T (condensing)	13	13	12	13
Stanier 3MT 2-6-2T (std. boiler)	10	8	6	6
Stanier 3MT 2-6-2T (large boiler)	0	0	2	1
Midland Railway 2P 4-4-0	0	0	4	1
LMS 2P 4-4-0	0	0	0	3
LMS 4P Compound 4-4-0[1]	0	0	0	0
Midland Railway 1F 0-6-0T	3	0	0	0
Fairburn 4MT 2-6-4T	5	3	5	5
Fowler 4MT 2-6-4T (plain cab)	2	2	2	5
Stanier 2-cyl. 4MT 2-6-4T	0	0	6	4
Midland Railway 4F 0-6-0	3	3	1	1
LMS 4F 0-6-0	8	9	9	11
Stanier 5MT 4-6-0	14	13	18	16
Jubilee 6P 4-6-0	13	13	14	13
Rebuilt Royal Scot 7P 4-6-0	0	0	0	4
Johnson 3F 0-6-0T (condensing)	7	8	8	7
Johnson 3F 0-6-0T (non-condensing)	5	5	2	1
Fowler 3F 0-6-0T	5	6	6	6
Midland Railway 2F 0-6-0T	2	2	1	1
BR Standard 4MT 2-6-4T	8	9	0	0
Britannia 4-6-2[2]	0	0	0	0

<u>Notes</u>

[1]. No. 41118 was based at the depot for a spell during 1957. Personal memory recalls that 41114 was similarly allocated for a period.

[2]. The handfull of Midland Britannias, drafted in from Eastern Division of the Southern Region, the Scottish Region, the Great Western and The Great Eastern in 1958, were mainly based at Trafford Park, Manchester. However, one or two, such as No 70017, were at Kentish Town for a while.

later Fowler version seemed to be less favoured; being heavier at the front end it may not have ridden as well. On one occasion an ex-Midland 4-4-0 with seven foot diameter driving wheels was called upon in an emergency, and seemed to be doing quite well with a three car peak period train, which may have been shortened for its convenience. The locomotive concerned was No.40421. Tender locomotives were only used on the suburban services in emergencies; there were problems turning them at Barking.

In the early and mid 1950s, LTS line Stanier three-cylinder 2-6-4Ts had regular turns, but later they only appeared when the rostered Midland division locomotive of a through train to Southend was unable to return. Very rarely, such occurrences also brought LTS division BR Standard 2-6-4Ts to the line.

Derby built diesel units started trial running over the line on Sunday 31st October 1959, and took over completely early the next year, apart from a very few through workings to Southend which remained steam-powered, normally by Kentish Town based Fairburn 2-6-4Ts, for a while longer. Regular interval working was introduced at the same time as the diesels. The new dmus reduced the Upper Holloway-Barking time from 36 to 30 minutes. In steam days, some Tottenham and Hampstead line suburban services originated from St Pancras or Midland main line stations, but as from the start of the diesel services, Kentish Town was standardised as the starting point.

Motive power for other passenger trains

The Tilbury boat trains were powered by Cricklewood depot, and could be seen with Black Fives, Ivatt 4MT or Crab 2-6-0s, 2-6-4Ts and even, when locomotives were in short supply, 4F 0-6-0s. Rarely, more exotic locomotives could be seen, such as Compound 4-4-0s (until around 1957) and Jubilee 4-6-0s (from that time on). Diesels first made an appearance from 1960, in the form of BR Sulzer Bo-Bos (Type 24) or Metropolitan Vickers Bo-Bos (Type 28). Motive power for excursions to Southend from Midland main line stations tended to be much the same as that used on boat trains.

Troop trains and other special passenger. workings mainly originated on the Great Eastern section or at various points on the Southern Region. From the Great Eastern K1 or K3 2-6-0s and B1, B2, B12 and B17 4-6-0s appeared, whilst the Southern normally sent unrebuilt light Pacifics, but occasionally N or U 2-6-0s, BR standard Class 5 4-6-0s or even Q1s. Many of the troop trains from the Southern Region Hwere hauled by locomotives from Stewarts Lane depot, and might have originated at a Channel port. By using the Tottenham and Hampstead line, a long detour around central London was involved.

In the summer of 1958, the Great Eastern section sent Metropolitan Cammell diesel multiple units over the line on excursion workings, but this didn't become common.

Specials from the Western Region were repowered in the Willesden area, due to the clearance problems with some ex-Great Western types.

References

H. White, *Long distance commuting from the north of London*, published in Railways South East, Harrow Weald, Middlesex; edition for winter 1989/90.

B. Anwell, *The west London lines*, parts 1 and 2, published in Trains Illustrated, Ian Allan Ltd., Hampton Court, Surrey; editions for September and October 1952.

G. Kitchenside, *The North London line*, parts 1 and 2, published in Railway World, Ian Allan Ltd., Shepperton, Middlesex; editions for April and June 1967.

Ian Allan Ltd., *ABC Locoshed book*, different editions. (Source of data on which Table 2 was based).

Ian Allan Ltd., *The dieselised St. Pancras sub-urban service*, published in Trains Illustrated, edition for February 1960.

R. Cogger and R. Kirkland, *Transfer freight trips to Southern /Region,* part II, published in The Railway World, Cricklewood Broadway, London; edition for January 1954.

G. Allen, *The North London route across the capital*, parts 1 and 2, published in Trains Illustrated, Ian Alan Ltd., Hampton Court, Surrey; editions for March and May, 1954.

Colin Marsden, *BR Diesel & Electric Locomotive Directory*, Oxford Publishing Company, Yeovil, 1991.

Edwin Course, *London Railways*, Batsford Ltd., London, 1962.

H. White, *A regional history of the railways of Great Britain: Volume 3 — Greater London*, Phoenix House, London, 1963.

C. Coles, *Railways through London*, Ian Allan Ltd., London, 1983.

C. Austin, *Snow Hill — London's only cross-city link*, published in Railway World, Ian Allan Ltd., Weybridge; edition for October 1985.

British Rail, *Passenger timetable*, 12th May to 28th September 1986, published by British Railways Board, London.

British Railways, *Passenger service (Eastern Region edition)*, British Railways, edition for 13th June to 18th September 1955.

J. Russell, *A pictorial record of Southern Locomotives*, published by OPC, Yeovil, 1991.

G. W., *Recollections of Bow Works and the North London Railway*, published in Railway World, Ian Allan Ltd., Shepperton, Middlesex; edition for November 1978.

E. Barnes, *The Midland drive for London*, parts 2 and 3, published in Railway World, Ian Allan Ltd., Hampton Court, Surrey; edi-tions for September and November 1962.

Borley and C. Lee, *The North London line*, published in Railway Magazine, Tothill Press Ltd., Westminster; edition for February 1964.

West London Link, photo feature in Railway World, Ian Allan Ltd., Shepperton, Middlesex; edition for December 1973.

Ian Allan Ltd., *Resignalling the London, Tilbury and Southend line*, published in Modern Railways, edition for February 1962.

Ian Allan Ltd., *Three Years of Dieselisation at Devons Road depot*, published in Modern Railways, edition for October 1962.

Tothill Press Ltd., *New Signalboxes at Hackney Downs and Barking,* published in Railway Magazine, edition for May 1960.

New multiple units for the L.M.R., published in The Locomotive Railway and Carriage and Wagon Review, July 1959.

J. Van Riemsdijk, *The London suburban tank engine,* published in Railways South East, Harrow Weald; edition for Summer 1988.

R. J. Essery, *Charlie Smith and the London freights*, published in *Railways South East,* Harrow/Weald; edition for Summer 1989.

J. Morss, *The Palace Gates to North Woolwich line*, published in The Railway Magazine, Tothill Press Ltd., Westminster; edition for September 1962.

Ian Allan Ltd., *The north-east London electrification of the Great Eastern line and the transformation of the Cambridge line*, Trains Illustrated, edition for January 1961.

P. Paton, *The London Tilbury and Southend line since the war — 2*, published in Railway World, Ian Allan Ltd., Hampton Court, Surrey; edition for April 1962.

E. Course, *The foreign goods depots of South London*, published in The Railway Magazine, Tothill Press Ltd., Westminster; edition for November 1958.

B. Perren, *Liverpool Street*, published in Railway World, Ian Allan Ltd., Hampton Court, Surrey; edition for October 1958.

Ivatt 4MT 2-6-0 No.43031 waits to leave St Pancras station in March 1961 with a boat train for Tilbury

THE GREAT WESTERN 2-6-2 TANKS

There were 175 members of the '45xx' Class, of which the first 75 came out with straight-top side tanks holding 1,000 gallons. Nos.4575-99 and 5500-74 came out with sloping-top side tanks enabling them to hold 1,300 gallons. Nos.4500-54 were built between 1906 and 1913, the remainder coming out of works between 1924 and 1929. Initially some of the later ones were allocated to the London area but all had left by 1931, a handful, displaced by dieselisation, returning to Southall to end their days. Essentially branch line engines, they were widely spread throughout the system. No.5531 was recorded at Plymouth Laira shed, 25th September 1960, in lined green, although in early BR years they were black and most remained so until withdrawal.

This typical contribution comes from Dick Riley, one of our regular contributors whose camera skill is matched by a deep knowledge of the subject recorded. In this feature he concentrates attention on a wheel arrangement particularly associated with the GWR and of which many examples were built to a variety of different designs.

With the passage of time 'historical colour', properly described and interpreted, becomes an increasingly important reference source and I have tried in the colour sections of this work to encompass something of the variety which has managed to be recorded in colour down the years — Ed

Sapperton banking engines at Brimscombe Shed, 25th June 1962. These are Nos.4100 and 4124 of the '51xx' Class. The '41xx' were the later-built members of the class which was introduced in 1928 when Collett rebuilt a Churchward '31xx' type to a heavier form. Most of the '51xx' and '41xx' engines were built new to a modified version of this rebuild.

The '61xx' Class, of which 70 were built between 1931 and 1935 to work accelerated London suburban services, were allocated to London Division sheds including Oxford. They were also familiar on Paddington empty stock workings having replaced the '45xx' engines on this duty. They were similar to the '41xx' and '51xx' Class in most respects but had 225psi boiler pressure against the 200psi of the older engines, although construction of these 180 engines, including 50 older engines rebuilt, was phased over a long period from 1929 to 1949. The London suburban services were reorganised in 1955 and following the introduction of diesel multiple units, the 2-6-2Ts began to be allocated elsewhere than London in BR days. No.6135 was at Old Oak Common shed, 23rd June 1957 while in the second picture, former London Division engine No.6119 heads an up stopping train, the 11.40am Newton Abbot to Exeter, past Parson & Clerks Signal Box, near Dawlish, 14th July 1959.

The largest 2-6-2Ts were the original '3150' Class built 1906-8. They were primarily used on banking or piloting at Severn Tunnel Junction, Newton Abbot (for the South Devon banks) and Gloucester (for Sapperton bank). In 1938 it was decided to modernise them with new front ends, 225psi boiler pressure and smaller driving wheels (5ft 3in rather than 5ft 8in). Because of the advent of war, only five were so treated, No.3101 being seen at Stratford upon Avon shed, 21st April 1957.

The earliest series of the '51xx' Class were built as the '3100' Class between 1903 and 1906 and altered to conform, to a degree, to the later '51xx' Class between 1928 and 1930, when taking numbers in the '51xx' series — see earlier view. In 1938 it was decided to update these engines too, and rebuilding had begun, but again the programme was cut short by the war, only ten engines having been rebuilt to the '81xx' Class. As rebuilt they had 5ft 6in as opposed to 5ft 8in driving wheels and their allocation was widespread for such a small class. In the traditional '51xx' Class territory No.8109 was recorded at Leamington Spa, 8th April 1958.

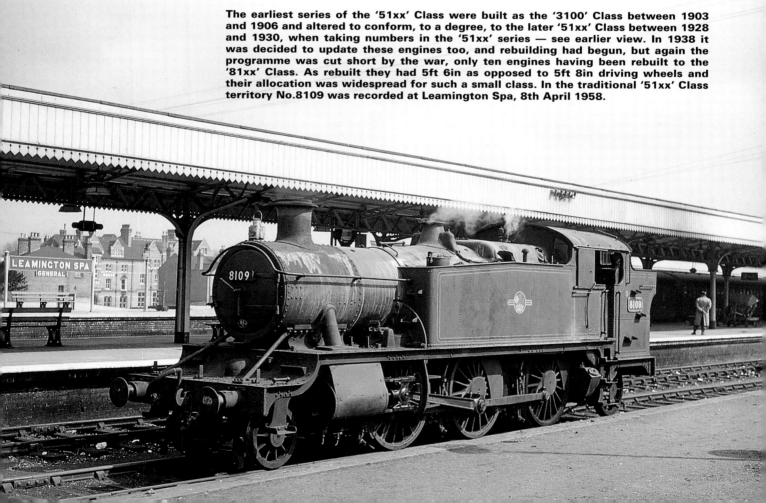

One advantage of these early images is 'rarity value', well exemplified by this example of a very unusual wheel arrangement in Great Britain, the 4-8-0, albeit in tank engine form. Ten were introduced to a North Eastern Railway design in 1909 (NER Class X, LNER Class T1) with five added by the LNER in 1925. No.1350 (one of the original NER examples) was photographed at Hull Dairycoats c.1938.

This picture shows No.3215, an example of the last GWR design of 4-4-0 when the engine was only a couple of years or so old. Their old-fashioned appearance was a consequence of their origins: they were introduced in 1936 as a

VINTAGE COLOUR SCH

The use of colour photography was not widespread until after the British system was nationalised which makes early colour images all the more valuable to the student of railway history. The four views on this page are but a small part of a large collection of early colour pictures recently acquired

'rebuild' using 'Duke' boilers and 'Bulldog' frames — see also 'Great Western Veterans' elsewhere in this book. Known, hardly surprisingly, as 'Dukedogs' they were later

and which will form an important part of a complete colour book of 'pre-BR standard' images which we expect to publish some six to nine months after Bedside Backtrack appears.

In appraising such pictures it is important not to compare them with modern photographic material, for

renumbered in the 9xxx series, No.3215 becoming 9015. In this view, the engine is in plain GWR green with 'shirt button' tender emblem.

ES 1938-48

most of them have been copied from original colour transparencies whose original technology does not permit direct reproduction without an intermediate copy. Nevertheless, their historic interest outweighs any shortfall in photographic quality; and they do have their own charm too.

A particular appeal of some of these early colour pictures is their almost 'oil painting' quality, well exemplified in this view of a down LMS express leaving St. Pancras c.1938 and oozing period atmosphere. The unidentified train is headed by a pair of equally unidentified compound 4-4-0s, a not uncommon pairing on this route in historical terms but getting a little more rare by this time, given that many new 4-6-0s had by now been drafted onto the Midland Division.

Period atmosphere of a quite different kind is represented in this 1948 view, whose slightly out-of-focus original detracts little from the historical value of the scene represented. The picture shows former Southern Railway 'Lord Nelson' Class 4-6-0 No.30856 *Lord St Vincent* and train (stated to be at Poole in August 1948) both in one of the short-lived 1948 experimental BR liveries. The engine is in 'LNER' apple green with 'LNWR' style lining while the carriages are 'plum and spilt milk', again derived from the pre-1923 LNWR.

Former GWR 'Hall' Class 4-6-0 No.4992 *Crosby Hall* in the snow at about 9.00pm, 19th January 1963, on a down Class 'C' freight, probably for Plymouth and/or Penzance, standing on the through road at Exeter St David's between what was then Platforms 2 and 3. This through road was also used for up trains via Exeter Central and the Southern Region — see next view.

Southern Class Z 0-8-0T No.30952 piloting Class N 2-6-0 No.31860 standing in the through road at Exeter St David's and waiting to tackle the steep bank to the nearby Exeter Central (SR) on 3rd November 1962 with the up 5.25pm freight from Torrington to Nine Elms. This picture was taken in the same location as the last view but because of the route configuration at St David's, Southern and Western region services faced opposite ways when heading for London, so 'up' became 'down' (and vice-versa) depending on which route was being taken.

EXETEF

Improved photographic equipment and material allowed cameramen to be ever more venturesome in capturing passing events, but only a few tackled colour at night in the 1960s. If successful it allowed the recording of scenes of a

BY NIGHT

*...particularly appealing and atmospheric kind and in this feature, **A. B. Jeffery** has put together a collection of a few such moments which he witnessed at Exeter during the bitter winter and early spring of 1962-3.*

GWR '14xx' 0-4-2T No.1471 on the 8.05pm Exeter-Dulverton push-pull train (Exe Valley service) in the bay Platform 1 (no longer used for passenger services) at Exeter St David's also on 3rd November 1962. The auto coach at the far end is believed to have been either *Thrush* or *Wren* (built as part of a series of new auto-trailers in the early 1950s) after transfer from the Thames Valley area.

It is hard to remember that some of the preserved locomotives in the National Collection were restored to working order and ran excursion services long before the demise of steam and a decade or more before the establishment of a National Railway Museum. Drummond ex-LSWR Class T9 4-4-0 No.120 was at Exeter Central, c.10.00pm, after working the 'North Cornishman' railtour (Exeter-Wadebridge/Padstow-Exeter) on 24th April 1963. The T9 was painted (incorrectly, since it was not superheated until SR days) in LSWR livery at the time but in more recent years, still in working order, it has been seen in both the correct SR and BR liveries.

All change at Bushey

There has never been a time when change has not affected the railways, but the period of steam-diesel transition was perhaps the most dramatic. It probably 'peaked' in the early 1960s and these views of the scene at Bushey Troughs on one day in 1961 are reasonably typical. The weather was fickle, hence the dull light in one of the pictures, but to record the scene at all 'beggars could not be choosers' in those days; time was running out for some types.

Bushey is at the London end of the celebrated London and Birmingham Railway which, absorbed into the LNWR from 1846, became so successful that it had to be progressively widened, first to four tracks and then (at the southern end) to the six seen here, the nearest pair being the electrified suburban lines to Watford. In this first view, one of the soon-to-vanish LMS 4-6-2s No.46248 *City of Leeds* is in charge of a Liverpool express composed of BR MkI coaches on the 'fast' line and is overtaking a down electric composed of fairly new BR standard multiple unit stock which had also gradually replaced the older LNWR multiple unit stock and its LMS successors.

In this second picture, however, although the down 'outer suburban' service on the 'slow' line, probably for Bletchley or Northampton, is already in charge of recently-introduced diesel power in the shape of an unidentified Birmingham/Sulzer Type 2 (later Class 26), the train itself, apart from the first carriage (BR MkI) is wholly composed of former LMS compartment stock of 1930s vintage. In the foreground can be seen a southbound London Transport Bakerloo Line train of 1938 tube stock. Bakerloo trains used the old LNWR electric lines north of Queens Park during rush hour periods at this time, a legacy of the fact that tube trains on this route were once jointly owned by the LNWR and London Electric Railway. The lines still remain but the trains are now very different. (Cliff Woodhead — 2)

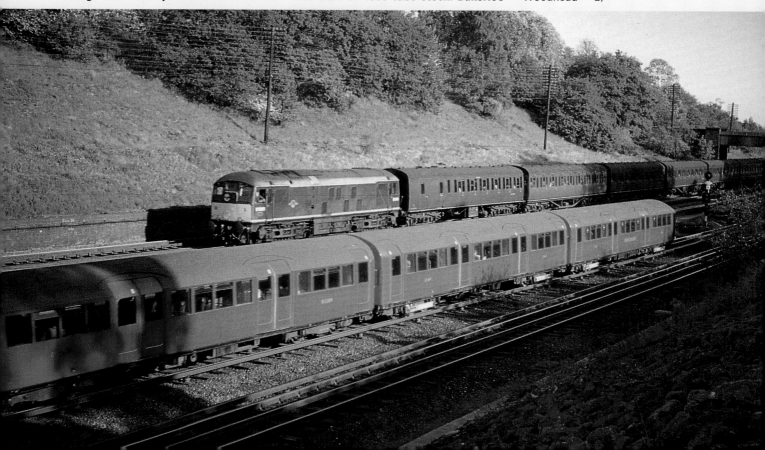

HIGH DRAMA ON RANNOCH MOOR

From time to time we get offered slightly 'offbeat' contributions, sometimes light-hearted, sometimes not, but often contributing to our understanding of the railway story. This feature is one such — an account of a day in the life of one **Jack Ray**, *an author far better known for his railway modelling activities but who, on this occasion, fell victim of a full size railway accident, happily more farcical than tragic in its nature. He was unable to take pictures, for reasons which will become obvious; but it is tale worth telling so we have illustrated it with a choice trio of vintage views of the area in which the events took place.*

The story I am about to tell will hardly find its way into the propaganda handed out by British Rail, for it reflects little credit on some of those concerned. At the time, however, it was infuriatingly frustrating, while in retrospect, like so many things, amusing,.. The incident is recorded in *The Railway Observer,* issued by the RCTS, Volume 44, no.548 for October 1974, and while the gist of that report is true, it

is inaccurate as to detail and naturally contains none of the human aspects of the inci-

Bridge of Orchy Station, North British Railway, on 27th July 1914 at the 'fin de siecle' of the pre-grouping era when railway activity was at a higher level than when the events recounted in this article took place. (H. Patterson Rutherford Collection — NRM)

dent. As one who inadvertently became personally involved in the whole affair, I would like to put the record straight, at the same time relating an entertaining story.

In August 1974 my wife and I were enjoying a Scottish holiday, the first week of which saw us travelling by car, and the second by train, availing ourselves of the touring passes known as *'Freedom of Scotland'* tickets, which allowed us to travel anywhere in Scotland. During the first week, we found ourselves one morning in Pitlochry, a crowded tourist centre from which we escaped by means of the road which ran by Loch Tummel and Loch Rannoch (but *not* Loch Aber — for we were fully aware of that Scottish joke!) – in fact the 'Road to the Isles', immortalised in song. It was a typically Scottish August day, alternating between spells of sunshine and sudden squalls which come racing out of the hills and up the river valleys and then disappear as quickly as they came. The narrow road twisted and turned, bringing us at length to Kinlochrannoch and then on to the remote station of Rannoch on the West Highland Line between Glasgow and Fort William.

The scene was one of utter desolation, awesome in its wild beauty, with miles of undulating moorland and distant mountains. On these bog-infested stretches of barren moorland, many an Irish labourer had become lost whilst seeking employment on the building of railway. Just how that lonely line was built has been told elsewhere — how it does in fact 'float' on the moor, with first a layer of brushwood being put down, covered by a foundation of rocks, and finally thousands of tons of ash upon which was laid the single track. No

writer of romantic fiction could ever conjure up a more desolate scene, or a more unlikely place for a railway station, for there was nothing here but a lonely inn, perched up above the station. The station itself, by Highland standards, was not without importance, boasting not only a long island platform with the usual offices and a passing loop, but also a siding. Signalling, as I remember, was pretty basic — a distant, a home and a starter, possibly an advance starter, but I cannot be sure. Just north of this station the line entered a long viaduct which carried the line over a shallow depression and thereafter climbed up towards the highest point of the West Highland line at Corrour station. To the south the line dropped away in long, sweeping curves on to Rannoch Moor and Bridge of Orchy, the next station towards Glasgow. The whole scene enchanted me and if it looked abandoned and desolate on a fine summer day, what would it look like in the depths of a Scottish winter!?

We arrived at the inn in time for lunch, the only other occupants of the room being a kilted gentleman with a shepherd's crook, a railway employee and possibly one or two others. Very soon we were chatting, such is the warmth of Highland hospitality, and naturally I asked the railwayman about the station and the trains which passed through it. It was not long before I fished out photographs of my 'O' gauge model railway of 'Crewchester', which were passed

round the room and discussed with great enthusiasm and interest. I do not known exactly the official status of my railway friend, but I suspect he shared the duties of porter, signalman and station master. After lunch we joined him on the platform where his wife, apparently also part of the station staff, was attending to the various duties, from sweeping the platform to controlling the signals. I was shown how on these Highland stations the signal levers were housed in the signal box at the north end of the platform, while the block instruments were in the station office which also contained the telephone. While we were there a northbound train was due, so we stopped to watch, although before it arrived another rain squall hit us and passengers took shelter — not in the station building but in the signal box! This cabin was built at platform level and was obviously used as a waiting room. The signal-lady, clad in a blue overall coat, handled the signal levers deftly and with the east of familiarity. The train came and went, winding its way north from the station in a downpour of torrential rain, adding considerably to the bleakness of the scene.

Taking leave of our new-found friends, we continued our journey, now in brilliant sunshine, until a week later we found ourselves in Fort William — and this was in the days of the old station at the southern end of the town. At that time we were based in Perth and had driven across from

there to Crianlarich where we had left the car, intending to be back there in time for dinner at the Crianlarich Hotel at 6.30pm. We had accordingly booked a table for that time. A poet, not unknown in that part of the world, had shrewdly observed that "the best-laid plans of mice and men gang aft up the spoot". and so it was on 2nd August 1974! Our train was the 2.05pm from Mallaig, leaving Fort William some time after 4.00pm and our journey was picturesque but uneventful as far as Rannoch where, to my delight, I saw my signal-lady friend on duty. She seemed, however, somewhat preoccupied for, after a pleasant greeting, she hurried into consultation with the guard of our train. It appeared that there had been a derailment down on the moor between Rannoch and Bridge of Orchy, with the result that the line was blocked.

At this juncture, a new figure emerged on to the scene, a fussy little man clad in the uniform of a stationmaster. He appeared to be in something of a 'flat spin', anxiously disappearing and re-appearing from his office at rapid intervals, obviously at a loss to cope with the situation. The first positive action taken by anyone was a sort of *ad hoc* strike engineered by the kitchen staff of the buffet/restaurant car and the kitchen was closed down. I joined the handful of passengers who had alighted, trying to find the reason for the delay and the blue-clad lady came to me and gave

LNER Class K2/2 2-6-0 No.4674 *Loch Archaig* **on an up express near Bridge of Orchy in 1935. The K2s were to a Gresley GNR design, 4674 itself dating from 1918 and during early LNER days, 1924-5, many of them were transferred to the West Highland section where they proved highly appropriate to the task in hand. Some few years later (1933-4) thirteen of them were also given names of local lochs and fitted with new side-window cabs (as seen in this view), the latter to afford added protection for the crews.** (NRM Collection ML230)

A phone call from Corrour station reported two stranded passengers and, as there was no guarantee of any more trains, could Rannoch help? Signal lady to the rescue again! "Why" she asked the station master, "don't we send the timber train engine up to Corrour to collect the stranded people?" And so the light engine set off for the summit, returning an hour later with two men, the first of whom was not only decidedly the worse for drink, but clutched to himself a full head of antlers. His condition occasioned much mirth among the passengers, but seemed to add considerable anxiety to the man 'in charge' of the situation. Meanwhile, many passengers, weary of the long wait, had made their way up to the inn. Time was getting on; it was now nearly half past seven and we had been stranded here for over two hours. The station master had now taken up a semi-permanent position in the office with the telephone glued to his ear. From time to time he would make negative noises into the instrument, but apart from this there was no sign of human life from him. I stood there, exchanging desultory conversation with the lady who seemed have resigned herself to the fact that her master was now dedicated to a course of masterly inactivity. From time to time the guard looked in to see if there was any news and carried on a whispered conversation with the signal lady, doubtless exchanging comments about the man at the phone. Just after the two left the office I heard the block bell ring 3-3-5 (line cleared). The man reluctantly set down the phone, came over to the instrument but responded with 3-5-5 (Warning Acceptance). He looked at me uncertainly, obviously wondering what I was doing there (and so, for that matter, did I!) I ventured "That was 3-3-5 from Bridge of Orchy — not 3-5-5. I think the section is now clear". He looked as if he were about to burst into tears and hurried to his anchor — the telephone.

I returned to my wife in the train. By now we were beginning to be aware of our lost meal, as, I suspect, many others were. The buffet car now being declared out of bounds to passengers by the staff, there was little we could do about it. I went back to the platform where the guard and the lady signal-person were in glum conference. She turned to me. "The down train has been down at the wreckage for over an hour now — waiting for this train to meet it. I'm going in to see what he is playing at". And she left me with the guard who added his own personal character of the station master.

At length the Master came out on to the platform, walked up to the driver and apparently issued his decision. I heard the driver call out "Half the passengers are up

me the details. A timber train, bound from Crianlarich to Corpach had come off the road down on the moor at about 5.05pm. The driver of the train had gone back through the wreckage to find the guard, still on the verandah of his brake-van, completely demoralised and obviously in shock. He had brought the man in his locomotive up to Rannoch station where he was being tended. The locomotive was still standing in the siding on the down side.

Delay followed delay; people came and went, with no-one quite seeming to know what was happening or what should be done. I joined the signal-lady who had sought refuge in the signal box, and she said "Station-master-huh! He is frightened of his own shadow. If he'd only leave this to me, I'd have this train on its way in half an hour'. She continued "Glasgow have organised a fleet of buses from Pitlochry to come and take London-bound passengers by road to Glasgow, but they won't be here for an hour or more. The guard should be going down the train making a list of London passengers now and telling them that buses will be here soon. Then all we have to do is get this train down to the wreckage, where the down train will be waiting, transfer passengers from one train to the other, and that's it. But that hopeless man can't make up his mind to do anything". Then she said "Come into the office and we'll see what's going on".

We went to the office where the

harassed little station-master was still arguing with the guard about what to do, until the signal lady (I do wish I had known her name!) could bear it no longer, and ignoring the station master she asked the guard "Have you got a list of all passengers for London? They're holding the sleeper at Glasgow until the buses get there". No, the guard had not done anything about that list and nearly an hour had gone by. Tired or waiting for an instructions from Napoleon of Rannoch, he want off to start that list and told me later that almost half the passengers did not understand English (a slight exaggeration, I suspect), but it was the height of the tourist season when many foreign visitors would be on the train. From time to time I went back to report progress — if any — to my wife and, incidentally, the rest of the passengers in our compartment. It was the best-informed compartment in the entire train! Returning to the platform and rather enjoying my unsought but privileged position as 'persona grata' in the office, I met a very worried young man who told me he had to get back to Clacton the next day, and I tried to re-assure him that the buses would soon be there. "Ah, but will they be in time to catch the night sleeper? – I've got a berth booked on it". With an assurance which I did not entirely feel, I told him that the train would be held at Glasgow and made my way back to the office, where our hero was coping with yet another crisis.

in the pub". This obviously brought stalemate to the situation. Having by now established myself as an unauthorised busybody, I went to the window of the locomotive, where the driver grinned at me. "He hasn't a clue, has he!?"

"Try a couple of blasts on your hooter", I suggested and, grinning even more widely, he reached for his lever and sent the echoes flying over the moor with a fanfare to wake the dead. Like a scene from *M. Hulot's Holiday,* a stream of people came running from the inn, across the footbridge, down the steps and back on to the train. The London passengers, thanks to the efforts of the guard, had been safely deposited in the inn to await the buses. We were off — at last: twenty to nine and the sun very low in the sky. I leaned out of the window, chatting to the blue-clad lady, and waited for the sound of the locomotive revving up. Nothing happened. After some further five minutes I said to the lady "If we don't get going soon it is going to be dark by the time we reach the scene of the accident and I do not fancy a stroll over Rannoch Moor in the dark." She agreed with me. "You'll never believe what he's doing now — he's looking for his pilot's arm-band and he can't find it". It took the man less than twenty minutes to unearth the badge of authority and he entered the cab of the locomotive. The time was nine o'clock — three and a half hours after arriving at the station. I hung out of the window to catch my first sight of the wreckage and in about ten minutes the driver eased up to a crawl; the other train could be seen in the distance, standing beyond a few timber wagons and the brake van. As we drew closer I saw the wrecked wagons lying alongside the track, and saw how the track itself had been distorted. We

Gresley Class J39 LNER standard 0-6-0 No.2788 and dating from 1930 in charge of an up through freight between Bridge of Orchy and Tyndrum c.1939. The lack of any signs of human activity, save for that associated with the railway, typifies the landscape of this remote region. (NRM Collection ML231)

came to a halt and the guard unbuckled steps from the end of the corridor and climbed down on to the ballast. I went down with him to lend a hand and soon we had several sets of steps down on to the moor. There was only a very narrow margin of ballast beside the track, and it was only too easy to slide off this and into the spongy bogland. Passengers from the other train were already making their hazardous way along to where our train was standing, many of them encumbered by heavy cases, rucksacks, &c. It was a most peculiar experience, up on that wild moor, with only the sound of the two engines ticking over, and the somewhat forced laughter of weary passengers as they fought their way through the wrecked wagons. The two crews exchanged roles, our driver and guard taking over the other train, and vice versa. We worked for some fifteen minutes in the gathering gloom, for dusk was now falling fast. The highlight of the exchange was when the gentleman with the antlers, helped by his companion, staggered along the track, falling from time to time into the bog but, like the youth who "bore through snow and ice the banner with the strange device", clinging valiantly to his trophy. I shall not forget our combined efforts to get that man and his burden up the steps and into the train — the guard, the companion and myself — and his progress down the

corridor sent passengers flying back into their compartment to avoid mortal injury.

We were propelled through the twilight by our locomotive, the guard leaning out of the end coach with a red-and-green lamp at hand, and I saw something I had never seen from the train before. The red deer, who never ventured near the railway during the day, had come down to feed and we saw them quite clearly — their heads up, ready to flee as this unscheduled train passed — a magnificent sight. At Bridge of Orchy our locomotive ran round and coupled on to the front of the train, so our progress through the famous horeshoe pass and up over Tyndrum Upper was at normal speed. We arrived at Crianlarich at ten o'clock and, after collecting the car and phoning our Perth hotel to warn them that we would not be in until after midnight, repaired to the Crianlarich Hotel, all hope of dinner abandoned. The grille had just been lowered in the bar, but a kindly hotelier offered us turkey sandwiches and hot drinks, which we consumed gratefully before the long drive back to Perth.

A week or so later my son was on holiday in Scotland and passed over the scene of the accident. The wrecked wagons were still lying where they had come to rest and he took one or two photos of the wreckage.

I suppose such dithering ineptitude must be uncommon, but as I never went to Rannoch again, except to pass through, I never again met the good lady or her husband who had made me feel so much a part of that astonishing day. There are no staff now at Rannoch, and footbridge, signals and signal box have all disappeared, the whole thing controlled by some faceless being at Banavie Junction, Fort William. 'Sic transit' ...

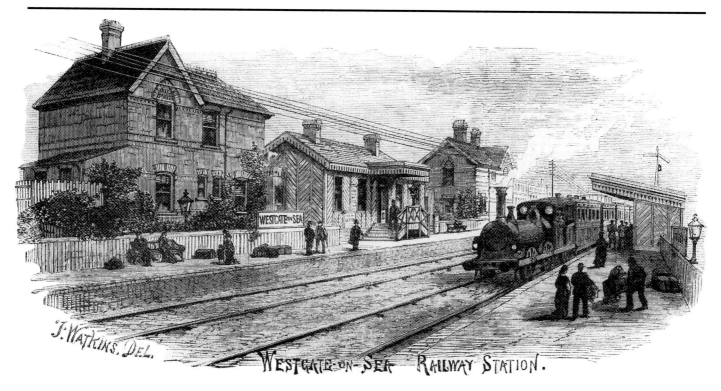

Westgate-on-Sea, a print of 1879. The station buildings are much the same today. (M. D. Mirams)

DOWN THE LINE TO RAMSGATE

A vignette of the early days of railways in the Isle of Thanet

By MICHAEL MIRAMS

The Kent coastal towns of Margate and Ramsgate have figured high in the league table of popular English seaside resorts for many years now, with Margate having celebrated its 250th anniversary as a 'watering-place' during 1986. Until the mid-19th century, travel from the big cities to East Kent was extremely difficult for holidaymakers, and even the Royal Family, who used both towns as summer retreats. The usual means of travel from London to Margate was either by steamship or the hoys, ancient sailing vessels with very basic facilities, which were patronised by those on a tighter budget. These creaky craft took up to three days to make the journey in inclement weather, and passengers arrived at Margate Jetty much the worse for wear.

Making the journey by road was even more hazardous, with the risk of highwaymen and stagecoach accidents preventing many faint-hearted travellers from spending a month at the seaside. So when the Southern Eastern Railway Company decided to extend its London-Dover line from Ashford through Canterbury and on to Ramsgate, shopkeepers and lodging-house proprietors in the Isle of Thanet rubbed their hands in gleeful anticipation. The prospect of numerous visitors and daytrippers stepping out of third-class carriages at Ramsgate, pockets bulging with money begging to be spent, was very pleasant.

The SER line from Canterbury to Ramsgate was opened on Easter Monday 1846 with the first train, consisting of seven first-class carriages, being hauled out of the Bricklayer's Arms terminus in London by an engine of the 'Shakespeare' class. Most of the passengers were SER Company Directors and their friends, but

Ramsgate Town Station, opened in 1846 and closed in 1926. (M. D. Mirams)

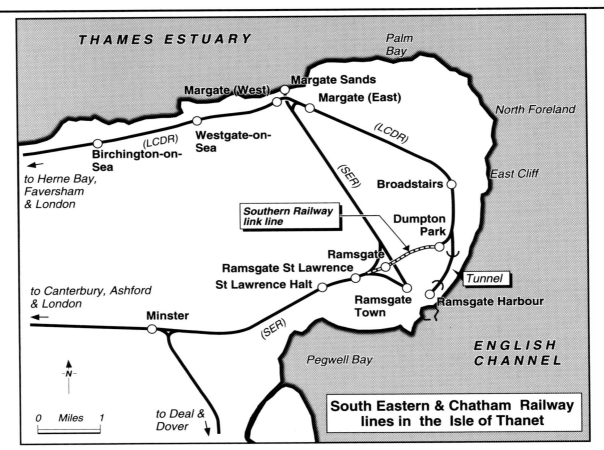

THAMES ESTUARY

Palm Bay

Margate (West)
Margate Sands
Margate (East)

North Foreland

(LCDR)

Westgate-on-Sea

(LCDR)

Birchington-on-Sea

East Cliff

to Herne Bay, Faversham & London

(SER)

Broadstairs

Southern Railway link line

Dumpton Park

to Canterbury, Ashford & London

Ramsgate
Ramsgate St Lawrence
St Lawrence Halt

Tunnel

Minster

Ramsgate Town

Ramsgate Harbour

(SER)

ENGLISH CHANNEL

Pegwell Bay

0   Miles   1

to Deal & Dover

South Eastern & Chatham Railway lines in the Isle of Thanet

The railway shed at Ramsgate Town, showing the extremely narrow central platform. (M. D. Mirams)

at Canterbury the train linked up with a 'special' from Ramsgate, filled with excited townspeople as a treat of the directors. At the new Ramsgate station (the name was changed to Ramsgate Town in 1899), a great crowd of people met the combined trains, and a colourful procession marched through the town to the Albion Hotel, where a banquet was held.

An extension to Margate was opened in December the same year, and this was the end of the SER line. A humble wooden station erected virtually on the sands at Margate was replaced by a fine brick building in 1858. There were no intermediate stations on the Ramsgate-Margate line, which was nearly four miles long. But there were several level-crossings, and a halt was provided at the celebrated Tivoli Pleasure Gardens.

Travellers boarding a Margate-bound train in London faced a long, roundabout journey via Redhill and Tonbridge as well as a tiresome ordeal at Ramsgate, where all trains had to reverse to continue their journey to Margate. A spur to allow through running was not provided until 1863, and this was no doubt prompted by the arrival of another company, the Kent Coast Railway, in Thanet. At the same time a new SER station, St. Lawrence, was opened just a half mile west of the Ramsgate terminus.

After the initial euphoria surrounding the arrival of the railway, disillusioned passengers began levelling complaints against Ramsgate Town, which was one of

A fatal crash at the Harbour Station in August 1891. A Ramsgate oyster-seller was crushed by the engine. (M. D. Mirams)

A schoolboy poses at the East Margate signal box in 1900. The station was closed in 1953. (M. D. Mirams)

tracks crept gradually eastward until Faversham was reached in 1858. An extension to Margate and Ramsgate was authorised in 1861, and the line from Herne Bay onwards was opened two years later.

The first Thanet station was Birchington-on-Sea, close to the village it served, and this was the only stopping place before Margate until 1871, when commuters at the rising resort of Westgate-on-Sea were given their own station. By this time the Kent Coast Railway had become the grandly-styled London, Chatham and Dover Railway. Margate Station stood on the site of the present building (the original water tower has survived), but the LCDR had the audacity to build another station right next to the SER's Margate Sands terminus! It was never used, and became a glorified cafeteria, and then the site of the town's first funfair.

The next station was East Margate, a simple halt serving the outskirts, and then a long run through chalk cuttings and open country brought the line to the present Broadstairs Station. The rails then veered southwards into a 1,638 yard-long, steeply inclined tunnel which emerged on the seafront at the oddly-named Ramsgate & St. Lawrence-on-Sea Station (St. Lawrence village was a long way from any sea!) This building, the terminus of the LCDR line, was built on the site of a Coast Guard Station. It was planned to link the railway with the steamers berthed at the east pier via a horse tramway to the harbour, but this never materialised.

The SER and LCDR lines operated quite separately from 1863 to 1926, although a working agreement in 1899 ended the long feud between the two companies, who joined forces as the South Eastern & Chatham Railway. Some rationalisation brought about station name changes, but it was another quarter of a century before the lines were 'merged', which resulted in the closure of Margate Sands, Ramsgate Town and Ramsgate Harbour stations. The treacherous tunnel was rendered obsolete,

the most inconvenient SER stations in Kent. It consisted of two short platforms with four tracks between them, and a twin-span overall station building with adjacent booking hall. It seems that two platforms would have been quite sufficient, one each for arrivals and departures, but in time an extremely narrow platform was squeezed between the innermost tracks. It was used only for local trains, presumably because local people, unlike visitors, were familiar with the hazards of the central platform. The geographical restraints imposed on the station meant that it could never be much

improved or enlarged, although there was a small station yard running parallel with the main road to Margate.

The Kent Coast Railway reached Thanet in 1863 almost by accident. Originally the North Kent Line was a small project, its main aim to link London with the Medway Towns via Gravesend, but the

St. Lawrence Station, opened in 1846, and closed on rationalisation of the Thanet lines in 1926. The Newington Road bridge has since been rebuilt, a view of c.1911. (M. D. Mirams)

Ramsgate Harbour station on a busy summer's day, an aerial view from the Augusta Steps. This steep incline from the Dumpton area, descending through a tunnel to the station, was the cause of many accidents. The picture is undated. (M. D. Mirams)

A passenger train begins the steep climb from Ramsgate Harbour Station, shortly before the First World War (August 1914). (M. D. Mirams)

and the old lines were linked via a stretch of track between the new Dumpton Park and Ramsgate stations, over a viaduct built from 2,000,000 bricks; this is still the situation some 60 years on.

As with all railways, accidents were frequent on the Thanet lines in the early days, although the SER was generally considered safer than the LCDR. Ramsgate Town however did have its share of mishaps. The first serious accident occurred on 11th August 1858, when a train was being rope-hauled from the ticket platform to the terminus. The ropemen lost control and the carriages piled into the buffers, injuring twenty people.

On 1st August 1864 Margate Sands was the scene of a fatal crash, when a stationary train was hit by another out of control. The last accident of any note at Ramsgate Town was in March 1913, when a goods train locomotive's brakes failed as it entered the station. The guard's van and several trucks smashed through the station building, but there were no casualties.

Accidents were much more common at Ramsgate Harbour, where the line ended at a turntable surrounded by a high brick wall. They were usually caused by engines failing to stop after entering the station, having gathered too much speed in the steep tunnel; and wet weather made things

In March 1913 a goods train went out of control and crashed into the station building at Ramsgate Town. (M. D. Mirams)

Another accident at Ramsgate Harbour Station during the First World War, caused by an engine overrunning the turntable, and then demolishing the boundary wall. (M. D. Mirams)

worse. There was a tragedy on Bank Holiday Monday in August 1891, when an empty excursion train, hauled by a Kirtley L Class 2-4-0 engine, roared through the station, demolished the wall and came to rest on the other side of the road. An oyster seller was crushed to death by the tender. The cause was inadequate braking, as the LCDR locomotive had no vacuum pipe at its leading end to connect with the brake-pipes on the GNR carriages. The two-man crew jumped clear in time, and considering it was holiday time, the number of deaths could have been much greater.

A similar accident happened in March 1915, when a D Class 4-4-0 with ten goods wagons was unable to stop because of the greasy rails. But on this occasion the engine was travelling so slowly that the Stationmaster was able to send warnings to people on the other side of the turntable wall that it was about to be demolished!

Such accidents earned the LCDR the local nickname of the 'Undone, Smashem and Turnover', whereas the ponderous but safer SER line was called the 'Slow, Easy and Comfortable'. No-one was too upset when Ramsgate Harbour Station was closed in 1926, but it proved a devastating blow to the town's holiday trade. The new station was a long way from local amenities and guest houses — a great inconvenience for passengers with heavy luggage; and who could afford taxi fares in the 1920s?

Undated view of the station buildings and turntable at Ramsgate Harbour, which was closed in 1926. (M. D. Mirams)

These two views of Ramsgate Harbour were taken on 4th August 1924 and show the same trains from different angles. They make an interesting comparison with the somewhat similar views in this account taken some ten or more years earlier. (Patterson Rutherford Collection — NRM/2)

BROMSGROVE

and the
LICKEY
INCLINE

A road approach view of Bromsgrove's distinctive buildings before demolition in 1969. The town lies about a mile West of its station along New Road, and until recently open fields intervened. This must have played a part in the decline of passenger traffic. Aston Fields, the area around the station, was once a railway village. (R. C. Swift)

*During steam days, there can have been few more active places than Bromsgrove, at the foot of the famous 1:37 Lickey incline between Bristol and Birmingham. Few, if any, northbound trains failed to take banking assistance and the provision of supplementary power — some of it pretty substantially dimensioned — was the main reason for the presence of a motive power depot at the foot of the bank. In this photo-feature, **Clem Huzzey** takes a look at the scene in its heyday.*

...and the railway side at the same period. The station was opened in June 1840. It enjoyed a brief heyday in its early years as loco centre and engine changing point for the Birmingham & Gloucester Railway. Under the Midland it settled down as a minor node of the system and the interface between the railway and North Worcestershire. Note the start of the fearsome 1 : 37.7 for two miles to the North. In the 1950s the traffic and trains were little changed in principles since late Victorian times, serving and blending with the rural market town. (R. C. Swift)

Fowler 4MT 2-6-4T No.42419 double heads a down local. The sharp curve into the down platform line had to be negotiated with extreme caution, lying as it did at the foot of the incline.

Just as Longbridge dominated local industrial employment, and was reached by bus or car, Central Birmingham was the local focus of office and commercial work. There were well-patronised local trains, from the 0747 arriving about 8.30am in New Street, to the rather grand semi-fast from Malvern Wells, which was distinctly for late starters and shoppers. The former also gave Worcester its first morning service to Birmingham, formed of corridor stock, but sometimes hauled by a 4F 0-6-0. The latter often had a utilitarian-looking but thoroughly competent Ivatt 4MT 4-6-0. Starting at Malvern Wells was a throwback to Midland running powers connecting with the Malvern-Ashchurch branch. (W. N. A. Thompson, courtesy W. H. A. Thompson)

One of the early consequences of nationalisation was the transfer to Bromsgrove of the solitary 2-8-0+0-8-2 LNER Garratt, BR No.69999, rendered redundant in its design role (banking at Worsborough) thanks to electrification of the LNER (ex-Great Central) route across the Pennines via the Woodhead Tunnel. By all accounts it was not as well liked at Bromsgrove as the 'native' power but in these two views in April 1949 it was performing well enough on both freight and passenger duties. It is worth noting that it was orientated so as to work 'cab first' up the bank, whereas former LMS bankers — and all other steam types tried on Lickey for that matter — operated chimney first uphill. (BR — 2)

52

In this attractive May 1949 view, No.69999 is seen running light between turns at Bromsgrove. One reason for its arrival was because of the perceived need for a replacement for the existing Lickey banker, the now elderly ex-MR 0-10-0, BR No.58100, more familiarly known as 'Big Bertha' or 'Big Emma'. There were always other banking engines to be see at Bromsgrove, but after the 0-10-0 was built, there was always one big one available. In the event, the Garratt did not prove a wholly suitable substitute and the eventual long-term replacement for the famous ten-coupled Midland engine was a BR Class 9F 2-10-0. (BR)

The Worsborough Garratt on the move while 'Big Bertha' stands at the bankers' coaling stage. Garrington's bridge is prominent in the background. The solitary four-cylinder 0-10-0 lasted from 1919 to 1956, but in the suburb of Aston Fields around the station a difficult or impossible task was and may still be referred to as 'Firing the Garratt'! Reliable local sources say that this engine was sabotaged because of its appetite for coal. An ex-GW 52XX 2-8-0T and 72XX 2-8-2T were tried at banking for a time but the big Midland engine was eventually replaced by 9F 2-10-0s, notably No.92079. This engine took over the electric headlamp for buffering up to the last vehicle of trains at night. (W. N. A. Thompson, courtesy W. H. A. Thompson)

Class 9F No.92234 banks through the up platform line. This was also the only approach to the incline from the South. Up calling passenger and parcels trains attached their bankers at the platform. Only the very lightest trains were allowed to climb unassisted. The majority of bankers in 1950 were the LMS copies of the Midland 3F 0-6-0Ts, but 94XX pannier tanks appeared later as part of a process of Westernisation. (W. H. A. Thompson)

'Black Five' No.45430 restarts a 'non-stop' express after taking assistance. Bankers ran forward from their stabling point below Garrington's bridge to buffer up to freights in the loops and 'non-stops' such as this on the up main. Wherever the push started, the little tanks would have huge fires, built up while waiting for duty. The red-hot cinders were blown clear out of their chimneys when they ran at the lower part of the Incline. Pyrotechnics were added to the noise, smoke and steam of the bankers working flat out, and onlookers' cars and scenery could be liberally showered. (W. H. A. Thompson)

A 'Black Five' double-heads a 'Jubilee' on an up express. These two classes covered most expresses in the fifties, although 'Patriots' could also be seen. The coaching stock could be Fowler, Gresley, Stanier, Collett, Hawksworth or BR Mark 1. (W. H. A. Thompson)

Ex-Midland Class 2P 4-4-0 No.40426 at the down platform with a 'Blood and Custard' local. Midland diagonal fencing lies behind the platform. The variety of power was remarkable. Compounds were also regulars on lesser trains, or as pilots. The Class 3F Midland 0-6-0s were common sights together with the LMS and MR Class 4F 0-6-0s. The diminutive and venerable MR Class 2F 0-6-0s also paid visits. At the other end of the freight scale were the standard Class 9Fs, while 'Crabs' were seldom assigned to anything which needed to move fast. (W. N. A. Thompson, courtesy W. H. A. Thompson)

A Class 8F 2-8-0 No.48668 heads a mixed freight through the down platform while its train snakes off the Incline. Stanier standard LMS types abounded with these 8Fs and 'Black Fives' at the top of the roster. The Class 5s were the most versatile and arguably the most common class between Birmingham and Bristol on the ex-Midland route. (W. N. A. Thompson, courtesy W. H. A. Thompson)

LMS Class 4P Compound No.41049 wheels a local South beyond Garrington's Works. With the decline of local passenger travel and ticket issue on trains, it is hard to appreciate the work the local service generated. This began early for the station workers. The booking clerk had to open his office about 7.15am. First he date-stamped a good supply of workmen's tickets for the first departure to Birmingham, as the rush of passengers would otherwise delay the train. At around 7.45am there was also a departure to Gloucester. The clerks worked early and late turns with their supervisor on a middle turn. Powder was mixed with water to make the ink, and the dip pens still bore the initials 'M.R.'.

Ten passenger trains stopped in each direction including one each for York and Great Yarmouth. The scope of connections at New Street was huge. To the South, the Somerset & Dorset was reached via Mangotsfield and Bath, giving connections to the Hampshire coast. Bristol was the gateway to destinations in the ex-GW South-West.

Bromsgrove booking office paid out about 120 wage packets per week, for which the cash was collected in a team led by the Stationmaster. Balancing the cash after the packets were made up was satisfying when achieved, but exasperating when under way, because of the many interruptions. (W. N. A. Thompson, courtesy W. H. A. Thompson)

Stanier 'Jubilee' 4-6-0 No.45639 Raleigh at the down platform with an express. Freight vans stand in the background as a reminder of the greater part of rail revenue of the day. There were few originating freight movements. The 3.27pm to Washwood Heath moved salt from nearby Stoke Works. Worcester men and engines hauled the London-bound salt via ex-GW metals. The second departure for Washwood Heath was at 9.50pm. The Wagon Works adjoining the passenger station generated damaged wagons inwards and repaired outwards. Regular messages passed over the telegraph in the station signalbox to Derby about materials for repairs and building dates. Sand originated from nearby Marlbrook destined for mould making in foundries. Tipped from a lorry into the wagons at Bromsgrove, no matter how well it was spread, the weight compacted in one area of the wagon floors. It eventually ceased because of the safety hazard of uneven weight distribution. (W. H. A. Thompson)

Tailpiece:

Bromsgrove regenerated. The station at its smallest was a single up platform, reached from the down main by crossovers. In 1990 two new services were superimposed on the sparse commuter trains. Class 156s started to ply between Birmingham and Cardiff, calling at Bromsgrove. This picture shows the first train of the new service. The footbridge, erected to serve the new wooden down platform, was swung into position only hours before the shot was taken. There was also a new Worcester-Barnt Green shuttle connecting into Birmingham trains. 1992 saw cuts in the shuttle, justified by poor ridership. The service was inadequately publicised and very unreliable. The Cardiff service has now been extended to Nottingham.

So in many guises Bromsgrove station has continued to serve the community. The trains are faster, but few travel. In the fifties people's and railway ways could be very old. Who now would pull up in a chauffeur-driven car to catch a morning train to New Street in top hat and spats? It seems more than 40 years ago! (R. C. Swift)

A Driver's Eye View

By Peter Rawson

Many ex-footplatemen have recorded their working environment in words but very few of them did so with a camera as well. The author is one who did and in this contribution, we feature some of the results. They all date from the 1950s, the last flowering of traditional steam operation before the diesel invasion, and are accompanied by a few of Peter's own stories by way of background.

ABOUT MYSELF

I began work on the railway in July 1942 at Mirfield shed, an ex-Lancashire and Yorkshire Railway motive power depot. After working as a cleaner and passed cleaner, I transferred to Hillhouse shed at Huddersfield to become a fireman. Hillhouse was an ex-London and North Western Railway shed, and there was great rivalry between the men of each depot. Mirfield men, or 'Lanky' men as they were nicknamed, thought that all 'Wessy' men were slovenly, shoddy workmen, while Hillhouse men used to say that if Mirfield men lost sight of the parish church clock, they were lost!

I had been interested in photography for quite some time, but it wasn't until I was given a plate camera by a driver that I got started. Thereafter I often carried a camera with me at work, and occasionally made off-duty visits to other depots, such as York, Old Oak Common or Doncaster. The pictures with this feature are the results of some of my efforts.

During those years none of us realised that steam engines would soon be gone forever and become part of history, so too the 'characters' who worked on them; they were something special with a loyalty to each other not often found today.

To set the scene: two typical views at Leeds Central station in 1956, the heart of the territory in which I worked. The first view (2nd March) shows a pair of former LMS 'Patriot' Class 4-6-0s, original No.45505 *The Royal Army Ordnance Corps* and rebuilt No.45531 *Sir Frederick Harrison* **leaving Leeds with a Newcastle-Liverpool express. This train was routed via Ripon and Harrogate and reversed direction at Leeds, having been brought from Newcastle by former LNER motive power.**

The second view, at the opposite end of the station on 28th September, shows former LNER Class D49/2 No.62765 *The Goathland* **just after joining its train of LNER non-corridors and before the running headlamp had been set in position — the one in view is the rear lamp for the light engine movement. This engine was based at Starbeck, near Harrogate, but the departure from the east end suggests that the train was going to take t**

A Mirfield-Ordsal Lane through freight leaving Mirfield sidings on 7th August 1953 in charge of 'Austerity' 2-8-0 No.90375.

LMS design but BR-built Class 2 2-6-2T No.41264 passing Heaton Lodge with a local passenger working on 19th March 1955. Two LMS brake thirds flank a former L&Y composite.

On the same day, one of the very early LNER Class B1 4-6-0s, now No.61002 *Impala*, passes Heaton Lodge Junction in the Manchester direction with an express formed from ex-LMS stock. On the left can be seen the footbridge over the ex-LNWR line to Leeds.

A Leeds-Liverpool express passing Hillhouse (Huddersfield) in charge of LMS "Jubilee' Class 4-6-0 No.45668 *Madden* on 17th October 1954. The engine is working back in the direction of its home base, Patricroft, and the train is mostly comprised of the still very new BR MkI coaches.

FREDDY

'Austerity' 2-8-0 No.90321 in the up loop at Huddersfield on 30th April 1955 with an ex-LYR saddletank pilot, possibly even Freddy's engine, seen on the left. The impressive signal cabin and the seemingly permanent Rippon Brothers coach works are now long demolished.

The pilot's domain: Hillhouse sidings from the top of the coaling plant on 14th June 1957. Both coaling plant and Hillhouse sheds have now disappeared

Hillhouse shed at Huddersfield, like all other steam sheds on the railway, had its assortment of characters, with outside interests ranging from ballet to boozing. All were good railwaymen, but some were more dedicated than others.

Freddy was a young hand passed cleaner, a quiet shy lad who never got mixed up in the rough and tumble of the cleaning sheds, but seemed to keep himself to himself. During meal breaks in the messroom he could be seen sitting in a corner and reading a book — a film book. Freddy was not only an enthusiast, he was an expert on movies.

When he was not at work he was at the cinema; when the show finished at one, he would go on from there to another. At that time there were about five or six cinemas in Huddersfield and every week Freddy would have seen the show at every one of them — plus some in outlying areas. There wasn't much that Freddy didn't know about the fantasy world of celluloid.

Harold was a young driver, a dedicated railwayman. Apart from being a local scoutmaster, his main interest in life was railways. He attended mutual improvement classes on Sunday mornings and he knew his rule book almost word for word — backwards, forwards and sideways!

But Harold was unhappy; he wanted to educate the rest of us; he loved his rule book in the way the local vicar loved his bible.

And so it came to pass that one fine day Harold was the driver on Hillhouse pilot with the old L&Y saddle tank and Freddy was acting as his fireman. This was Harold's great opportunity to improve on Freddy's edification.

He began by asking him if he had read his rule book lately, to which the reply was "No."

From then on, Harold was in his element; he went through the book, rule by rule, and each time he put a question, Freddy didn't have a clue!

It went on for hours, and poor Fred began to feel smaller and smaller. Finally Freddy said, "Can I ask you a question Harold?"

"Certainly — anything you like," was the reply. Then Freddy dropped his bombshell. "Who was the first Tarzan?" he asked.

...And Harold's face was blank!

THE 'ROMAN CANDLE'

Having spent the first five years of my railway career at Mirfield engine shed which was an ex-Lancashire and Yorkshire railway depot, I got some experience working on ex-L&Y engines. Passenger trains being worked by 2-4-2 radial tank engines and goods trains by 0-6-0 Class A engines.

These ancient machines, built in the late 1800s, needed skillful handling by both driver and fireman. Mirfield men were proud of their engines and of their own expertise in handling them. All enginemen on other companies were lesser mortals, and Hillhouse men, ex-LNWR or 'Wessy' men were classed at about the same level as football hooligans. I must admit however, that firing a radial tank with a Mirfield driver was easier, although there were occasional struggles.

It was some time in the late 1950s that a radial tank arrived at Hillhouse to everyone's dismay. Having been used to Stanier Class 3 2-6-2 tanks for local passenger trains — where the mere sight of a shovel would make the safety valves blow off — this was a disaster.

If she had been in tip-top condition it wouldn't have been so bad; but she was well past her prime. This engine was used for working a Huddersfield to Wakefield express with two coaches to connect with the West Riding Limited. I think the time allowed from Huddersfield to Wakefield Kirkgate was twenty minutes: then we had to run round the train at Kirkgate in order to take it to Westgate station.

The journey to Wakefield wasn't too bad, but the return trip was an all-out struggle. With a white-hot fire to leave Wakefield, a full boiler and the safety valves blowing, we departed in a blaze of glory.

By the time Horbury junction was reached, the fireman was anxiously waiting for the driver to shut off for the junction, in order to put the injector on; she gave us a choice — steam or water — but not both.

The whole journey was spent juggling with the injector and the pressure gauge. It wasn't long before she got the nickname 'The Roman Candle'. It was said that all the firemen who had worked on the 'Roman Candle' were round-shouldered from looking down into the gauge glass, trying to find the water.

The brakes would only work for a few applications before becoming non-existent. This was because the threads on the pull-rods were worn. Drivers developed the art of using the reversing wheel to stop when running light engine — it was easier than trying to slide one's feet!

A fireman told me of a time when they were working the morning trip to Wakefield running bunker first. It was the custom to 'dip' at Thornes troughs to avoid having to put the bag in at Wakefield. The water scoop was worked by a vacuum control, the usual procedure being to move it to 'in' position, then 'out' and 'in' again, and so on, in order to skim the right amount of water from the trough without getting the scoop stuck.

On this occasion, Jack the fireman wasn't quick enough and the scoop refused to come out. Within seconds the tank lids lifted and water shot skywards: the four

Ex-LYR 2-4-2T No.50865 passing through Mirfield en route to Sowerby Bridge on the afternoon Normanton to Sowerby Bridge turn, composed of a mixture of LMS and LYR stock (LYR brake third in the middle). This engine and its sister (see next picture) were both nicknamed 'Roman Candles' by Hillhouse firemen.

vent pipes at each corner of the cab were like the fountains of Rome and great waves crashed over the tank sides down into the cab, cascading on to the floor and through the handrails.

Jack said that his mate stood to attention with his back to the boiler face and his hand on the regulator, with water pouring on him through the roof, "Just like a captain going down with his ship".

As a schoolboy I used to hear my father talk of working trains of eight to ten coaches to Blackpool with a radial tank; he was an honest man, but I don't think he would have managed it with the 'Roman Candle'.

One bright sunny morning I signed on and was given the job of taking her light engine to Crewe to be broken up. We threw out the fire, raked the ashpan and smokebox, and as we started to walk to the station. I looked back at her there standing on the pit. I could well imagine some railway preservationists with tears running down their cheeks; ... but I only had that glorious feeling of revenge!

LYR 2-4-2T No.50725 stands at Hillhouse shed on 15th July 1955 — innocent enough at the moment ...! Note that the engine still carries the old LMS shedcode for Huddersfield — 25B; soon afterwards it became 55G in the NE Region list.

Cab view from No.50725 near Cooper Bridge with a Wakefield to Sowerby Bridge local c.May 1950.

The opposite side cab view taken after arrival at Sowerby Bridge.

HILLHOUSE MEN

Driver Frank Cooper and fireman Clifford Peace turning No.73165 at Stockport (Edgeley) after working an express from Bradford. They then worked the 1.40pm connection with 'The Comet' express back to Bradford. Frank was a magician and escapologist in his spare time. During the war he was offered the chance to go on tour with ENSA but preferred his job on the railway.

The date of these pictures was 5th September 1955 and No.73165 was one of the still fairly new BR Standard Class 5 4-6-0s, developed from the Stanier LMS version and fitted with self cleaning smokebox. By now, Hillhouse carried the 55G shed code, following the transfer of many former LMS/LM Region sheds in the old West Riding of Yorkshire into North Eastern Region administrative control.

A familiar enough sight at Mirfield, albeit of 'Wessy' origin, were the former LNWR 0-8-0s. This is No.49116 'on shed' on 1st March 1954. Funnily enough, they had never carried smokebox number plates during most of their LMS life and this 'feature' remained the case during BR days.

A CURE FOR TOOTHACHE

The job title of 'engine cleaner' was misleading, because engine cleaners rarely cleaned engines. Cleaners were used for just about everything that needed doing in the shed, from floor sweeping, tube sweeping to coal stacking.

I used to like working with the steam raiser, or collecting spares from the station, and even 'knocking up'; but one job I used to dread was helping the coalman when his

One of the pre-grouping 'home' team: former 'Lanky' Class A 0-6-0 No.52236 leaving Mirfield Shed on 1st September 1954.

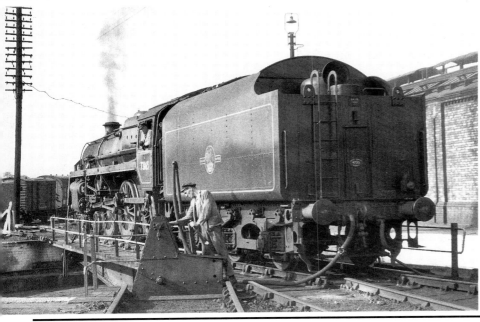

mate failed to turn up for work. Mirfield shed didn't have a coal hopper, but a coaling stage instead. This was a building, open at both ends with a water supply tank on top and a ramp going through the middle.

Wagons full of coal were pushed up the ramp and engines to be coaled came on a track alongside. To start on a full wagon required an engine with a low tender, such as a 'Lanky' Class A 0-6-0, in order to enable the wagon door to be dropped. The two men would stand either side of the door with one foot on the tender and the other on the axlebox of the wagon; they would knock out the door pins, the door would drop and coal showered down on to the tender. When the shower stopped they had to start to dig their way into the wagon, still balanced between wagon and tender. This was hard work, and in addition to the dust and danger was the problem of smoke. Engines went into the coaling stage after having the fire cleaned and made up again. Often there wasn't enough steam left in the boiler for the driver to use the blower to lift the smoke; so that it drifted across the coal stage, choking the coalmen with sulphur fumes.

I arrived at work one afternoon for the 4.00pm to 12.00am shift and was given the job of assisting the coalman, and to make matters worse I had come to work with a raging toothache!

Joe, the coalman, was a cheerful, good-hearted man with a figure that reminded one of a barrel on short spindly legs. He always wore a flat cap and chewed tobacco which he cut at intervals from what looked like a block of chocolate — He said that it helped to keep the dust down. He was well into his fifties and in spite of his size, he was extremely agile as he jumped over the side into the coal wagon.

I followed him and the misery began. We shovelled away together for what seemed to be hours. What with fumes, the uneven floor of the wagon and the awkward working position, it was not long before my shirt was wet with perspiration and I began to ache in every joint. I also began to think that the tender had a hole in the bottom, as it never appeared to be getting any fuller whenever I looked over the side.

Just when I was beginning to think that

The LNER B1s were quite a familiar sight at Mirfield and a fair number of them were from the early batch named after antelopes. This is No.61016 *Inyala* passing Mirfield on 28th September 1956 with a York to Manchester train of mixed LMS and LNER stock.

it would never happen, the driver shouted "She'll do now." We retired to the stuffy little cabin, lit by a gas mantle and heated by a glowing red coal-fired stove, to wait for the next engine to come in.

Joe asked me why I was looking so miserable and I told him that I had toothache. "That's nowt", he said, "I'll soon cure that."

He cut a lump of his chewing tobacco and passed it across. I hesitated, I had never tried chewing tobacco before and didn't fancy it now. "Go on, take it; it'll cure thy toothache," he said. I put it gingerly into my mouth and slowly started to chew.

It was the most terrible and bitter taste that I have experienced, either before or since. As I chewed it became worse and I began to feel a bit strange. We heard the driver shout that he was waiting for us with the next engine and as I followed Joe over into the wagon it was like climbing into a boat ... I was sure that it was swaying up and down!

Looking over the side, I was horrified to see a Stanier Class 5 with an empty tender; it was like gazing into the hold of the *Queen Mary*!

We began shovelling coal which echoed as it hit the steel floor of the tender. It seemed that I had been shovelling coal all my life and would end my days doing nothing else: to make matters worse, the hole in the side of the wagon appeared to be moving from side to side and the gas lamps above began chasing each other about among the smoke.

Then my stomach began to heave and I felt sick. Before midnight arrived and the shift finished we had coaled eight or ten engines and I was firmly of the opinion that the devil himself didn't have premises anywhere near as terrible as the Mirfield coaling stage ... but my toothache had gone!

I started with a picture of rebuilt 'Patriot' No.45531 *Sir Frederick Harrison* so it seems appropriate to conclude with a view of the same engine (now on its own) passing the shed where I started my railway career and with the 'reverse' working of that shown in the first picture: a Liverpool-Newcastle express on 6th July 1956. Behind the train is the coaling stage where I cured my toothache!

Charles Trubshaw

A Victorian Railway Architect

By **S. John Dixey**, RIBA

Apart from the early railway engineers, most locomotive chiefs, a fair number of general managers and a handful of other exalted folk, the actual names of those who were closely involved with the building and evolution of our railways are not often widely known. This is especially true in the field of architecture, that important part of the railway infrastructure which often gave the railway its most obvious and pubic outward presence. This account attempts to redress the balance for just one British railway company which did place great store on such things — the Midland.

Contemporary portrait drawing of Charles Trubshaw. (Author's Collection)

O n the 12th June 1992 Leicester London Road Station celebrated its centenary. On Monday 12th June 1892 the then Mayor of Leicester, Alderman Wright, opened the first part of the completely new station, the booking office. The remainder of the works were completed over the following two years and the old Campbell Street Station of 1840 was closed. Only the stone gate posts remain of the first station in Station Street. Of the 1892 construction the porte-cochére and adjacent offices remain. The booking hall structure is hidden behind 1980s alterations and leads to the recently restored original footbridge and stairs down to the platforms.

The Architect for the station was the Midland Railway Company Architect, Charles Trubshaw, not well known like some of his contemporaries in private practice but responsible for quite prodigious amount of construction work. The company architects were not in the public eye and generally carried out the more mundane tasks. Only very large companies could justify employing them and even then most employed private firms to carry out the more prestigious work. However, the Midland was quite different.

So who was Charles Trubshaw? He came from an architectural family. In 1856 he started his professional education in the office of his father, also named Charles Trubshaw, who was the Architect and Surveyor to the County of Stafford. He was elected an Associate of the Royal Institute of British Architects in 1865. The previous year, 1864, he had joined the Engineering and Architectural Staff of the London and

North Western Railway Company. We do not know of any work he specifically completed with that company though he was there for ten years until 1874 when he was appointed Architect for the Northern Division of the Midland Railway. In 1882 he was elected a Fellow of the Royal Institute, one of his proposers being John Holloway Sanders who was the MR architect for the whole railway up to 1874 and the Southern division until his retirement in 1884, when Trubshaw took over the whole railway. Trubshaw remained with the MR until his retirement in 1905, when he had faithfully served the company for over 30 years. He passed away at Derby on 15th February 1917.

J. L. Randal in his Proposer's statement for Trubshaw's Fellowship of the RIBA in 1882 put forward as examples of work executed under the Candidate's superintendence with which he was acquainted, Skipton and Hellifield Stations, costing respectively £15,000 and £11,000. Trubshaw's statement tells us that between 1874 and 1882 he had been engaged upon:

> "Many passenger stations, dwellings for the company staff ... Goods, Grain and Bonding Warehouses, Engine Shops and Sheds at Leeds, Liverpool, Manchester, Sheffield etc."

Skipton Station was renewed and completed in 1876 and must therefore have been one of his first projects for the Company. Hellifield was later in 1880 when the Lancashire and Yorkshire Railway Branch from Blackburn was opened.

The station is the public face of the railway. Here the travelling public congregate prior to and at the completion of their journeys. Architecturally it is therefore a most important statement. The ease of use and the comfort afforded to the passenger, particularly in the days of competitive travel, could give the edge. This is why major stations were often designed by the important architects of the day. Let us therefore look at the stations being designed by the railways with which Trubshaw may have been involved.

During the latter part of the 1860s the LNWR was an established main line railway and seems to have been content to take over other companies to expand. Twenty-one were absorbed between 1864 and 1874 extending its range of operations into Wales, Cumbria and Derbyshire. These railways came complete with buildings. Any additional buildings to be added were of the LNWR standard timber design which had been evolving from around 1860. Thatto Heath on the Liverpool to St Helens line opened in 1872 is typical of the style. Major work taking place during the period involved the complete rebuilding of Liverpool Lime Street by the Engineer William Baker, the hotel being built to the competition winning design of Alfred Waterhouse.

It would therefore seem unlikely that Trubshaw would have had much involvement with stations whilst with the LNWR.

The Midland, on the other hand, was at the start of an exciting era in the early 1870s. Having been guided by the able managerial hand of James Allport since the 1850s it had opened its own magnificent

Road and platform side views of Skipton station, completed by Trubshaw in 1876 and not very different, apart from such ephemera as posters and notice boards, when photographed here in 1966 and 1970 respectively. (BR LMR, John Edgington)

terminus, St Pancras, in London in 1868. Its hotel, opened in 1873, had been designed by George Gilbert Scott, one of the most prominent Architects of the day. 1873 also saw the appointment of S. W. Johnson as Chief Mechanical Engineer. His beautiful locomotives in their new crimson livery were to enhance the architectural work of Trubshaw and help establish the richness of the Midland's public image. In 1876 the Settle and Carlisle railway was opened and the Midland was now able, in conjunction with the G&SWR, to deal with its own Anglo-Scottish traffic without recourse to agreements with the LNWR and its party.

It is interesting that around the time of Trubshaw's arrival, the Midland was developing a timber frame design. The new platform waiting rooms at Glenfield and Ratby were erected in 1876 and the engine shed at Skipton was completed in 1877. As we know Trubshaw was responsible for the station, it is quite possible that he was involved with the engine shed too. The triangular station at Ambergate was also completed at this time. The majority of the timber buildings constructed were used on platforms under the glazed canopies which became the hallmark of the Midland at its intermediate and larger stations.

Since the early 1860s the Midland appear to have developed a standard layout

Thatto Heath, a typical LNWR standard structure of 1872 and much as built when photographed over a century later in 1984. (Author)

A splendidly evocative view of the imposing frontage of Bradford Forster Square, opened in 1890 and seen here just after the railway grouping in 1924. (John Edgington Collection)

for its small station buildings which was used all over the system, only the elevational treatment varied. The intermediate stations showed more individuality, Mansfield of 1875 was built in an Italianate style being entered through an impressive Venetian entrance.

1880 saw the opening of Manchester Central Station. Sir John Fowler designed the overall roof which still exists. The station offices never materialised in a permanent form and temporary wooden buildings were erected which lasted until the station was rebuilt as an Exhibition Hall (see BACKTRACK Vol.6 No.3). Opposite stands Trubshaw's most well known building, the Midland Hotel. Designed in 1897 following a trip to America with William Towle, the Midland Hotels Manager, to see some big hotels, it was completed in the summer of 1903. A grand design, ten stories high, the building is a mass of vitrified terra-cotta mouldings built upon a foundation of red and grey Aberdeen granite. Other hotels designed by Trubshaw for the company were in Leeds and Bradford.

The major stations built by Trubshaw include Bradford 1890, Gloucester 1896 and Sheffield in 1904. Bradford, Forster Square was built on the site of the old Market Street station. An arcaded screen led into a porte-cochère which fronted the station. An octagonal tower marked the corner of the building. A taller tower of the same design at the other end formed the corner entrance of the hotel. The style is Italianate. Leicester London Road, which followed two years later, was on a similar principle. Heavily ornamented with terra-cotta the porte-cochère has a balustrade interrupted by gables over the arrival arches and by an octagonal clock tower at the city end. The platforms were covered by a three bay steel roof which was completely glazed and spanned between two side walls. The screen wall of glazed yellow and red bricks gave the whole platform area a light and lofty feeling. In the same year

Interior and exterior views of the arcaded screen and port-cochére at Leicester London Road, opened in 1892 and clearly influenced by the Bradford example two years earlier. The pictures were taken during the centenary year in June 1992 and the general state of repair reflects highly creditably upon its present day custodians. (Author — 2)

Derby had its front rebuilt for a Royal visit to the town. A porte-cochére of 1872 was moved to the front of the new building, the design of which blended well with it. However, the octagonal tower was included, though the exuberance of terra-cotta was not. Sheffield used the same arcade for the porte-cochére as Leicester but looked flat. It did not have a tower.

A new design for a standard smaller station had been evolving since the opening of Ilkeston Town in 1879. The chimneys were particularly fine being decorated with terra-cotta plaques and stonework. They show a leaning toward the Arts and Crafts movement style. The style culminated with Saxby in 1892-3 though Coalville Town rebuilt in 1894 showed the same influences. Non-standard buildings also continued to appear. Irchester on the Highham Ferrars branch of 1894 was a half-timbered structure with herringbone brickwork infill. Crosshill and Codnor had a half timbered central section built off a brick plinth.

When Charles Trubshaw retired in 1905 he could look back on a career of some achievement. His buildings had helped enhance the prestige of the Midland Railway from a growing provincial railway system to a vast commercial organisation which was ultimately to shape the destiny of the LMS at grouping. As an architect he was aware of the continuing architectural debate of his day and this was reflected in his work. As a Company man he does not seem to have received the credit he should, the Architect's office being subservient to the Engineering Department. The fact that Leicester Station reached its centenary and the local management are sufficiently proud of it to have celebrated the fact by commissioning a painting to be unveiled by the present Lord Mayor of Leicester, is a tribute to Trubshaw and his work.

Intricate ornament and detail on the impressive Midland Hotel, Manchester, opened in 1903 but still looking good in 1985. (Author)

Arcaded symmetry in the screens at Sheffield, opened 1904 and seen here some eight years later. (BR LMR)

KEADBY

A LOCOMOTIVE COLONY OF THE 'SHEFFIELD COMPANY'

The rapid growth of the iron and steel industry to the south of the Humber estuary in later Victorian years created a great increase in railway traffic and led to more than a few problems which were never wholly solved. In this account, extensively illustrated and including a number of rare and early views, **Bryan Longbone** *outlines the story.*

HISTORICAL BACKGROUND

When the South Yorkshire Railway & River Dun Company opened its railway extension from Thorne to Keadby in 1859 it had no further thought than a service to and from Trentside at Keadby. This short terminal branch ran adjacent to the same company's canal and was initially intended to supplement the existing waterborne traffic from South Yorkshire to the Humber. Being a terminal branch it was deemed necessary to erect an engine shed at Keadby near to the goods yard. The single road structure built was sufficient for the services which passed to and from Doncaster and points west.

On the other side of the river, events were rapidly taking place which placed this railway on to a more industrious footing, the effects of which the Manchester, Sheffield & Lincolnshire Railway (the SYR vesting in this concern by 1874) and the later Great Central Railway, were unable to overcome. For six miles away, at Frodingham, the re-discovery of ironstone and consequent development of a series of ironworks led to the laying down of the local Trent, Ancholme & Grimsby Railway which served this infant industry. These developments required the use of more engines. But operations policy on the MSLR was such that the two large engine sheds at Grimsby and Mexborough provided such engines, the extent of each varying over time.

Keadby was of similar nature to its neighbour at Wrawby Junction (Barnetby) at the other end of the TAGR. During the 1880s both serviced purely local pilot workings with an odd passenger and goods turn daily.

Engines began to be out-shedded to Keadby from Mexborough sometime during the 1886-92 period, taking over a similar function undertaken earlier by Grimsby. By the beginning of the twentieth century, traffic matters at Frodingham, in particular light engine mileage costs, crews' hours of duty, overtime, &c, dictated that engine facilities be located at Frodingham. However, the GCR was unable to afford the cost of land or, alternatively, unwilling to pay the high prices demanded by the landowner. The Great War then intervened and put off further development with

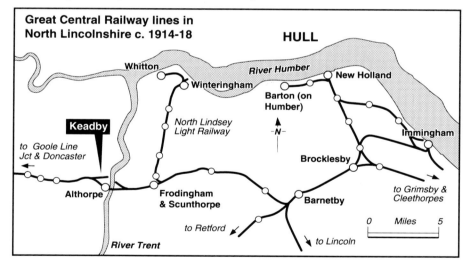

Great Central Railway lines in North Lincolnshire c. 1914-18

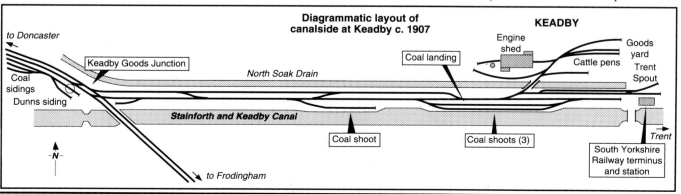

The original Keadby swing bridge across the river Trent, replaced 1916. Two MSLR 0-6-0s (one a pilot engine) on a down train, the first wagon for cattle, the second a coke empty. The bridge signal box is high above the river, and was used for river craft purposes. (Scunthorpe Museum)

A late 1920s view of the rear of the shed area with the North Soak drain crossing the foreground. Q4 No.5356, the nearest engine, was allocated at Keadby from October 1929 onwards. Another example, though, with cut-down chimney and dome, is behind, with a J50 tank and three J11 Pom-poms also beyond. The roof of the shed building is behind. (R. Carpenter)

engine shed at Frodingham. It was not until 1932, and even then with government assistance, that a replacement was opened at Frodingham.

The following account is an attempt to record the activities of the local shed staff at Keadby in putting up with such atrocious local working conditions, the prime example being that only one engine could be under cover at any one time. Keadby may be taken as an example of what could be called 'railway colonies' in this part of the country, for the 'Sheffield Company' possessed similar communities at New Holland and Barnetby which were primarily of railway nature.

Keadby Shed

The shed itself was a simple one-road brick dead-end structure with no frills and sufficed for the demands of the initial single line branch. A turntable was soon laid down at Keadby Junction after the line was opened and work began on the connection with the TAGR. This was in accordance with recommendations of the Board of Trade. Other basic necessities were added but no dates are available and the only detailed picture derives from the period of the 1914-18 war. By this time the coaling of engines was performed under a spartan shelter on top of a coal staith adjacent to the nearby canal, hand-loading being used from a coal wagon direct into the tender below on the running line. Water could be obtained from the nearby canal at the junction where an old locomotive boiler powered a steam pump which extracted from the waterway into an overhead cylindrical storage tank. Water was then gravity fed into the engine tenders and tanks. However, canal water is not the best of raw materials for a boiler, especially at Keadby. Here it was notoriously dirty, hard, as well as saline, due to ingress from the River Trent via the river lock some half-a-mile away. Engine crews, if possible, topped up supplies well before the Keadby/Frodingham area at such localities as Barnetby.

Not until the Great War was there a railway water supply at Frodingham. The

finance difficult to come by. It took an avalanche of protests over the severe congestion at Frodingham from the local iron and steel traders, who had by now a very much larger industrial hold in the area, to impress upon Sir Sam Fay, the GCR general manager, the severity of the problem. Again, with grouping of the railways in one form or another inevitable after the war, the question of engine facilities was further delayed with the LNER inheriting the problem. By this time the single-road shed building and adjacent sidings at Keadby were hosts for upwards of seventy engines or so at weekends. With the bulk of traffic to be moved some five to eight miles away, operating costs were an increasingly heavy charge.

The post-war boom was followed by a slump in all traffics and such events did not prompt the LNER into erecting an

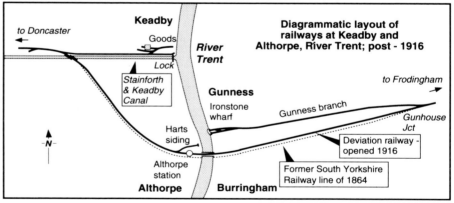

Diagrammatic layout of railways at Keadby and Althorpe, River Trent; post - 1916

Keadby Locks on the South Yorkshire canal. Photograph taken from the Trent bank. This is a LNER-period view with a J11 and a Q4 visible in the sidings. The coaling stage can be seen in the distance on top of a coal staith alongside the canal. (E. Carter Series)

Not Keadby, but no apologies, just a few miles away at Frodingham in 1947. However, J60 No.8962 had been a Keadby stalwart since the 1920s. The van is of interest, displaying — Loco. Running Dept., Packing Van, Keadby — this would accompany any breakdown between Stainforth and Frodingham in GCR days. (C. H. S. Owen)

MSLR Class 23 No.199, built 1865. (Real Photographs)

villagers of Keadby prized a tenderful of 'good' water from areas such as Sheffield and assisted in emptying the odd tender in order to serve their household needs, there was no mains water supply in the area at this time. In fact the 'big men' of Mexborough shed who worked into and lodged at Keadby refused the local brew and had supplies bought in by train from their home area. The turntable at the junction was never enlarged from 43ft 7in and the later engines of GCR design had to journey to Frodingham in order to turn at the North Lincoln Angle. A 'Pom-pom' 0-6-0 was just capable of being turned but larger types were forced to undertake the costly and wasteful trip up to Frodingham.

Old coaching stock and a redundant gasometer were the office and fitting ancillaries. They were located at the rear of the shed and were very much a make-do affair. The company's hesitancy in spending money reflected the GCR's endeavours to purchase a site at Frodingham.

The limited layout of the shed as well as the goods yard was approached via a single line bridge over the North Soak Drain. However, it got to the point where engines had to be accommodated in the sidings alongside the canal. The North Soak Drain separated the 'old main line' from the shed and the goods yard. Adjacent to the canal an ashpit was set down for the then new Class 8A 0-8-0 engines. At weekends, further space was found for engines in the coal sidings across the junction. Here the coal dump was sited and the loading of wagons

during a cold winter was an often-used punishment for a wilful cleaner.

Keadby's Early Engines

Prior to the bridging of the Trent in 1864 the engines which would have worked this branch were a selection from the 28 engines which the SYR possessed at this time. This year also saw the beginning of the MSLR takeover of the SYR. The MSLR was already to the east, at Barnetby, and also to the west of the SYR, at Penistone, and consequent interchanging of the two companies' engines became rapidly evident. This is borne out by observations recorded at the Trent Bridge site, near Keadby, during 1864. This bridge was only open for goods traffic at this period. During the month of May MSLR engines No.23 *Whitmore*, a 0-6-0; No.39 *Mars*, a 0-4-2; and No.74 *Centaur*, a 2-4-0, were recorded. No.39 made the first crossing over the Trent with westbound pig iron on 29th May. This engine was built for the Sheffield, Ashton-under-Lynne & Manchester Railway in 1848. No.74 was a former Great Grimsby & Sheffield Junction engine. The late George Dow, in his history of the Great Central, Volume 2, relates that the four MSLR Class 15 2-4-0 tender engines, originally built for the Sardinian Railway by Beyer Peacock, were used on this Doncaster-Barnetby branch but it is unlikely that they would have been allocated to Keadby being mainly used on through passenger trains.

TABLE. List of MSLR engines noted in the diary of W. Alvey which worked the Mexborough-Frodingham goods

No		Built.
44	Former SA&M Rly. 2nd Class 0-6-0	1849
108	MSL 1st Class 0-6-0	1852
114	MSL 1st Class 0-6-0	1853

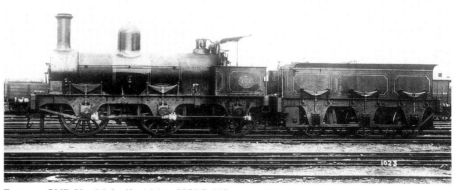

Former SYR No.20 built 1861, MSLR NO.171. (Real Photographs)

Former SYR No.9, built 1844, MSLR NO.160. (Real Photographs)

William Alvey's engine for many a long day, former SYR No.25, built 1864, later MSLR No.176. (Real Photographs)

Early passenger engine. Grimsby locomotive shed hosts MSLR Class 15 No.215. This was one of a series of four 2-4-0s purchased from Beyer-Peacock. According to Dow (_Great Central_ Vol. 2) they were used initially on passenger services between Doncaster and Barnetby, thus along the newly-opened Trent, Ancholme & Grimsby Railway with stations at Keadby. (Real Photographs)

119	MSL 1st Class 0-6-0	1853
124	MSL Class 23 0-6-0	1860
155	Former SYR No.4 0-6-0	1849
157	Former SYR No.6 0-6-0	1849
159	Former SYR No.8 0-6-0	1849
160	Former SYR No.9 0-6-0	1849
165	Former SYR No.14 0-6-0	1856
169	Former SYR No.18 0-6-0	1859
171	Former SYR No.20 0-6-0	1861
172	Former SYR No.21 0-6-0	1861
	(Reb. Class 23 1869)	
173	Former SYR No.22 0-6-0	1862
178	Former SYR No.27 0-6-0	1864
179	Former SYR No.28 0-6-0	1864
195	MSL Class 23 0-6-0	1865
197	MSL Class 23 0-6-0	1865
199	MSL Class 23 0-6-0	1865
200	MSL Class 23 0-6-0	1866
201	MSL Class 23 0-6-0	1866
207	MSL Class 23 0-6-0	1866
283	MSL Class 18 0-6-0	1872
302	MSL Class 18 0-6-0	1872
310	MSL Class 18 0-6-0	1873

The above engines were noted for the years 1867-77 and would have been serviced on many occasions at Keadby shed.

From the 1867-77 diaries of a Mexborough engineman, a William Alvey, a very good idea of the engines utilised on the Mexborough-Keadby goods and the Mexborough-Barnetby pick-up can be gained. The same engine was in use, day-in, day-out, by Alvey on such turns, in particular MSLR Class 23 0-6-0 No.176. other members of this ubiquitous class noted were Nos.174, 175, 195, 196, 202 and 206. Some of these engines were rebuilds of former SYR types. Two other previous SYR engines were very evident, Nos.165 and 173; again, both 0-6-0 tender engines. In addition, two Class 18 0-6-0s, Nos.156 and 322 were later used on the pick-up and Class 6A 0-6-0 No.388 was similarly noted

in 1877. This naturally is only a snapshot of the engines used through and to Keadby. These engines were worked out and returned with their crews with shifts as long as eighteen hours worked, with fifteen to seventeen hours being quite normal. Servicing of these goods engines from Mexborough would have been undertaken at the Trentside shed. On these two services the engines noted in use were all 0-6-0s, this wheel arrangement was rapidly overtaking the earlier and smaller 0-4-2s for ordinary usage and with traffic increasing, the addition of a coupled wheel enhanced the adhesive weight of the engine.

From a survey undertaken by the MSLR during March 1886, only three engines appear to have been allocated to Keadby. One such was No.173 and was engaged as the Keadby pilot engine, shunting and sorting traffic at the junction and for the various coal drops. The driver was C. Mawson and the fireman F. Geeson. They signed on at 5.00am and worked with the engine from 6.00am to 7.00pm, 72 miles being clocked up. The second engine was No.156, a 0-4-2, formerly SYR No.5 _Albion_ of 1848. With this engine, driver W. Adsetts and fireman W. Hock signed on at 5.00am and left for Gunness across the river. Its duty from here was the workmen's train up to Frodingham arriving at 6.20am. Twelve hours shunting was performed at Frodingham and they then returned to Gunness, finally signing off at Keadby shed at 8.15pm. The final engine recorded was Class 18 0-6-0 No.322 built at Gorton in 1874. On this occasion, driver G. Freeman

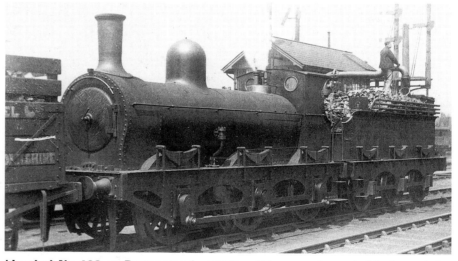

'Jumbo' No.462 at Doncaster in 1902, with a goods probably bound for Marshgate sidings, from where the first wagon, a Frodingham Iron & Steel Company coke wagon, would be worked to Frodingham. No.462 is possibly a Mexborough engine but from this shed, many engines, including 'Jumbos' were outshedded to Keadby. (Ken Nunn Collection)

Class 6C No.45, a 'Jumbo' with later Belpaire firebox and rebuilt cab. This was a Keadby engine from before Grouping until scrapping. (Real Photographs)

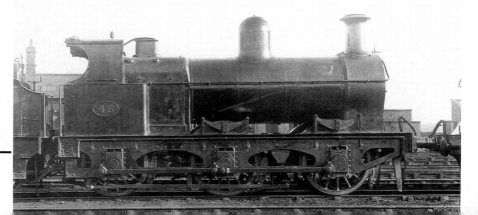

A local engine from the mid-1920s, 'Pom-pom' No.6051 went to Immingham in 1930, here photographed at Gorton. (Real Photographs)

GCR Class 8A No.1144 at Guide Bridge. From Grouping until 1930 this engine was Keadby-based. (Real Photographs)

and fireman John Beech signed on at 6.30am and left with the engine at 7.05am for Hexthorpe, to the west of Doncaster. There followed a return trip to Gunness, back to Doncaster, with intermediate shunting, then a return to Keadby by 4.40pm. Two Doncaster trips were worked in this case compared to the more local work of the two older engines. Additional details are given for these engines:

Engine	Tallow (lbs)	Oil (qts)	Waste (lbs)
156	1	1½	2
173	½	1½	2¼
322	1	2¼	2

This table directly reflects the nature of the engine and the work done by each and the crew. Tallow was a natural lubricant used on wagon axleboxes.

During the nineteenth century the engine facilities and railway staff were relatively small in number. The ironworks at Frodingham and much of its related traffic was worked by South Yorkshire and Grimsby based crews with Keadby engines and men working the local pilots and trips. In 1861 there appear to have been only two drivers based at Keadby but over the next ten years their number increased to six. Of course, the earlier year was prior to the opening of the TAGR and reflected Keadby as a branch terminus. In 1881 there was a decrease to four local drivers but from this period separate maintenance categories are also listed. In this year there were two boilermasters, two engine fitters and a fitter's labourer. The well-known former SYR driver, Joshua Slowen, was one such local man in 1861, still there in 1871 but by 1881 working at Barnetby shed. Some of the drivers were born locally but others came from the nearby industrial areas of Yorkshire and Derbyshire. It is an interesting detail that surnames crop up in later years, even today, through sons going on to work for the railway.

Goods tank engines of the 0-6-2 arrangement principally the Class 9F, and in later years associated with Staveley shed, were based at Keadby during the last

years of the century. Two such engines were involved in a fatal collision in fog at Gunhouse Junction in November 1899.

World War I and later

Moving on to 1915-20, further details become available of Keadby's engine stock. Mexborough engines were still outshedded to Keadby but some of the larger goods types were known to have an enamel plate, lettered 'K', inside the cab. What is in no doubt though was that there were more engines. The expansion of the Frodingham iron and steel industries, coupled with increased outputs during the 1914-18 war, warranted a much larger and more permanent stud of locally-based engines. Assistance from engines and crews based at Immingham shed in working services from the Frodingham area in the easterly direction was resorted to. The predominant types working the goods traffic were still the various MSLR 0-6-0 tender engines: Class 6C 'Jumbos', Class 18, Class 9 'Claddies' with the Class 8A 0-8-0 'Tinys', Class 8K 2-8-0s and Class 9J 0-6-0 'Pom-poms' on the increase. Just prior to and after Grouping many of the 'Jumbos' were replaced by 'Claddies'. These classes made way for the 'Tinys' and finally the ROD/O4 classes.

'Jumbos' recorded during this period include Nos.3, 30, 34, 35, 45, 46, 463, 472, 488 and 493, some still with their original round-topped fireboxes. 'Claddies' recalled include Nos.566, 568 and 571. In addition there were some 9F 0-6-2 tank engines which worked the workmen's trains and local passenger services on the North Lindsey Light Railway up to Winteringham and Whitton. Engines of this class remembered were 530, 745, 746, 1059 and 1063. Engines employed on the Keadby pilot duties were Class 18T 0-6-0 saddle tanks. Nos.345, 413 and 418 were rebuilds of earlier tender engines; they possessed a handbrake only and this worked on wooden blocks. These engines rapidly gave way to the LNER J50 tanks after the Grouping.

The GCR Class 1B 2-6-4 'Crab' tanks, locally known as 'Zeppelins' (this possibly dating their introduction to the area) were represented for a time. Initially they worked coal trains into Frodingham from South Yorkshire. However, they lacked braking power on such trains but, otherwise, they were excellent machines and for the remainder of their early stay at Keadby were employed on the heavy pilot and banking duties at Frodingham. In 1916 some of the oldest drivers still had their own engines, for example Fred Groves with No.3 and John Beech with No.34, both engines being 'Jumbos'.

The influx of ROD 2-8-0s on to the GCR and LNER accelerated the decline of the former MSLR 0-6-0 engines. Class 6 'Tinys' and the Class 7 2-8-0s (this being a power classification), along with the larger boilered GCR 8M/LNER O5 2-8-0s from Mexborough became fixtures.

After the 1923 Grouping, so-called 'foreign' engines began to appear including various former GNR types, Class 'A' and 'B' 0-6-0s and the 'Long Tom' 0-8-0s; others were examples of former GER and NER classes. These visitors were not often appreciated by the local railwaymen. They preferred the sturdy and comfortable Robinson designs, engines which were less fickle and did not require as much attention. Also they could be more readily

A latter-day GCR period photograph (note pop valves) of 'Tiny' No.139. A short period was spent at Immingham, but otherwise No.139 was a Keadby engine from 1923 at least and moved up to Frodingham shed in 1932. (Real Photographs)

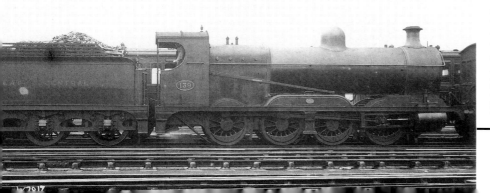

'Tiny', or LNER Class Q4, No.5151 at Ardsley engine shed. This was from October 1929, a Keadby/Frodingham engine thereafter. Note the blast furnace of the West Yorkshire Iron Company with in the background. (Real Photographs)

Another Ardsley photograph from where Q4 No.6073 was based from 1927. Two years later the engine moved to Keadby and remained there into Frodingham shed days. (B. R. Longbone Collection

thrashed, this possibly having something to do with Robinson's boiler and frame design.

During the Great War there were about 50 engine crews with a further 50 or so other staff of all grades at the shed. The earliest known senior position at Keadby shed appeared to be fitter-in-charge; a J. T. Booth had this job from January 1901 to December 1903 (his wage rising from £2-10-0 [£2.50] to £2-17-6 [£2.87] per week) when he transferred to Lincoln as a foreman. G. J. Johnson followed as foreman at Keadby, coming from Mexborough, with his payment rising from £130 to £145 per year when he left for Wrexham during January 1905 as Assistant District Foreman, the GCR having recently taken over the Wrexham, Mold & Connah's Quay Railway. A T. E. Morris followed as foreman at Keadby and he remained until September 1916 with his salary rising from an initial £177 per year to £180 upon leaving to be foreman at Lincoln. Another Mexborough man followed, one Sammy Hoole; he had been the Assistant Locomotive Foreman at Mexborough shed. His background was as a fitter, something of which the Keadby staff took advantage; when the shed fitters pretended ignorance of a job, Sammy would 'muck-in' and do the job himself. Hoole's position as Locomotive Foreman at Keadby shed initially earned him £180 per year but with war rises and inflation he was earning £350 per year by August 1919. He was still in charge with the change to the LNER and

with the locomotive facilities moving to the new shed at Frodingham during 1932.

By the war of 1914-18, and shortly after, six fitters were employed at the shed, one on the night shift and the remainder on days. One or two worked as required on stopwork, that is such work as front end, valves and brakes. In 1915 there were about fifteen cleaners per shift, two shifts per day of ten hours each; one boilersmith on days and another on nights, each with a mate. In addition, working days, was Tommy Maud, formerly of New Holland shed, changing tubes on stopped engines along with two wash-out men. The day foreman was in charge of the cleaners and shed shunting; no doubt in Keadby's case, this would be continuous. His corresponding number on nights worked out the relief roster and saw to it that all the jobs arising were adequately covered with engines and men. In this year Dick Mawson was the shed clerk in the office, making out the daily roster and with him was the telephone lad, who also booked the men on and off duty.

Many railwaymen moved up to the Scunthorpe area when the new shed was completed. The shed at Keadby was then used as a store but, even before this, the roof was apt to drop in. No doubt the shed staff and train crews appreciated the change in conditions and facilities at the new Frodingham site at first, but it wasn't long before the exigencies of World War II affected an increasingly busy traffic centre. And by the 1950s the reinforced concrete shed at Frodingham was well under attack from the corrosive chemical dust and fumes emitted from the nearby melting shops, coke ovens and mills. The fresh air of Trentside was all but a memory for most.

Even in such a relatively short article as the above there has been much information from former Keadby enginemen, now, alas, no longer alive. If individuals have to be named then Bill Leeman was paramount but others included Les Amery, Fred Digby, Harland Phillipson and George Fussey. The many chats the author had with these gentlemen was always informative as well as entertaining.

In addition, Scunthorpe Central Library, Gainsborough Library and the Archives of the Great Central Railway Society have been most helpful. Lastly I would like to thank Ron Fareham and David Jackson for hints and assistance.

Examples of the GCR Class 1B had been used in the area during GCR ownership, but it was not until June 1929 when No.5367 moved from Immingham to Keadby. However, it did not remain long, returning five months later, but recorded on many occasions by G. R. Spence. It returned to Frodingham during 1948. (Real Photographs)

THE GOODS GUARD AND HIS BRAKE

*Right until the end of steam — and for more than a few years afterwards — the loose coupled goods train was a familiar sight on the railways of Britain and the 'goods guard' had a vital role to play — often more important than the driver if truth be told. Right at the end of the story, **Dr M. H. Yardley** recorded a few typical examples with his camera and they are offered here as a pictorial memory of the sort of practices which dated back for almost a century and which were near-archaic during most of that time!*

Most freight traffic for the Bootle branch was tripped from Edge Hill's Park Sidings or Exhibition Junction Sidings, neither of which gave direct access to the branch. Trains were marshalled with a brake van at each end, and would set off toward Manchester, the locomotive running round at Pighue Lane Junction. On 22nd April 1968 Class 8F No.48692 pulled a trip working to Alexandra Dock out of Park Sidings as the guard looked back along his train.

Arranging and shunting the train at minor sidings and depots was the responsibility of the train crew. A flask of radioactive waste from Sizewell Power Station was picked up by Class 31 No.5861 on 16th April 1969, to be placed in the middle of a short rake of empty coal wagons from Leiston for the run back to Ipswich, the first leg of its long journey to Sellafield.

Sometimes the guard was assisted by a travelling shunter. The remains of the Ellesmere/Wrexham branch, then extending only as far as Cadbury's Factory near Bangor-on-Dee, had several sidings in its few miles, but it was surprising to see two shunters climb aboard as Pannier tank No.9610 restarted the freight onto the branch at Wrexham Central on 25th July 1966.

After closure of a line, point mechanisms were often disconnected, even if signals remained in position. The demolition train on the Somerset & Dorset line behind Hymek Class 35 No.D7003 waited at Midsomer Norton as the guard wedged the facing point before proceeding down the hill to Radstock and Bristol, on 28th March 1968.

An essential part of the guard's duties was to ensure that the driver knew the length, weight and brake power of his train. The driver of Class 52 No.1016 *Western Gladiator* waited for the guard to give him the details before leaving Radstock with the 1.20pm coal train to Portishead on 23rd February 1970. Since closure of the direct route to Bristol the route was via Westbury, Bath and St Philips Marsh.

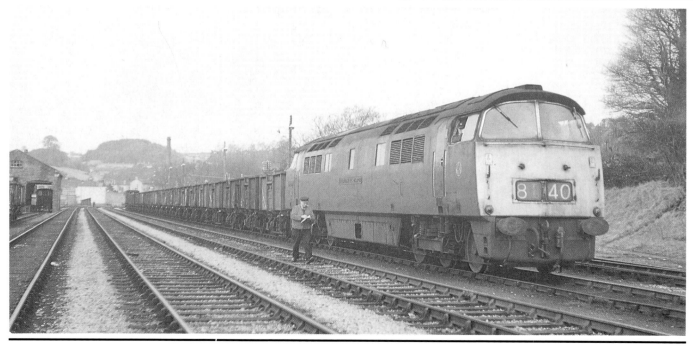

Many level crossings, even over minor roads, kept their gates long after the loss of crossing keepers which followed closure to passengers. There were no less than seven such crossings in the three miles from Brymbo to Minera on the branch from Wrexham. Normal practice was for the fireman to open the gates and the guard to close them behind the train. On 18th June 1966, traffic was heavy enough to need a pannier tank at each end of the train, and the guard hitched a lift on the banker, No.9610, as it followed the train over Berwig Crossing where the passenger service, withdrawn in 1931, terminated.

At small depots and sidings the guard was in charge of shunting operations, his shunter's pole being an essential item of equipment in the days of loose-coupled vehicles. As Class 8F No.48754 shunted the sidings at Rhydymwyn, near Mold, on 18th April 1967, the guard walked toward the top of the yard, shunter's pole over his shoulder, ready to uncouple wagons for the locomotive to propel back into the sidings.

In minor locations the guard had to check which wagons were ready for despatch. At East Rudham, on the former M&GN line, Class 31 No.D5638 backed into the sidings to pick up its train for return to Kings Lynn as the guard checked wagon labels.

It was the responsibility of the guard to ensure that his train had enough brake power to descend gradients safely, which included pinning down brakes on individual wagons when there were not enough continuously-braked wagons. After propelling a load of iron ore out of the sidings at Ullcoates Mine, Workington's Ivatt Class 4 2-6-0 No.43008 re-started its train down the steep branch onto the Whitehaven Cleator & Egremont line as the fireman and guard, wielding brake sticks, made sure that all wagon brakes were pinned down securely on 14th December 1967.

When things go wrong away from a main centre the train crew has to sort them out if possible. The branch to Beckton Gasworks crossed the approach road to the Woolwich Ferry at Backton Crossing, which was unmanned. As Class 11 No.12130 drew its train of empty mineral wagons across the road on 21st May 1969 a crossing gate swung back into the train, fortunately without derailing the wagon, but holding up traffic while the guard and second-man cleared up the mess.

EARLY PULLMANS
A REVISIONIST HISTORY

By **Anthony Bower and Charles Long**

Much confusion (a fair amount of it recorded in print) surrounds the story of the early introduction of Pullman cars into Britain and Europe and much ill-researched speculation has often become set in 'tablets of stone' in consequence. In this newly researched contribution to the story, the authors have wisely gone back to prime sources in order to separate fact from fiction and their findings may well surprise more than a few who thought they knew all about Pullmans!

Because the bulk of the British Pullman Car Company's own records were destroyed during an air raid in World War 2, later chroniclers of the early years of Pullman operations in Britain have sometimes drawn on second- and third-hand evidence, some of which has subsequently proved to be of very questionable value. In recent years, however, a number of complementary primary sources of information have become more accessible — although, inconveniently for the lone researcher, they are divided between Britain and the United States. Until 1907, it should be remembered, the British company was a subsidiary of the American Pullman organisation.

Unbeknown to each other, the present writers had for some time been independently exploring different areas of this 'new' archive material. For various reasons, each of us had begun to have nagging doubts about a number of published statements on the provenance and the subsequent history of some of the earliest American-built Pullman cars that saw service on Britain's railways. But it was only when we eventually met (through membership of the Pullman Society) and compared notes that the individual pieces of a complex jigsaw finally began to fall into place,

and a more coherent and, we trust, a more reliable picture started to emerge.

In this article, we have identified all sources of 'new' information and, where there remains uncertainty, we have said so. Although our central thesis is essentially based directly on our own research, some supporting evidence and incidental information has been drawn from two recent American publications themselves largely derived from unimpeachable primary

source material. The first is *Palace Car Prince*, by Liston E. Leyendecker (Colorado University Press). Rather surprisingly, perhaps, this is the first-ever full-length biography of George Mortimer Pullman, founder-President of the organisation that was to make him one of the most powerful figures in American industry and brought the Pullman name recognition throughout the western world. The book draws extensively on the diaries of Pullman's wife, Harriet (Hattie), and other private family papers to which Professor Leyendecker was given privileged access. The other publication we consulted is *The Palace Cars*, by Ralph L. Barger (Kalmbach-Greenberg). The second in a projected seven-volume history of all 22,000-plus vehicles built by (or for) the American Pullman company, Mr. Barger's book surveys all the wooden-bodied Pullman cars (including export cars) constructed between the late 1850s and the early 1900s, based mainly on data taken from the original Pullman works Lot Books now lodged in the Newberry Library, Chicago. This material supplements our own, separate, examination of other Pullman records in the Newberry Library.

In February 1873, the Midland Railway became the first British railway to invite George Pullman to supply, and operate under contract, American-style sleepers and parlor[1] (semi-open saloon) luxury day cars over its system. Pullman's prospectus had been warmly commended to the MR's Board and shareholders by the railway's General Manager, James Allport, who had made a fact-finding visit to the United States and Canada the year before, and had evidently been much impressed by what he had seen. Previous British accounts of Allport's North American trip have always given the impression that it had been undertaken solely on his own initiative, but it now appears that it had probably been directly prompted by Pullman himself.

Accompanied by Hattie, George Pullman had made *his* first trans-Atlantic crossing to tour Britain and Europe between August and October 1870.[2] While this was primarily intended as a holiday trip, it would have been wholly uncharacteristic of the man not to have been alive to any opportunity that might present itself to extend his business interests overseas. It was on the voyage from New York that he had made the acquaintance of Colonel Georges Gourand,[3] who was later be become his first resident representative in Europe. And, right at the end of their tour, the Pullmans returned to Liverpool from London via Derby, where, on the morning of Thursday 6th October, George Pullman had arranged to meet James Allport.[4] While, so far as we are aware, there is no surviving record of their conversation, it is surely inconceivable that it did not centre on their mutual interest in the railway business. While it is more than likely that Pullman had also approached other key railway managers during his trip, it was

At a time when 'footwarmers' (containers of hot water hired from principal stations) provided the only form of train heating in Britain, the American-built Pullman cars introduced the circulating hot-water system diagrammatically illustrated here. According to an American source, the safety valve was set to a pressure of 150lb.

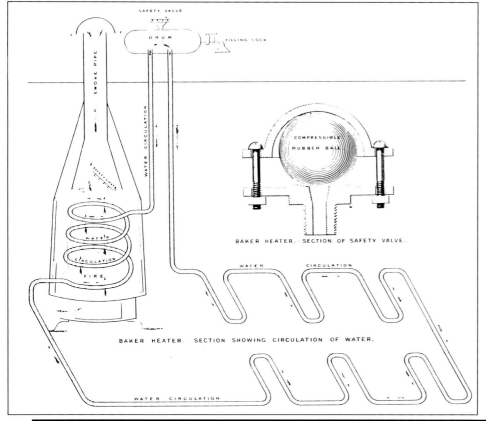

BAKER HEATER. SECTION OF SAFETY VALVE.

BAKER HEATER. SECTION SHOWING CIRCULATION OF WATER.

An 1871 advertisement for the Baker heating system.

the seeds sown by his contact with Allport that, just over two years later, were the first to bear fruit.

Under the 1873 agreement with the Midland Railway, Pullman initially contracted to supply three sleeping cars and three parlor cars, plus eight non-supplementary-fare day cars (four first/second-class composites and four van thirds).[5] These substantial, end-entrance bogie vehicles, equipped with toilets and coke-fired boilers supplying hot-water heating coils, were considerably larger and heavier than the unplumbed and unheated lightweight six-wheel side-door compartment coaches then usual in British main-line service. The new cars were built, largely in pre-fabricated sections, at the Pullman Car Works in Detroit, Michigan, under the following lot numbers:

• Lot 19/Plan 38 sleepers: *Enterprise; Excelsior; Midland;*
• Lot 20/Plan 39 parlors: *Britannia; Leo; Victoria;*
• Lot 21/Plan 41 composites: *Nos.5-8;*
• Lot 22/Plan 42 van thirds: *Nos.1-4.*[6]

The construction was sectionalised because the various parts were to be shipped to England in knocked-down form for final assembly at Derby, in sheds leased to the Pullman company by the Midland Railway.[7] Work proceeded quickly and by late-June/early-July 1873 the first consignment of 200 bundles and 70 boxes of car timbers were taken from Detroit across the Canadian border to Montreal, and loaded on the ss *Missouri*, one of five Dominion Line vessels used to convey the materials to England. The *Missouri* tied up at Huskisson's Dock, Liverpool, on 21st July, where the cargo was received by Albert Pullman, George's brother and Second Vice-President of Pullman's Palace Car Company,[8] and Aaron Longstreet, Superintendent of Construction at Detroit, who had both arrived earlier from New

Cross and longitudinal sections of a standard Pullman sleeping car of the mid 1870s, showing both 'day' and 'night' positions. In Pullman terminology, each seating/berth bay was known as a 'section'.

Scale ³⁄₈ in = 1ft.

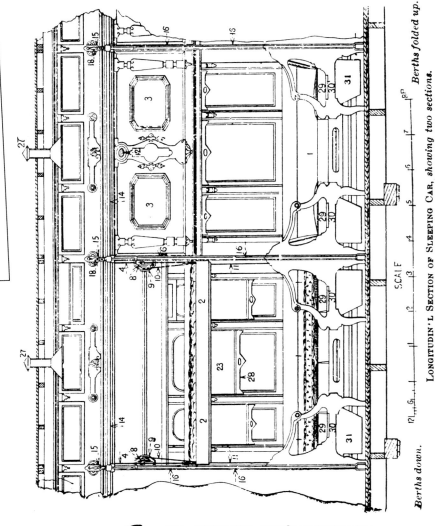

Berths folded up.

LONGITUDIN'L SECTION OF SLEEPING CAR, *showing two sections.*

Berths down.

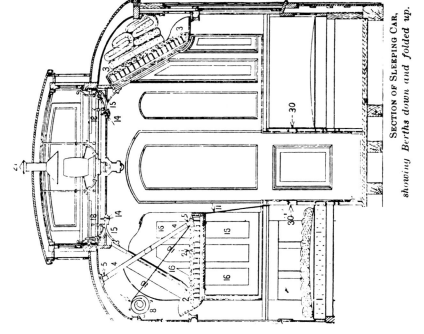

SECTION OF SLEEPING CAR,
showing Berths down and folded up.

PULLMAN DRAWING-ROOM CAR FOR THE MIDLAND RAILWAY.

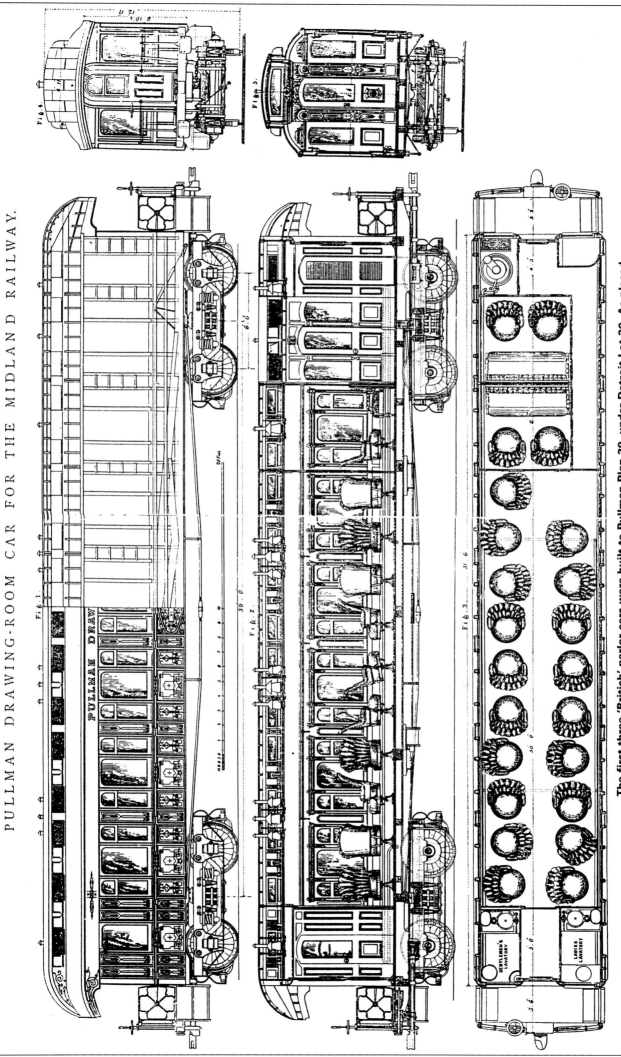

The first three 'British' parlor cars were built to Pullman Plan 39, under Detroit Lot 20. As placed in service, the car had two fewer revolving seats in the saloon area than shown in this well-known drawing first published in the issue of *Engineering* for 2nd April 1875. Scale: 4mm = 1ft.

York on the ss *Baltic*. They arranged for the transfer of the materials to Derby, where Longstreet was to remain to supervise the assembly of the cars.

Later consignments on Dominion Line ships from Montreal can be identified from the Customs records:

- Liverpool, 1st August — ss *Neera*, with "51 bxs [boxes], 163 pkgs [packages] & 44 ps [parcels] car timber. 112 car springs";
- Liverpool, 15th August — ss *Palestine*, with "30 pkgs carr timber";
- London, 2nd October — ss *Palestine*, with "575 pkgs car materials";
- Liverpool, 13th October — ss *Memphis*, with "12 buffers, 21 bdls [bundles] springs, 74 pkgs car materials, 20 equalisers, 6 draw bars";
- Liverpool, 24th October — ss *Mississippi*, with "12 bxs car materials, 16 draw bars, 10 equalisers, 92 pedestals" (presumably for parlor-car swivel chairs).[9]

During the same period other ships had arrived direct from New York with small unitemised consignments specifically for the Midland Railway; while one cannot be certain what these contained, it seems likely that they included tools and other workshop equipment from Pullman's maintenance facility at Elmira, New York State.

Contrary to the impression given in a number of accounts published in recent years, it is not possible to specify precisely when the first cars emerged from the Derby erecting shops, or the order in which they appeared. What is clear, however, is that at least two cars must have been available by early January 1874 (some weeks earlier than commonly supposed), since, on the 20th of that month, James Allport reported to the Midland Railway Board that, in order to check clearances through bridges and tunnels and "passing each other", they had already run "on every portion of the line, with the exception of the part between Ambergate and Leeds".[10] The earliest positive identification of individual vehicles we have been able to trace are of the sleeping car, *Midland*, and the parlor car, *Leo*, which, on 5th February, were "accidentally" discovered by a Northern newspaper correspondent "in an obscure siding" near St. Pancras, where they were being prepared for a trial run to Bedford and back the following day.[11] With Albert Pullman and Col. Gourand conveniently on hand to answer questions, this curious incident has all the hallmarks of a tip-off to a favoured journalist! *Midland* and *Leo* were again named in an account of a demonstration run for invited guests over the same route on 21st February.[12] Besides representatives of the trade press, those on board included Sir Daniel Gooch, James Staats Forbes and "gentlemen interested in the Russian and other foreign railways". Yet another press report claimed that *all* the sleepers and parlor cars had been completed by 28th February — and listed their names.[13]

Although none of the newspaper reports we have seen identifies the two sleepers and two parlor cars[14] used on the celebrated general press trip between St. Pancras and Bedford on 21st March (about which the *Daily News* correspondent opined, "Literally, nothing seemed left to desire"), it is now clear that *Midland* was *not* part of the formation as has often been claimed.

That would have been impossible, because the car was no longer in England.

In its issue of 28th February, *The Railway Record* had reported that Albert Pullman and Col. Gourand were staying at the Midland Grand Hotel, St. Pancras, drawing up plans "for the adoption of [the Pullman] system on all the principal railways of Europe". As a follow-up to the promotional run on 21st February, a Pullman sleeping car was to be taken on an extended tour of Continental railway systems. The vehicle chosen was *Midland*. On 7th March, it was recorded that the demonstration car was to be transported as deck cargo on a barge to be towed from London's East India Dock to Dunkirk.[15] The Midland Railway's shipping agents, Chinnery & Johnson, made the detailed arrangements for the voyage, and Customs clearance was noted on 19th March.[16] This is more than *three months* earlier than the date generally quoted for the car's transfer. By the first week of June, when the MR's first Pullman service was publicly inaugurated between Bradford and St. Pancras, *Midland* was already in Italy.[17] The car's Continental wanderings, under the care of Col. Gourand, were to take it through France, Italy, Austria, the German states, Russia (with a change of bogies to suit the 5ft gauge), and Belgium. But all this effort produced only two new contracts, both in Italy. *Midland* arrived back in England on 18th June 1877.[18]

A contemporary description of the first batch of cars for the Midland Railway reveals the interesting detail that the bogies under *Victoria* were originally equipped with American Allen patent paper wheels — not with the British wooden-centred Mansell pattern otherwise standardised.[19] The Allen wheels were claimed to offer "advantages in safety, freedom from noise, smoothness of travelling and other important points."

The so-called 'paper', which formed the wheel centre, was in fact a compressed strawboard. Around 120 discs of this material were glued together and sandwiched at high pressure between ¼in iron facing plates, which were themselves bolted to each other through the strawboard core and secured to the steel tyre by projecting flanges. At that time, such wheels were standard equipment on Pullman cars built for American service. George Pullman had a major financial stake in the Allen Company, and it is scarcely surprising that he attempted to promote use of the patent wheels on his export vehicles as well.[20]

The official American records provide no support for claims that some of the first 'British' cars had previously seen service in the USA. The relevant plan numbers were unique to these vehicles, which were clearly tailored to suit a more restrictive loading gauge than the American norm, their overall height being almost 1ft less and their width some 6in less than the standard dimensions of contemporary US cars. There is, however, an intriguing possibility that some of the Midland vehicles had originally been destined for exhibition in Austria.

On 15th March 1873, *The Chicago Tribune* had reported that "The four Pullman cars to be sent to the Vienna Exposition are now almost ready. They are being built at Detroit. Two are sleepers and two are parlor cars and they will be the most magnificent specimens of cars ever exhibited". On 1st April, the same paper draw attention to George Pullman's recent trip to Europe and successful negotiations with the Midland Railway, but then went on to say: "He does not intend to exhibit at Vienna. The Austrian Patent law is not satisfactory and if his patents were violated, he could never obtain adequate justice because of vexatious legal delays".

The May 1873 issue of *The National Car Builder* also noted the Midland contract, asserting that the first cars would be shipped "in September". However, "Mr. Pullman also states that in view of his arrangements in England which necessitates construction and shipping abroad of so many cars designed for actual service, he has decided not to send any cars to the

Introduced in 1869, the Allen paper wheel was widely used in the United States in the latter part of the 19th century. From 1881, the main manufacturing plant was located alongside the new Pullman works established near Chicago.

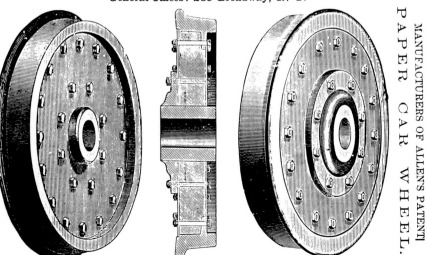

ALLEN PAPER CAR WHEEL COMPANY,
General Offices: 239 Broadway, N. Y.

MANUFACTURERS OF ALLEN'S PATENT PAPER CAR WHEEL.

Especially adapted for Sleeping and Drawing-Room Cars, Locomotive and Tender Trucks. Steel Tire with Annular Web—Strongest, Most Durable, and Most Economical Wheel in use. 74 manufactured in 1877; 60,000 manufactured to date; present facilities, 36,000 per year. Works at Hudson, N. Y., at Pullman, and at Morris, Ill.
W. H. FENNER, Jr., President.   J. C. BEACH, Treasurer.   C. H. ANTES, Secretary.

Vienna Exposition".

What, then, happened to the vehicles that had been reportedly "almost ready" in mid March? Was all the design work and preliminary construction of the first of the Midland vehicles really accomplished in less than five months from the signing of the contract at Derby in February? Certainly the Midland Railway appears to have been somewhat taken aback at quite how soon the first car parts would arrive from America, and the choice of site for the Pullman erecting shed, and the construc-

Plan 45 parlor car *Juno.* **This photograph is a rarity in showing one of the early 'British' cars in its original condition, with short-wheelbase bogies and Miller automatic couplings.** (B. Brough Collection)

Between 1875 and 1877 no fewer than 21 parlor cars were constructed to Pullman Plan 45 — four under Detroit Lot 25, and seventeen under Detroit Lot 31. Characteristically for this period, the official Pullman body plan does not show the end entrance balconies. Many of these cars were remodelled (sometimes more than once) during the course of their sometimes lengthy working lives. Although much rebuilt, *Jupiter*, of 1875, was destined not to be withdrawn until December 1932, as 'Car No.1 Third Class'. Scale 4mm = 1ft. (C. M. Knoll Collection)

tion of the shed itself, seems to have been undertaken in some haste.[21]

There is, incidentally, no truth in the claim that has sometimes been made that Pullman's British operations pioneered the use of parlor cars. The American records clearly show that when the Midland cars first took to the rails, there were already some 50 vehicles of this description in service in the USA.[22]

The next series of Pullmans to arrive from Detroit for assembly at Derby, in 1875/6, were four parlor cars and five sleepers:

• Lot 25/Plan 45 parlors: *Jupiter, Mars, Saturn, Venus*;
• Lot 26/Plan 46 sleepers: *Norman, Princess, Saxon, St. George, Transit*.[23]

Mars was the first Pullman car to enter service on the London, Brighton & South Coast Railway, in November 1875.[24] In the long term, this was to prove a most significant development because, without the LBSCR's enthusiastic support of short-haul parlor-car operations from the 1880s onwards, Pullman activities in Britain could scarcely have remained viable. *Mars*, it should be noted, *was* a standard parlor car — not a sleeper made up permanently in the 'day' position as has invariably been claimed in previous British publications.

Two further lots, of 17 parlor cars and five sleepers, quickly followed in 1876/7. Indeed, from the dates recorded for entry in service, it appears that assembly of the first of these vehicles at Derby may have overtaken that of the last cars in the preceding series:

• Lot 31/Plan 45 parlors: *Adonis, Albion, Alexandra, Apollo, Ariel, Aurora, Ceres, Comet, Diana, Eclipse, Globe, Juno, Mercury, Minerva, Planet, Vesta, Vulcan*;
• Lot 32/Plan 48 sleepers: *Australia, Castalia, Germania, India, Scotia*.[25]

The names *Diana* and *Vulcan* have not previously appeared in any lists published on this side of the Atlantic. Soon after they were completed in 1877, the two cars concerned were renamed *Albert Edward* and *Alexandra* (II) respectively and joined *Mars* on the LBSCR.[26] The naming of a second car after the then Princess of Wales while *Alexandra* (I) was still in service on the Midland line is noteworthy. While the recycling of car names was to become quite common over the years, concurrent duplication was very rare — if only because of the potential confusion in day-to-day book-

keeping (and Pullman's central stock register was, after all, held some 4,000 miles away from the company's British outpost!). One can only hazard a guess that, in this case, the replicated name was chosen as a fitting companion for *Albert Edward*, named after the Prince of Wales (later to become King Edward VII), and that the renaming itself was prompted by some Royal event in the South of England in which the LBSCR played a supporting role.

In the summer of 1876, the English-born James Bower (grandfather of one of the present writers), who had previously been employed by Pullman as a Dining Car Conductor in the USA, returned to his homeland — evidently charged with the task of organising on-board train-catering facilities in Britain.[27] More than three years were to pass, however, before that aim was to be achieved. Nevertheless, one particularly intriguing item, unloaded from the ss *Adriatic* in mid-December 1876 might be noted here: "One stove for Great Northern Railway!"[28]

Readers familiar with earlier published accounts of the spread of Pullman services in Britain may indeed be rather surprised that, up to this point, there has been no mention of the Great Northern, or of any

James Bower, in early Pullman conductor's uniform, photographed in Leeds in 1876. (A. J. Bower Collection)

cars named *Ohio* and *Ocean*, with which — supposedly — the GNR, jointly with the Manchester, Sheffield & Lincolnshire Railway, inaugurated a 'saloon car' service between King's Cross and Manchester in 1875. But no reference to any export cars so-named has been found in the American company records. Not only do these car-names also nowhere appear in a Great Northern Railway 'Pullman correspondence' file, now lodged in the Public Record Office at Kew (ref: RAIL 236/678), there is no mention there either of the GNR/MSLR joint London-Manchester service prior to 1883 — when the MSLR strongly opposed a suggestion that the operation of a proposed dining car should be contracted out to Pullman.

While it does make passing reference to an earlier contact, the first letter that survives on the Great Northern file is dated 18th December 1877. This is from Herbert Shenstone Roberts, who had been Pullman's London Manager for just over a year, to the GNR's General Manager, Henry Oakley. It describes the plan of a sleeping car specifically drawn up to try to persuade the GNR, and its principal East Coast partner, the North Eastern Railway (for which the GNR acted as intermediary in negotiations), of the potential attraction of Pullman sleepers on overnight services between King's Cross and Edinburgh. Had the design ever been realised, it would have been some 6ft shorter and, at an estimated weight of 17 tons, around 5-6 tons lighter than the cars previously supplied to the Midland Railway. But, although the plans had evidently been prepared to meet GNR objections to the "cumbersome" nature of the Midland vehicles (again, the contemporary record offers no evidence of domestic experience of Pullman working), the Great Northern Board remained wary of entering into any long-term agreement.[29] The official documents indicate that the NER originally had even stronger doubts about Pullman operations, but these had softened in the face of the abstraction of Anglo-Scottish overnight traffic by the rival Midland/North British Waverley Route partnership, whose

James Bower at the time of the inauguration of the first British dining-car service in November 1879. (A. J. Bower Collection)

Pullman sleepers had, in the two years since the Settle & Carlisle line had been open, offered a standard of accommodation far superior to that of the three somewhat cheerless saloons the East Coast companies could then muster between them. Nevertheless, the East Coast authorities remained hesitant about the principle of contracting out services, and the GNR Board, meeting on 3rd July 1878, again deferred a decision.[30]

Later the same month, however, a Pullman car did come to the East Coast Route. Since mid June, George and Hattie Pullman, accompanied this time by their young daughter, Florence, had again been touring Britain and France.[31] On 21st July, the Pullman family, with a group of friends and colleagues, including Col. Gourand and H. S. Roberts, embarked on a three-day round trip from London to Edinburgh, travelling north from King's Cross and returning to St. Pancras, making additional sightseeing stops en route to visit York Minster and Abbotsford House, the home of Sir Walter Scott.[32] For this trip the parlor car *Globe* was employed as a private saloon, with James Bower in charge.[33] This vehicle, completed in November 1877, had not previously been in traffic, and its sudden removal from Derby at the end of June had evidently taken the MR's Carriage & Wagon Department wholly by surprise.[34] (Past British accounts have always claimed that *Globe* went direct to the LBSCR — and stayed there.)

While in London, George Pullman had, not unnaturally, involved himself in the negotiations with the GNR. Because of the railway's continued reluctance to enter into any long-term commitment, and anxious to set up the basis of a deal before he left for home, he offered a major concession. He stated his terms in a letter dated 25th July 1878:[35]

"I have considered our recent conversations with a sincere desire to do what I can to meet your Company's wishes and I think I can afford you a temporary arrangement which will be satisfactory to you.

"I understand that your Board and that of the North Eastern hesitate to enter into an agreement (on the basis of that with the Midland) submitted to you by Mr. Roberts because they have not had any experience of the suitableness of our carriages for your traffic, but that the two Boards are favorably [*sic*] inclined to the system and if a fair trial of it were allowed them and turned out satisfactory they would be prepared to enter into a contract for an extended term.

"It has not been usual with my Co. to send their carriages on to any Railway without a contract for a term of years but I have so strong a persuasion that an experiment will in your case lead to a contract that I am disposed to make an exception of my Co's ordinary practice.

"You are aware that we have no carriages in this country of which we can dispose without consulting other parties — I think I shall be able to make arrangements with them, but I of course write subject to that contingency."

Plainly, *had* the GNR (partnered by the MSLR) been running two Pullman cars between King's Cross and Manchester for three years past, these remarks would make no sense at all. Pullman went on to

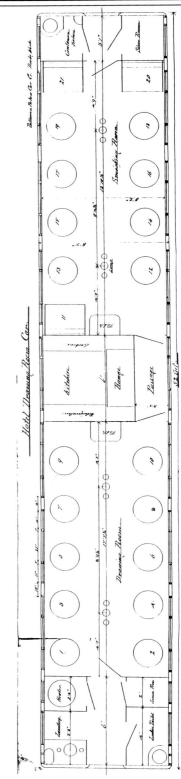

Project plan of a dining car (based on a Plan 45 bodyshell) for the Great Northern Railway drawn at Pullman's Derby Works, possibly towards the end of 1878. In practice, a central kitchen layout was never adopted by Pullman in Britain (and it is not clear how access would have been gained to the kitchen in this case). What is styled as a 'refrigerator' would have been a simple ice-box. The British-drawn plan is noteworthy as being the sole example known to the authors where the Pullman company itself has used the term 'drawing room' to indicate an open saloon area. Scale 4mm = 1ft.

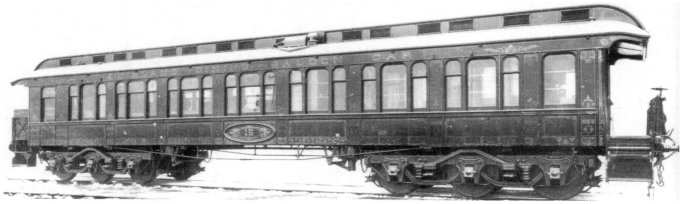

propose that two sleepers should operate over the East Coast main line for one year "by way of experiment", with a third available as a spare. He also scouted the idea of providing "two or three" parlor cars "should you desire them". The GNR Traffic Committee, meeting on 8th August, resolved to accept only the offer of two sleepers (with no designated spare), and then initially just for six months. The two cars selected were *Germania* and *India* which, before entering service, passed through Doncaster Carriage Works to be fitted with the vacuum brake.[36]

Following Pullman's return to the USA, H. S. Roberts persisted in attempts to persuade the GNR (and NER) to accept the offer of three parlor cars, suitably modified to provide on-board dining facilities. He suggested that one should run each way in the main 10am Anglo-Scottish service (presumably with one spare), stating his belief that "a car of this kind ... would pay very well".[37] This offer was firmly "Declined" by the GNR Board.[38]

Notwithstanding this rebuff, work started at Pullman's Derby workshops (evidently on a private-venture basis) on the conversion of an existing parlor car into a diner, and a group of GNR Board members went to inspect it in January 1879.

There are no known surviving photographs of the first British Pullman diner, *Prince of Wales,* **remodelled from the Plan 39 parlor car,** *Victoria.* **Nevertheless, apart from the fact this vehicle was not remounted on six-wheel bogies, the conversion doubtless formed the model for the transformation of the other two Plan 39 cars into diners for the Midland Railway. The illustration shows the one-time** *Britannia,* **originally renamed** *Windsor* **when it became a diner in 1882, and subsequently renumbered '15' after purchase by the Midland in 1883.**

According to Henry Oakley, the GNR party had felt that "something more should be done in the way of providing cooking accommodation than [the Pullman company] then proposed", and had voiced their reservations during the course of their visit. Nevertheless, it was agreed that, when the conversion was completed, the GNR would give the car an initial year's trial on the main daytime service from Leeds to London and back.[39] This was, of course, the vehicle that was to become famous as the pioneer British dining car, *Prince of Wales* — commonly claimed to

have been remodelled from the elusive *Ohio.* Nowhere in the GNR papers, however, is the car's former identity revealed, nor is there any indication that the chosen vehicle had previously seen service out of King's Cross. Indeed it had not, as Pullman records that survive on the other side of the Atlantic have now made clear.

In Chicago, the company kept an annual account of the Cost of Construction and Equipment of Cars in which the entire fleet of what was known as the Pullman European Car Association (PECA) was listed alphabetically. This covered the cars in service in England and in Italy and, where any name changes had been made, it noted the original names of the vehicles in question. In later lists, car locations and transfers were also recorded. An extract from the Cost of Construction list for the year ending 31st July 1880 is illustrated. It will be seen that *Prince of Wales* has been added to the end of the 'P's, with the name *Victoria* entered in the 'Original Name' column, while the original entry for *Victoria* has been deleted with *P of W* faintly alongside. (To the very end of Pullman ownership of *Prince of Wales,* the PECA lists confirm its former identity as *Victoria.* The car was sold to the GNR in 1885.)

Coincidentally, from April 1879, Augustus Rapp, who had been appointed Pullman works manager at Derby the previous August,[40] began to submit regular returns to the Midland Railway's Carriage & Wagon Committee, showing whether those cars allocated to the MR were 'in operating condition', 'in need of repair' or 'under repair'. On the lists for both 1st April and 1st July *Victoria* is among the cars "under repair", while on 30th September, it was reported "in good working condition", having been "repaired since 30th June 1879".[41] Thereafter, however, it disappeared from the record, signifying that it had (at last) officially been removed from the Midland roster.

Before *Prince of Wales* entered public service on the GNR on 1st November 1879 as Britain's first dining car, two press trips were arranged: one for London journalists on Saturday 18th October, and the second for those from Northern newspapers a week later, on 25th October. For these runs, an additional 'overflow' parlor car was also provided. Its identity is revealed in reports of the second trip: "The drawing room car was one ordinarily used by the company and named the *Globe*".[42] These press stories and a note about repairs to *Globe* recorded in the Doncaster Order Book 11 months later[43] serve to support a Bower family tradition that, for some two years after the Pullman family tour of July 1878, this car was retained on the GNR for

This well-known *Illustrated London News* engraving of the dining saloon of *Prince of Wales* shows James Bower emerging from the kitchen/servery area.

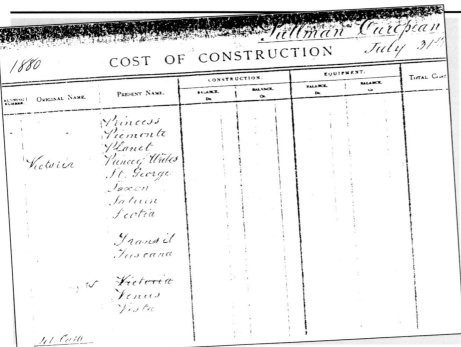

Extract from the PECA Cost of Construction account, dated 31st July 1880, showing that *Prince of Wales* **had originally been** *Victoria*. **Against the deleted name** *'Victoria'*, *'P of W'* **has also been entered.** (Courtesy Newberry Library)

special workings, and thereafter used as required with *Prince of Wales* during the year's dining-car trials, before being equipped at Derby with electric lighting powered by Fauré batteries, renamed *Beatrice*, and transferred to the LBSCR early in 1881.

Nevertheless, the GNR's continuous brake returns for the year ending December 1879 record that only one Pullman car — which would have been *Prince of Wales* — had been added to the two noted in July of that year (*Germania* and *India*).[44] The returns for the LBSCR are unhelpful in trying to determine whether any new Pullmans had been added to that line's complement during the year. But those for the GNR seem to indicate that, although it may have been retained for the initial one-year dining-car trial, *Globe* was never officially regarded as part of the Great Northern Pullman roster.

While one cannot be absolutely certain how the legend of the phantom *Ohio* and *Ocean* originated, it is likely that someone at some time simply assumed that engravings of two twelve-wheel cars so named that appeared in the 1878 edition of F. S. Williams' classic *The Midland Railway* (Bemrose) were illustrations of British cars and, since they could not be recognised as any vehicles in the well-documented MR allocation, jumped to the conclusion that they had run on the GNR. In fact the two engravings are of vehicles in service on the Pennsylvania Railroad and had almost certainly been lifted from a PRR publicity booklet of 1876, promoting travel to the US Centennial Exhibition.[45]

The official PECA record of the conversion of the original *Victoria* also disposes of another legend that has hitherto enjoyed wide currency in British publications: namely, that this vehicle had been converted into a buffet car — and renamed *Alexandra* (III) — for experimental service on the London & South Western Railway's Waterloo-Exeter main line from May 1880. As previously remarked, that there should have been *two* coexisting cars named *Alexandra* (one on the Midland and one on the LBSCR) was unusual enough, but that they should have been joined by a *third* borders on the incredible. Although there is no absolute proof, it is much more likely that, for the LSWR operation, *Alexandra* (II) was borrowed from the neighbouring LBSCR. If this theory is correct, it would also solve the mystery of the LSWR vehicle's disposal after the Exeter Pullman service was suspended. The LSWR's Traffic Committee pronounced this "a failure" and recommended that it should be withdrawn little more than a month after it started.[46] There must also be some doubt that, while it survived, it offered anything very special in the way of refreshment service: the promotional note that appeared in the June and July 1880 editions (only) of the LSWR public timetable makes no mention of this; there, the big selling point is that the car offered "separate Lavatories for Ladies and Gentlemen".[47]

It has been suggested that the South Western car went to France in 1882 or 1883 for a short-lived Pullman operation between Paris and Le Havre on the Chemin de Fer de l'Ouest. It is, however, more likely that the car used on this service was, in fact, *Mars*, which (at some date that we have yet been unable to pinpoint) was transferred to the Continent and can next be positively located in store in Amsterdam in February 1884, when it was offered to the GNR for conversion to a diner as a companion for *Prince of Wales* — the railway to pay transport charges and conversion costs![48] Presumably it was intended for the projected GNR/MSLR Manchester dining service — for which, a year later, the MSLR itself was to provide a very handsome twelve-wheel kitchen/diner. In the event, *Mars* was sold to the Compagnie Internationale des Wagons-Lits on 28th April 1884.[49] It subsequently became No.155 in the CIWL fleet and was employed on a 'voiture-salon' service between Amsterdam and Rotterdam.

Three other 'British' cars, all sleepers, were transferred to the Continent early in 1883, for further service in Italy. *Australia* and *Castilia*, from the Midland, and *Germania*, from the GNR, were overhauled at Derby and given "a more luxurious and inviting appearance than heretofore".[50] From Customs records, it would appear that they were shipped from London Docks to Dunkirk on 13th February.[51]

On arrival in France, the three cars were taken to Calais, where, with two luggage vans and "a sort of guard's car",[52] they were to form the Continental special train (leaving at 2.26pm on Friday 23rd February 1883) run to convey passengers on a one-off Thomas Cook/Pullman special excursion from London to Florence and Rome.[53] Basically this was largely designed to earn some revenue from what was essentially a necessary stock transfer move (the publicity implies that excursionists were expected to book their return journeys independently). Nevertheless the operation considerably angered CIWL (the Pullman company's increasingly powerful rival on the European mainland), which had recently concluded sleeping-car con-

The account of the introduction of Pullman cars to Britain given in the 1878 edition of *The Midland Railway,* **by F. S. Williams, was accompanied by these engravings of cars named** *Ocean* **and** *Ohio.* **The illustrations are probably the origin of the legend of cars so-named running on the Great Northern Railway. In fact they represent cars then in service on the American Pennsylvania Railroad. Note the fascia inscription 'Pullman Drawing Room Sleeping Car' on** *Ohio.*

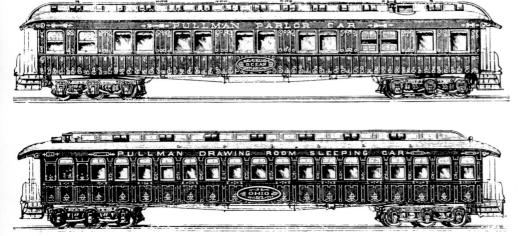

tracts with a number of the railway administrations involved.

Some earlier accounts have claimed that *Germania* had crossed the English Channel in 1880, but papers in the Public Record Office independently confirm that this car was still on the GNR until the end of 1882.[54] It has also been claimed that a parlor car was included in the formation of the Cook/Pullman special train. This has been assumed from the promotional handbill's reference to "Drawing Room and Sleeping Cars", but that is to misunderstand Pullman usage of the term 'drawing room' — as, indeed, it has been widely misunderstood on this side of the Atlantic for

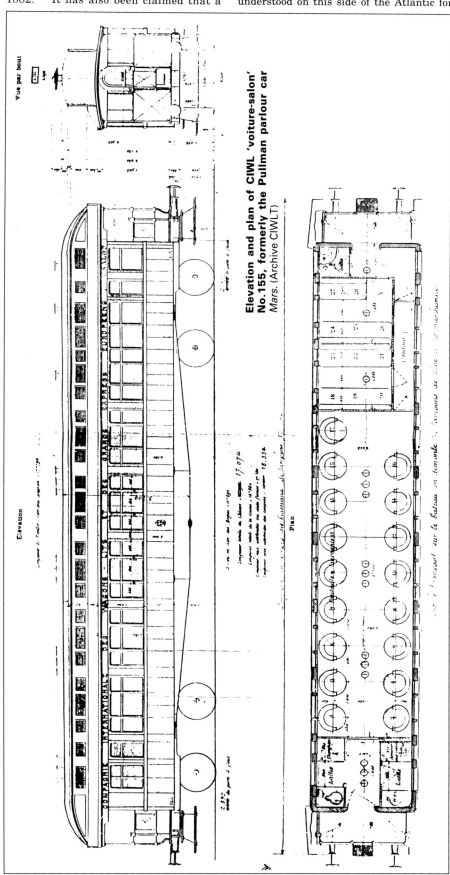

Elevation and plan of CIWL 'voiture-salon' No.155, formerly the Pullman parlour car *Mars.* (Archive CIWLT)

the past 120 years! Because the 1870s MR parlor cars originally bore the fascia inscription "Pullman Drawing Room Car", British commentators have generally taken it for granted that the 'drawing room' appellation was simply an Anglicised interpretation of the American 'parlor'. That assumption is false. Contemporary illustrations of American Pullmans and numerous official car plans clearly show that a 'drawing room' was specifically a *private compartment* — or, in its original sense, a 'withdrawing room' — whether in a parlor car or a sleeper.[55] In itself, the term in no way indicated that a vehicle was a day car. Some sleepers in American service even bore the fascia inscription "Drawing Room and Sleeping Car" or, more simply, "Drawing Room Sleeping Car". Interestingly enough, *The Times*, in its report of 23rd March 1874 on the Midland Railway's innovation, had clearly differentiated the car types as "parlour cars" and "drawing room and sleeping cars". And H. S. Roberts, in his approach to the GNR on 18th December 1877, had discussed the projected East Coast sleeping car's three-berth "drawing room" at some length.

Confusion about the terminology must also be seen in the context of the widely differing norms of ordinary passenger accommodation in the USA and Britain at the time. In comparison with a standard American day-car open saloon, a Pullman drawing room (in its proper sense) offered well-heeled travellers unparalleled privacy. But, in this respect at least, its superiority over the British first-class compartment was minimal. Over here, it was the saloon accommodation that provided the novelty and which, in the popular mind (and in the mind of user railways), was consequently associated with the 'drawing room' designation.

Following the successful demonstration of electric lighting on *Beatrice*, and on the LBSCR's four-car 'Pullman Limited' (direct ancestor of the 'Brighton Belle'), which entered service in December 1881, the GNR approached the Fauré Company in July 1883 with the idea of installing electric light in *Prince of Wales*. Although Patrick Stirling, the GNR's Locomotive, Carriage & Wagon Superintendent, was quite relaxed about the Fauré estimate of £250 for the proposed conversion, Henry Oakley regarded it as wholly unacceptable, compared with the 10s (50p) a week then being spent on oil for lighting the car.[56] As it happened, however, the patentees of an improved galvanic battery — British Patent 4990/83 — stepped forward to claim that their new system would cost only one-eighth of the amount demanded for the chemicals required in other battery systems. Their offer was accepted. Fitted with a twelve-cell battery providing power for six Swan incandescent lamps, *Prince of Wales* made its first run with electric lighting on the 5.40pm King's Cross-Leeds on Thursday 25th October 1883.[57]

Acknowledgements
We would particularly like to thank the following for their help in preparing this article: Prof Liston E. Leyendecker, State University of Colorado; Charles M. Knoll, Sonoma, Ca; Newberry Library, Chicago, Ill; Public Record Office, Kew; The British Newspaper Library, Colindale; HM Customs & Excise, London; Maritime Record Centre, Merseyside Maritime Museum, Liverpool.

References

1. The American spelling was invariably used in all Pullman printed documentation and, when shown, on the cars themselves until the severing of all ties with the US parent company.
2. Leyendecker: *Palace Car Prince*.
3. 'Gourand' is the form shown in most contemporary press reports that we have seen, although 'Gouraud' is also sometimes found.
4. Leyendecker: *ibid*.
5. Since *all* cars were fitted with handbrake controls, it is not really correct to single these out as 'brake cars'.
6. Pullman European Car Association (PECA) Cost of Construction & Equipment of Cars, 31.7.75 (Newberry Library, Chicago). Also Barger: *The Palace Cars*.
7. MR Traffic Committee minutes, 20.5.73 (Public Record Office: RAIL 490/150). The Pullman sheds were quite distinct from the later MR carriage works. See J. B. Radford: *The American Pullman Cars of the Midland Railway* (Ian Allan).
8. This was the registered title of the American parent company. However, the European subsidiary, when it was established, was known as the (non-possessive) 'Pullman Palace Car Company (Europe)'.
9. *London Customs' Bill of Entry — Bill A (Ships' Reports)*.
10. MR Board minutes, 20.1.74 (PRO: rail 491/22).
11. *The Leeds Mercury*, 6.2.74.
12. *The Railway Service Gazette*, 28.2.74. The special is also mentioned in *Engineering*, 27.2.74, although, in this case, the cars are not identified.
13. *The Railway Record*, 28.2.74.
14. Formation confirmed by report in *The Times*, 23.3.74.
15. *Joint Stock Journal*, 7.4.74.
16. *London Customs' Bill of Entry — Bill B (Imports, Exports and Shipping)*.
17. *Giornali di Napoli*, 5.6.74.
18. *London Customs' Bill of Entry — Bill B*.
19. *The Railway Record*, 28.3.74. Confirmation is provided in American Pullman company ledgers (Newberry Library). There is also a brief mention of the paper wheels in *Engineering*, 2.4.75, although no specific vehicle is identified.
20. For a more detailed description, see John L. White Jnr: *The American Railroad Passenger Car* (John Hopkins University Press).
21. MR Traffic Committee minutes, 20.5.73 (PRO: RAIL 491/150).
22. Barger: *ibid*.
23. PECA Cost of Construction & Equipment of Cars, 31.7.76 (supplemented by information in Barger: *ibid*).
24. LBSCR Traffic & Stores Committee minutes, 27.10.75 (PRO: RAIL 414/129). Also MR Carriage & Wagon Committee minutes, 6.11.77 (PRO: 491/251).
25. Barger: *ibid*.
26. PECA Cost of Construction & Equipment of Cars, 31.7.83 (supplemented by information in Barger: *ibid*). The transfer of the cars to the LBSCR (on 10.10.77) is mentioned in MR Carriage & Wagon minutes, 6.11.77 (PRO: RAIL 491/251).
27. Bower family tradition.
28. *London Customs' Bill of Entry — Bill A*, 12.12.76.
29. H. Oakley to GNR Board, 6.2.78; endorsed by Board, 8.2.78 (PRO: RAIL 236/678).
30. H. Oakley to GNR Board, 20.6.78; endorsed by Board, 28.6.78 (PRO: RAIL 236/678).
31. Leyendecker: *ibid*.
32. Leyendecker: *ibid*.
33. Bower family tradition.
34. MR Carriage & Wagon Committee minutes, 2.7.78 (PRO: RAIL 491/251).
35. G. M. Pullman to H. Oakley, 25.7.78 (PRO: RAIL 236/678).
36. H. Oakley to GNR Board, 7.8.78; endorsed by Traffic Committee, 8.8.78 (PRO: RAIL 236/678). At this date, continuous braking of passenger trains was still not universal, so the fact that *Globe* was, presumably, fitted with Westinghouse air brakes (and hand brakes) only would not have been a bar to its use on the GNR for the Pullman family excursion in July. Dual-braking became standard on East Coast Joint Stock to suit the vacuum-braked GNR and the air-braked NER and NBR.
37. H. S. Roberts to H. Oakley, 18.9.78 (PRO: RAIL 236/678).
38. H. Oakley to GNR Board, 23.10.78; endorsed by Board, 25.10.78 (PRO: RAIL 236/678).
39. H. Oakley to GNR Board, 5.2.79; endorsed by Board, 7.2.79 (PRO: RAIL 236/678).
40. MR Carriage & Wagon Committee minutes, 3.9.78 (PRO: RAIL 491/251).
41. MR Carriage & Wagon Committee minutes, 1.4.79, 1.7.79 and 30.9.79 (PRO: RAIL 491/252).
42. *The Bradford Observer* and *The Leeds Daily News*, 28.10.79.
43. GNR Doncaster Order Book, 12.10.80 (PRO: RAIL 236/688).
44. *Continuous Brake Returns*, 1879 (C. E. Stretton Collection, Leicester Library).
45. The same exterior views are reproduced in Barger: *ibid*.
46. LSWR Traffic Committee minutes, 9.6.80 (PRO: RAIL 411/249).
47. LSWR Public Timetables, 1880 (PRO: RAIL 947/18).
48. H. S. Roberts to H. Oakley, 22.2.84 (PRO: RAIL 236/678).
49. PECA Cost of Construction & Equipment of Cars, 31.7.84.
50. *The Railway Official Gazette*, 2.83. By this time two more bogie cars had entered service on the GNR (Detroit Lot 54/Plan 68: *Columba, Iona*), and two on the MR (Detroit Lot 155/Plan 68A: *St. Andrew, St. Mungo*). Four 'lightweight' six-wheel cars had also been supplied (Detroit Lot 158/Plan 130: *Balmoral, Culross* to the GNR; and *St. Denis, St. Louis* to the MR).
51. *London Customs' Bill of Entry — Bill B*, 13.2.83: "£6000 rlwy Carriages".
52. *The Railway Official Gazette*, 4.83.
53. For the text of the promotional handbill (preserved in CIWL archives), see George Behrend: *Pullman in Europe* (Ian Allan).
54. GNR account for oil used in Pullman Car lamps (including *Germania*), 5.7.82; also revised draft operating agreement submitted by H. S. Roberts to H. Oakley, 12.82 (PRO: RAIL 236/678).
55. Barger: *ibid*.
56. GNR Pullman correspondence, 7.83-10.83 (PRO: RAIL 236/678).
57. *The Pictorial World*, 1.11.83.

The Pullman 'hotel car' — essentially a standard convertible sleeper/day car, incorporating a kitchen — did not catch on (if only because of complaints about the lingering smell of food), and no examples were seen in Britain. Nevertheless, this engraving of 1869 serves to show that, in Pullman eyes, a 'drawing room' (in this case with fold-down berths and an intercommunicating door to a second drawing room) provided a measure of privacy lacking in the communal 'saloon' — which also served as the 'dining room' and 'sleeping room'

This 1901 Pullman drawing of alterations to parlor car *Beatrice* provides confirmation that a 'drawing room' was synonymous with the British 'compartment'. Scale: 7mm = 1ft. (C. M. Knoll Collection)

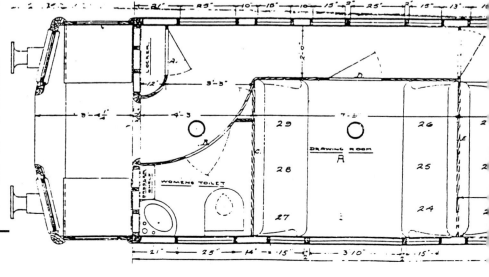

Cab, running plate and frames of No.6202 in the erecting shop at Crewe works in 1935. Already, the large size of the forward turbine (far side) compared with the reverse mechanism (near side) is making itself apparent — see text. (The late Gavin Wilson Collection)

TURBOMOTIVE
PROTOTYPE AND MODEL
BY JOHN HORTON

It should occasion no real surprise that many fine modelmakers are also excellent railway historians, for in order to make a good model it is usually necessary to have more than a passing knowledge of the prototype. This is the thinking behind the MODELLERS' BACKTRACK approach to the subject: the need for accurate details before models can be attempted, especially in terms of appreciating the outwardly visible changes which took place over time; and it is particularly pleasing when an account is prepared by one who is able to combine both sides of the subject in a single feature.

John Horton is such a person, combining a high level of modelling skills with prototype knowledge gained as a BR steam fitter in his early working life. Like many modellers, he likes to tackle less common prototypes by way of change and in this feature, has chosen to take No.6202, the famous experimental turbine driven 4-6-2 built by the LMS in 1935, as his subject. But the principles of his approach to the subject are widely applicable and form an excellent 'blueprint for action' of which many can take advantage.

PART I — THE PROTOTYPE

In January 1932, the LMS recruited William Stanier as its new Chief Mechanical Engineer, this post being a considerable enlargement from his previous appointment as Works Manager Swindon GWR. This, in today's parlance, was an inspired piece of 'head hunting' by the LMS board, notably by its President, Sir Josiah Stamp and his Vice President for Engineering, Sir Harold Hartley. As is well known, the LMS had severe personality crises in several of its departments and it must have been felt at Board level that a 'new broom' was the answer.

At the age of 54, with his superior on the

Left hand broadside view of No.6202 as built with domeless boiler. (BR)

GWR, C. B. Collett, only some five years older than he, in today's view it would be a sensible move for Stanier to make. However, in those days, GWR servants were, as the term implies, 'GWR Servants' and Stanier came from a long line of them. With this in mind, Sir Josiah must have been quite persuasive. It was an inspired move on the part of Stamp and Hartley to acquire this quiet and unassuming ENGINEER to weld and lead the factionalised LMS Motive Power and Design Departments, plus the hitherto all powerful Operating Department together. So Stanier came with his knowledge, plus a large chestful of Swindon drawings &c and, apparently, an extraordinary ability to transmit this knowledge to his team.

Strangely (at this distance in time) in February 1932 he was approached by Dr. Guy of Metropolitan Vickers on the subject of a turbine driven 2-8-0 on trial in Sweden which was producing very promising results. He was then despatched by the LMS Board to Sweden in the company of Dr. Guy with instructions to report back — probably even before he had visited his new empire's outstations! Possibly — and this is only a conjecture — the hand of Sir Josiah

Right hand broadside view of the locomotive in steam at an early date — note the much smaller reverse turbine casing above the footplate compared with the left hand side. (The late Gavin Wilson Collection)

and his never-ending quest for operational efficiency was behind this move.

The Swedish engine itself was unusual in that it was non-condensing, a result of collaboration between Ljungstrom of Sweden and Metrovick of Trafford Park, Manchester. Most previous examples had been of the condensing variety, which as its name implies, carried large condensers on board to return the waste exhaust steam back to water for re-use in the boiler. The British experience of the earlier condensing types though slight, had been both expensive and disastrous; but this non-condensing version appeared to offer the advantages of turbine propulsion without the mechanical disadvantages and weight

Detail view of right hand side after fitting with domed boiler. Note the changes at the top of the turbine casing. (The late Gavin Wilson Collection)

penalties of the hitherto unreliable condensing gear.

What were these advantages? Briefly they were smother drive — ie constant torque throughout the driving wheel revolution. With this smoother drive the 'hammer blow' effect on the rail by a normal reciprocating cylinder locomotive was lost. This, in simple terms, enabled a heavier and possibly more powerful locomotive to remain within the civil engineering restrictions on a given route. Another large advantage was the fact that reciprocating locomotives performance declined commensurate with the mileage done since the last valve and piston ring renewals. On stating this, one should perhaps think in terms of the LMS position in 1932 where many West Coast main line locomotives at the time were ex-L&Y Dreadnoughts and ex-LNW Claughtons, both well known for their fast wearing properties and already eclipsed by the LMS standard Royal Scots, relatively new but reaching very high mileages in short periods. However, none of these three types were masters of the job *when approaching shopping or simple ring replacements*. The turbine locomotive was felt to offer constant power throughout the

periods between shoppings for heavy general repairs.

A marginal saving both in coal and water was also expected, plus an extended firebox life through the loss of the pulsing effects of the blast.

The *known* disadvantages at the time were: higher first cost of construction, obtaining adequate power through a wide speed range, and the not inconsiderable problems of converting a fluid drive into probably the hardest non-shock absorbing ride imaginable! A further known disadvantage was that turbines in industrial and marine use generally were supplied with drier (hotter) steam than locomotives used in British practice normally provided. Nevertheless, the go-ahead was obtained from the LMS Board for MetroVick to prepare a pilot scheme for future use.

Stanier's design team at Derby on 'New-Work' had started on the '7P 4-6-2' as it was called and this design eventually emerged as the first and second 'Princess Royal' engines. At the same time *materials only* were laid aside for what at the time was known as '7P 4-6-2 Third engine' as described in the Derby Drawing Register for that period (1932-39). It is here in the register that possibly the most fascinating aspects of the development of No.6202 come to light, going through various arrangements of equipment and setting out. The decision to revert to roller bearings, having been discarded and partially reinstated, gives a final resting place to the myth, often quoted, that three sets of 'Princess Royal' frames were built and one set aside for No.6202. Because these 'Cannon' bearings and horn guides were considerably larger than the standard axle-boxes fitted to the rest of the 'Princess' class, No.6202's frames were considerably deeper than the rest; also, the frame stretchers and lightening holes bore little resemblance to those of any other Pacific.

A copy of the Derby Drawing Office register is held at York Museum and well repays the curiosity of all who like to trace the development and modifications applied to some classes throughout their lives.

This view of the left hand side of 'Turbomotive' from above, after fitting with a domed boiler — see text — shows a few early changes to the forward turbine casing — see also previous view. Those modifications below the smokebox are fairly obvious but also, faintly visible on the side of the casing about half way along the side of the firebox, is a new, c.18in diameter, circular washout plug access door. Note also the raised sheet steel cover angled upwards below the smokebox — again see text. (The late Gavin Wilson Collection)

Whilst Derby was engrossed in the 'flagship' Pacifics, Horwich quietly got on with the job of designing the taper boiler 2-6-0 and Crewe of course built the lot!

Design, having settled down over the preceding twelve months or so, hardened from the initial pilot scheme into incorporating it into the 'Princess Royal' class. A 2,600hp forward turbine was mounted in the left hand frameplate approximately

Front end detail of No.6202 entering Euston c.1936. (The late Gavin Wilson Collection)

where the outside cylinders would be on Nos.6200-1. This drove through triple reduction gearing of 34 : 1, permanently in mesh with the leading coupled axle, the final reduction gear on this axle being mounted on a flexible carrier to allow vertical travel and absorb the shocks &c found at rail and crossing joints. This 2,600hp was to be attainable at 62mph, so enabling 500 ton trains to be handled on the existing West Coast route and schedules. The reverse turbine was mounted on the right hand side directly opposite its counterpart. Smaller and less powerful than its forward big brother, it was only envisaged as a light engine and low speed shunting movement prime mover and consequently suffered throughout the life the engine in power, lubrication and transmission engagement problems. Some of these were overcome but not to a satisfactory degree. This unit was not in direct engagement with the main drive train, and had an interlocking mechanism to prevent its clutch engaging inadvertently. Likewise the steam supply was also interlocked, however the best laid plans would go astray — and they did!

All the gear trains were enclosed in a gearcase and together with the turbines were pressure lubricated by two steam dri-

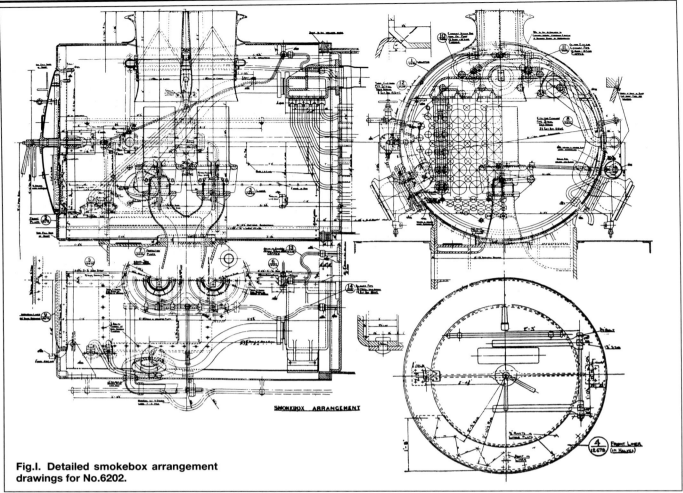

Fig.I. Detailed smokebox arrangement drawings for No.6202.

ven closed circuit oil pumps working all the time. These were backed up by a gear driven pump which of course only worked whilst the engine was actually moving. This gearcase and combined oil tank held about 60 gallons of oil which was circulated in about one minute. A large oil cooler was provided and was mounted between the frames, angled and provided with a sheet steel cover that could be set to provide a shield for the cooler matrix whilst cleaning the smokebox or, as usually seen in photographs, angled upwards to provide an air ram effect to enhance cooling when running.

From the start, No.6202 had a boiler with improved heating properties in the form of more superheater elements and a larger combustion chamber. These became the standard for the rest of the class, ie Nos.6203-12. It will be seen from the above remarks that No.6202 was always considered a bona-fide member of the class itself. Other innovations incorporated in this machine were a double chimney complete with twin variable blastpipes and a feed water heater combined with the exhaust steam injector. This feed heater was supplied by tapping off the forward turbine. As previously stated, Timken roller bearings throughout engine and tender were another milestone in efficiency.

On its emergence from Crewe Works in June 1935 it was obvious that this was something special. Like most things in engineering "if it looks right it probably is right" and right from day one, it proved itself capable of filling all its traffic requirements, except for the reversal of its empty stock trains on its arrival at Euston

where it was soon found that the reverse turbine was not powerful enough. The variable twin blastpipes were also not effective throughout their range and were soon fixed in the minimum position. As the controls of the 'Turbomotive' as it was now universally known differed from the other Pacifics, it was found advantageous to form a link of enginemen, complete with travelling fitter, to handle the locomotive. This soon settled itself down to the Euston to Liverpool service where it performed regularly and adequately.

Like all 'one-off' experiments, there were several learning curves to be followed and as always these were dependent on top management's will to follow these sometimes rocky paths. The LMS management certainly backed this one to the hilt and one feels that they felt that great kudos was obtained with this revolutionary machine. Certainly on looking at the history of No.6202 there is the re-occurring problems with the reverse turbine, or more particularly its control mechanisms which in themselves were found to be unreliable causing several expensive and disrupting visits to Crewe over the early periods.

Continuing on the 'down' side of the story of No.6202, Stanier soon found that the GWR policy of low superheat did not pay off on the LMS and was increasing superheat values throughout his range of standard taper boilers. At this point in time, some 60 years later, one can only wonder at the compliance of the Board to authorise the colossal expenditure that this entailed. Surely the achievements thus far achieved by Stanier held him in good stead at this crucial point, and was the firm guid-

ing hand of Sir Josiah still in evidence here? However, as far as No.6202 was concerned it meant going from a domeless and 32 element superheater first boiler to a second unit with a dome regulator and 40 superheater elements; and perhaps it would be useful at this point to amplify the story for any readers not quite up on the terms 'domeless' and 'domed' in connection with Stanier boilers.

'Domeless' means that there is no raised dome on the top of the boiler to collect the steam; it is collected at a high point, usually the front of the firebox and piped to a casting in the smokebox called a header. This header is compartmented into a regulator and a superheater unit. The dome-like cover on the boiler only covers the water top feed valves and the small manhole on which they are mounted. A 'domed' boiler is exactly what it says: it has a dome on the boiler which houses the regulator from which the steam then travels to the superheater header mounted inside the smokebox, actually of course on the front tubeplate. The top feed non-return valves are as on the domeless boiler, apart from the point that the manhole they occupy is separately mounted away from the dome. This although perhaps seeming elementary to some readers has very significant visual features when applied to the 'Princess Royals' with their various boiler changes during their lives.

A series of dynamometer car tests were performed against two of the standard Pacifics Nos.6210 and 6212, on the Euston to Glasgow route and as expected No.6202 came out slightly better on economy and slightly stronger than the standard locomotives — exactly as expected! An alteration to the superheater elements was made; these were changed from twin elements to triple elements to ascertain if any more worthwhile economies were in the offing, but the earlier arrangement was reverted to.

In the four year period up to the start of the Second World War there had been a policy of constant monitoring and improvements applied to the engine and this was shown in its gradually increasing mileages between 'incidents'. It is a recorded fact that as 'Turbo' was an experimental one-off machine, a good few of the stoppages were the result of over-cautious examining fitters! The author, having been in a similar position himself, can sympathise wholeheartedly, because in railway work the safety aspects weigh above all else, no matter the delays that may be incurred, irate Shed Foremen included!

Changes in appearance over this period were very few, being confined to the instantly recognisable domed and separate top feed second boiler. A few more access panels appeared in the side casings, together with their attendant hinges and locking clips and there were — of some significance — ventilating louvres cut in the tops of the control valve casings in an effort to reduce temperatures. This in conjunction with the increased oil cooling and pumping capacity gave a notable step forward in reliability. The only other but perhaps most notice-

A rare view of 'Turbo' running tender first with empty stock at Bushey, the engine still with domeless boiler. As a matter of interest, No.6202's tender was the very first of the Stanier marque to have the curved top side panels from new and was different from all later examples in having straight edges on both sides of the backplates to the side steps. Another interesting point is that No.6202 was the only LMS 4-6-2 never to be fitted with the later higher-sided ten-ton tender. (The late Gavin Wilson Collection)

able addition, was the fitting of smoke deflectors — or as the LMS called them 'Wind Plates' and the lengthening of the reverse control casing to house the extra oil pump in February 1939. The mileage accrued by this time was approximately 180,000.

At the outbreak of war on 3rd September

Smoke deflectors were added just before the war and the engine is seen in this condition in the post-war 1946 livery. (The late Gavin Wilson Collection)

This second c.1946 view clearly shows the extended turbine casing fitted on the right hand side in later years — see text. (The late Gavin Wilson Collection)

1939 the experiment was brought to a halt and No.6202 was duly withdrawn on the 21st of that month as it was felt that Metropolitan Vickers would be unable to 'fit it in' during war conditions should the need arise.

After lying in Crewe Works for nearly two years, the need for anything that could turn a wheel meant that the September 1939 decision was reversed and 'Turbo' duly re-appeared in traffic on 24th July 1941. Unfortunately the surmise that Vickers would no longer be in a position to co-operate as fully as before became fact within two months of its return to service when the reverse turbine developed a fault. This failure could be partly attributed to standing idle for a considerable period, a common complaint with heavy machinery lying dormant for long periods when the bearings and wear surfaces settle and can develop local pitting.

Spasmodic use during the war brought it up to its heavy general repair, at which time both turbines were reconditioned, but the 'gremlins' were about and shortly after returning to traffic the reverse turbine unit suffered a further failure, with oil passages blocked by cotton waste left in from its previous stripping. By this time the LMS Co.'s meticulous costings on it had been abandoned.

After the repair of this latest damage and delays No.6202 worked again with its mileage totting up to its heavy general repair time. This was a very protracted repair which lasted for over a year and in fact the engine was just lying out of use, its boiler being removed and fitted to No.6210. This was regained in due course and after the completion of the heavy repair (after some fifteen months or so) it was released for traffic. However, war conditions were certainly telling against this thoroughbred machine.

In the equally severe immediate post-war period the availability of the locomotive suffered even more and could best be described as erratic. The engine history cards show a general pattern of light casual visits to Crewe, but as the costing system had been abandoned there are no details shown as to their purpose. The end of a long period out of traffic from March 1946 to April 1947 saw No.6202 appear sporting the very attractive LMS black

with 'just a hint' of straw and maroon. The author believes that up to this date, 'Turbo' was still red.

To continue this now sorry saga, the frequent visits to works resumed; but the writing was on the wall for this brave experiment and it was possibly considered a rostering liability. During one of its four visits to Crewe in 1949 the ex-LNWR experimental BR livery was applied, the May visit is felt to be the most likely as the new larger Lion and Wheel emblem was applied.

May 1950 saw the final disappearance of 'Turbomotive', for the decision had been taken to 'rebuild to a reciprocating locomotive' as the history card laconically states. It was February 1952 before any drawings were filed for this conversion under Job No.5621 (Derby drawing office had been fully occupied up to this point with the new BR Standard Pacifics). These drawings show that it really was a minimal conversion resulting in a curious composite. The coupled wheelbase was reduced at the leading axle from 8ft 0in to 7ft 3in, this brought it into line with the 'Coronation' standard and enabled a complete front end of that class to be welded on. As these engines had

'Turbo' as BR No.46202 in LNWR lined black livery with the newly adopted BR emblem on the tender. The date was 1949, by which time the BR standard liveries and markings had been determined, so strictly speaking the engine could have been given the blue BR livery as applied to all other ex-LMS 4-6-2s. (The late Gavin Wilson Collection)

derived valve gear driving the inside cylinders the Princess Royal class now comprised of Thirteen engines sporting four motion variants between them! As stated the conversion really was kept to a minimum, resulting in the ugly drop in the platform at the half-way point. Perhaps even more curious was the provision of a new smokebox wrapper fitted with a single chimney, and the original 'Coronation' single blast pipe used, although the 'Coronation' double blastpipe was standard by this time. The author remembers seeing

The rebuilt 'Turbo' as No.46202 _Princess Anne_ seen in service at Crewe during its tragically short working life. (The late Gavin Wilson Collection)

her once in her new guise but was not at all impressed!

On 15th August 1952 No.46202 _Princess Anne_ started her short and dramatic career of eight weeks, only to end in the horrific Harrow disaster on 8th October of that year. Beyond economic repair, she lingered at Crewe for some eighteen months before being officially condemned and withdrawn on 22nd May 1954. The boiler was recovered, repaired and placed into the pool of spare Princess Royal units. Unfortunately no trace of the tender No.9003 has been found, so it is assumed that it was cut up.

The questions could be asked after all these years: "Was it a success?" Also, could it have promoted further examples? The authors belief is a cautious 'Yes'; it was a success but only until the outbreak of war. The reversal of the September 1939 decision to lay it up sounded the death knell of this remarkable machine. Could it have promoted further examples? The introduction of the 'Coronation' class in 1937 and their success in bringing power levels beyond that of No.6202 at less cost meant that it was destined to remain a lone experiment.

Furthermore, it is felt that a large com-

pipework and fittings were soldered, the complete detailed unit being screwed onto the real copper one. Again this enabled detailing and painting to be done to this item.

Having cut one's teeth on the back shape, the more complex front throat plate was attacked next. This is the point where nine out of ten models get it wrong; and I include some expensive professionally built models in this sweeping statement. The curves of this item are very graceful indeed and as this model's firebox shows above and below the platform it has to be right. Another piece of the faithful oak was carved and filed to the desired shape, incorporating the extension of the bottom half of the boiler cone as this part blends into the throat plate. This area is in full view and can make or mar it, and repays care. It took two attempts to get this right; however, perseverance wins in the end. When this front plate was soldered in the firebox, the unit became quite imposing, except for the joint line between the front and the sides. This of course is because .010in sheet in 7mm scale represents nearly ⅜in thick — not typical of cladding plates at all! The remedy became immediately obvious — flood a line of solder along those edges where it showed and cut it back until an apparent scale ½ inch was showing. A table of scale 7mm equivalents was included in MBT Vol.2 No.6.

It now remains to solder all these three units together in a straight line. The best way that I know is a very old method used in welding fabrication shops and indeed I would hesitate to say where it came from. By looking at the illustration it will be seen that the complete, pushed together, assem-

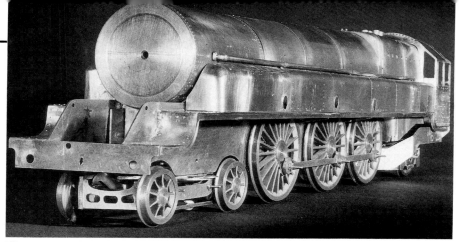

These two pictures show the engine 'coming together'. The side casings are still to be finally fitted to close the gaps around the smokebox. (Tony Wright)

bly is laid on paper using the foundation ring as a datum, the plan view centre line having been drawn on the paper first. By packing the smokebox and boiler until the base is horizontal the boiler centre line can be checked and established all the way round. At several points along the assembly the diameters of the components are measured and accurately drawn on the paper set equally about our centre already drawn. The points in this case need to be: front of smokebox, start of boiler cone, front base of firebox, rear base of fire box.

Plastikard templates or 'bridges' are cut out to snugly fit over the boiler at the same points, again these template apertures are halved exactly to coincide with the vertical centre line. Once more the boiler horizontal centre line measured from the bases of the bridges can be marked just as a check.

When all the bridges are pushed over the boiler and all the bases are touching the drawn parallel lines on the paper and by squinting or 'boning' along the vertical centre line the complete unit is in line, so tack it up before anything gets disturbed! Once tacked the remainder of the seams can be finish-soldered with confidence.

These descriptions about complete the potentially awkward items with particular reference to the 'Turbomotive', but it can be seen that a lot of it is relevant to say, LNER Pacifics, the GWR Great Bear and

Ready for painting — all items that are removable or to be glued on (eg the top feed casing) are left off at this stage. Note that the model is in domed configuration so the modifications to the casings — see prototype photographs — have been incorporated. (Tony Wright)

of course the BR Standard 9F 2-10-0 or 4-6-2s. The 'boning' technique is also applicable to Churchward taper boilers and in my opinion is well worth the time taken to set it up.

Perhaps a few lines on the use of machine tools may not come amiss at this point. I use a pantograph miller as my main machine. Readers may think, and quite rightly, that the use of this takes modelling out of the average person's reach and I would agree whole heartedly. However, the use of this machine is the only way that I can build a model to the squareness and clean finish that I desire; but for a one off model like No.6202 it can take longer than conventional scratch building methods. Let me qualify that statement by quoting an example. Using a pantograph first of all requires a template to be made, say two, three, or four times larger than the finished metal item. It follows that I can cut this out probably cleaner and more accurately than I could at actual size and in metal. Also any error incurred in the pattern is reduced in the finished part. Where the machine really scores is when there is more than one part per pattern to be made.

Acknowledgements must be made to the several people who lent me photographs to supplement my own collection during the building of No.6202, namely Nelson Twells, Don Rowland and Roger Carpenter. Special mention must be made of Fred James, an ex-Derby man who helped unravel several threads in the modification and conversion to *Princess Anne* drawings.

No.6202, as running 1937-8, completed after painting by Keith King. (Tony Wright)

GREAT WESTERN

VETERANS

By Paul Timothy

Now who, unless they knew, would immediately identify this mid-19th century classic as 'Great Western'? It would look equally at home on almost any railway of the 1850s, the fluted dome and safety valve casings being very characteristic of the time. In fact, it was a typical E.

B. Wilson engine of 1855, originally built for the Newport, Abergavenny & Hereford Railway in 1855 as No.28 *Reindeer.* In 1860, the NA&HR was one of several companies which amalgamated to form the West Midland Railway and No.28 became No.94 in the WMR lists. Three years later,

the WMR was then absorbed into the GWR and No.94 became GWR No.191 (as shown here), still a relative youngster of eight years old. The GWR must have liked it for it was twice rebuilt (1873 and 1893) and it did not go out of service until 1902. The picture is undated but pre-dates the rebuilding. (RCTS Part 3, page C32)

The GWR is often perceived as a railway which pursued locomotive standardisation in a big way and for those not imbued with a passion for Swindon it can often be seen as a bit 'boring' in consequence — rather like the post-Stanier LMS! Now it is true that the abolition of the Broad Gauge in 1892 gave it a 'once for all' chance to make a new start, a fact of which both William Dean and George Jackson Churchward took full advantage, but what is often forgotten is that the 4ft 8½in discipline had a long pre-1892 history and that even afterwards, not everything which ran on the 'narrow gauge' Great Western carried the stamp of uniformity. This rather fine set of official views serves as a timely reminder of a few of those exceptions.

Note: The author freely acknowledges extensive reference to *The Locomotives of the Great Western Railway* (RCTS), to which series, readers who wish for further details are referred. For the record, the Part No. and principal page reference for the types concerned are given at the end of each caption.

The 2-4-0 was arguably the most characteristic mid-Victorian passenger type and the GWR itself introduced many variants during Armstrong's and Dean's time in office. No.811 was an example of Armstrong's last 2-4-0 design, the '806' Class, of which twenty were built in 1873. They were similar to Armstrong's immediately preceding type but with larger (6ft 6½in compared with 6ft 0in) driving wheels, it being very common practice, then as in later days, to offer broadly the same type with several different sizes of driving wheel for different types of work. The picture shows the engine pretty well as built but during their long life, these engines underwent many changes. They were given cabs, brass numberplates, straight platforms and closed splashers, not to mention the several boiler and tender changes. No.811 received its first replacement boiler in 1889 (of a type similar to that shown on No.71 in the next picture) and was not withdrawn until 1918, after two further boiler exchanges. (RCTS Part 4, page D32)

This undated view (but see below) shows No.71 *Dee,* one of a small group of seven 2-4-0s — the 'River' Class of 1895-7 — with a truly venerable history. They were reconstructed from older 2-2-2s, dating from 1872-5, which carried the same numbers and were themselves renewals of a standard gauge 2-2-2 type introduced by Gooch in 1855. It should be appreciated that 'renewal' was an accountancy term which could cover anything from a minor rebuild to a brand new replacement and in this case, it is doubtful if anything remained of the original Gooch engines after the 1872-5 changes; but the 2-4-0s were genuine rebuilds. No.71 was built in 1855, 'renewed' in 1873 and reconstructed in 1895. It lasted until 1915 but had two different types of boiler during that time. From 1895-1903, and again from 1908, it carried the type shown in this view but from 1903-8 it had the similar version with the dome on the back ring. Given the elliptical roof carriage on the left of the picture, a style not introduced on main line stock until 1904, the picture must have been taken between 1908-15. (RCTS Part 4, page D43)

The GWR had no purely standard gauge lines until 1854 but thereafter, the 'narrow gauge' played an increasingly important role and by the mid-1860s the random collection of 4ft 8½in goods engines had become inadequate for the ever increasing traffic and the need was felt for a new standard type. From 1866 to 1876, hundreds were built of which No.682, shown here, came into service in 1872. Correctly known as 'Standard Goods', they were often referred to as 'Armstrong Goods' in later years when Dean's later design had to some extent usurped the original designation. No.682 is seen as built in this undated picture, but in later years a proper cab was fitted and in due course, replacement boilers of the same type as mentioned earlier for the 2-4-0s became the norm, No.682 receiving a 'front ring dome' replacement in 1887 and a 'back ring' version in 1906. The engine was withdrawn in 1915, somewhat ahead of the peak period for most of the class — the first few years after World War I. (RCTS Part 4, page D57 et seq)

Like most British systems, the GWR made considerable use of the 4-4-0 type but this wheel arrangement was relatively late to arrive on the standard gauge compared with many other railways, not appearing until 1894. This and the next two views show three progressively larger examples, starting with No.3527, one of 40 engines which surely had one of the most extraordinary origins of any British 4-4-0. The '3521' Class rebuilds, as they were called, started life as 0-4-4Ts dating from 1887-9, but they had a fearsome reputation for derailment and were therefore rebuilt to 4-4-0 form during 1899-1902. The rebuilding necessitated the reversal of cylinder and firebox positions, almost certainly involving new inside frames. Of them, 26 received the small boiler shown here, the rest getting the new Standard No.3 domeless raised Belpaire boiler. No.3527 took 4-4-0 form in 1900 and in due course (1915), did receive a more modern boiler — flush Belpaire with back dome position, as did the other 25, most of them rather sooner than 3527 and one as early as 1902. No.3527 was withdrawn in 1927 as one of but five of the original 26 small boilered rebuilds not to be subsequently superheated as well. (RCTS Part 7, page G45)

Along with his contemporary bogie singles, Dean's early 4-4-0s were amongst the most graceful late Victorian designs, well exemplified in this lovely view of No.3272 *Amyas,* a member of the celebrated 'Duke' Class (dating from 1895) a more detailed account of which, including drawings, was given in MODELLERS' BACKTRACK Vol.1 No.3. The 'Dukes' were an extremely versatile class whose relatively small 5ft 7½in driving wheels made them suitable for a wide variety of tasks save for the heaviest high speed work. Inevitably, they came in for their due share of reboilering of which the domed flush Belpaire type gradually became the standard form; *Amyas,* built in 1896, acquired one in 1913. Many of the 'Dukes' were later rebuilt as 'Bulldogs' — essentially a larger boilered 5ft 7½in 4-4-0 (most of which were built new) developed from the 'Duke' Class — but No.3272 remained in small boilered form. Superheated in 1930, it was withdrawn in 1938. The picture is undated but although it shows the pre-Belpaire form, it post-dates the change from straight nameplates on the side of the boiler to the standard curved form at the end of 1903. (RCTS Part 7, page G12 et seq)

This view shows an intermediate form of yet another GWR design whose origins go back into the 19th century — No.3298 *Grosvenor* of the 'Badminton' Class — a typical double framed 4-4-0, this time with 6ft 8in driving wheels. Like the small-wheeled examples already considered, the 'Badmintons' came into service during the Dean period with small parallel boilers, though they were the first GWR type to be built new with Belpaire fireboxes. The engines were built during 1897-9, No.3298 appearing in 1898. Like many types at the time, the 'Badmintons' were in the thick of Churchward's experiments with new and better boilers and in due course all but three of them were given new No.4 Standard boilers of the type first seen on *City of Truro* and her sisters from 1902, thus making them temporary 'Cities'. *Grosvenor* is seen in this form here, a condition which the engine displayed from 1905-11. In the latter year, a replacement (smaller) No.2 Standard (superheated) boiler was fitted and the engine ran thus until withdrawn in 1929. (RCTS Part 7, page G29 et seq)

The six-coupled pannier tanks were a distinguishing aspect of the GWR scene to the end of steam and it can therefore hardly occasion surprise that when a travelling crane was needed, the 0-6-0PT formed the basis for the engine part. In the case of 0-6-0CT No.17 *Cyclops*, the engine part was similar to the '850' Class 0-6-0PTs whose origins went right back to 1874. It will be noted, however, that the dome was omitted in order to accommodate the jib when in lowered position for travelling. Travelling cranes (or crane tanks as they were often known) were an interesting if unfamiliar aspect of the railway scene and No.17 was one of two built in 1901 (a third example was added in 1921). The rear extension above the four-wheel bogie was designed so that the whole of the crane to the rear of the cab (including the jib when raised) could be rotated through 360°, allowing for maximum flexibility of operation. In due course, changes in techniques were to make self-propelled travelling cranes less and less useful and No.17 and her two sisters were all withdrawn in 1936. The picture cannot be dated but as can be seen, the custodians of the equippage kept it in fine state. The 'H' spoke wheels, somewhat reminiscent of LNWR practice but unusual for the GWR, are also worthy of note. (RCTS Part 5, page E71)

The WC&P station at Clevedon on 25th June 1938. (The late H. C. Casserley by courtesy of R. M. Casserley)

The Weston, Clevedon & Portishead Light Railway was not one of life's financial successes. It was in receivership for all but twelve years of its forty-three year existence but, nevertheless, was one of Britain's delightfully eccentric rural lines which, in keeping with many other light railways, was at one time part of the 'Colonel Stephens' empire. **Martin Smith** tells the story.

A Light Tale – the WC&LPLR

I. Origins to Receivership

The Weston, Cleveland & Portishead Tramway Company, to give it its correct original title, was born as an indirect result of Brunel's strategies. That, however, does not imply that the master engineer had anything to do with the line's construction as the WC&P entered this world because of what was considered an oversight by the man himself. Instead of diverting broad gauge main lines, Brunel often preferred to serve towns near the lines by branches and, in Somerset, this practice manifested itself on the Bristol & Exeter Railway. This left the towns of Weston, Clevedon and Portishead at the end of branches and, although the distances between each of the towns were fairly short for the proverbial crows, mere humans had to undertake a series of laborious train changes to travel from one to another. The coming of the B&E heralded the growth of the holiday industry in the three towns and, although Weston was treated to a diversion of the main line in 1884, local businessmen felt that a direct rail link between the towns would further improve local fortunes.

Assent for a standard gauge tramway linking the towns was obtained in 1885 but, five years later, only a short section at the Weston end had been completed; the lack of action was due, not only to a sparseness of funds, but also because some landowners seemed to be vying for a Blue Peter badge for obstructiveness. An extension of time was granted in 1892, a condition being that the section to Clevedon should be completed by 1894 and the extension to Portishead by 1896.

Patience seems to have been unlimited. Despite the revision of completion dates, the section between Weston and Clevedon was not finished until 1897 and, even then, the Portishead extension seems to have been conveniently overlooked. The final stages of the construction work were undertaken by the company's own staff as, early that year, the contractor had withdrawn when payments had not materialised. The WC&P labour force was overseen by the company's general manager, one Edward Wintour, who had gained much of his engineering and administrative experience on the Severn & Wye Railway, a company which had been purchased jointly by the GWR and the Midland in 1894. It was Wintour himself who had the distinction of driving the

engine hauling the WC&P's ceremonial train to Clevedon on 7th October 1897.

The first train on the completed section had, in fact, run on 18th August but that had been solely for the benefit of the WC&P's engineering staff, and a considerable amount of work had still to be undertaken after that date in order to bring the

line up to Board of Trade standards. The BoT inspector had not been over-impressed by what he had first seen and, no doubt, had appreciated the irony in one particular clause in the WC&P's Act of 1892 which stipulated that no fares would be charged to members of the Royal Family. Although the company was, to all outward purposes,

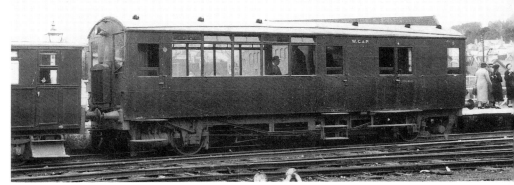

WC&P Drewry Railcar No.5, acquired from the Southern Railway in 1934 and which retained its SR livery — see also Section V. (The late H. C. Casserley by courtesy of R. M. Casserley)

Western Super Mare, 22nd May 1929, with WC&P No.5, a Manning Wardle 0-6-0ST in charge of the former LSWR 'Triplet' set — see also Sections V/VI. (The late H. C. Casserley by courtesy of R. M. Casserley)

WESTON CLEVEDON & PORTISHEAD LIGHT RAILWAY

As neither the engineering train nor the ceremonial train had been revenue-earning services, they had been legitimately operated without Board of Trade approval. By the time the necessary work had been done on the line, it was 1st December 1897 before it was officially opened for the serious business of extracting money from the fare-paying public. The locomotive which had been belatedly acquired for the occasion was a Kitson 0-6-0T named *Harold*, hired from Messrs. C. D. Phillips, the contractor engaged on extension work at the Alexandra Dock in Newport.

On the WC&P's unveiling to the public, *Harold* took 30 minutes to cover the 8¼ miles from Clevedon to Weston, stops being made at the seven intermediate stations. The service became standardised at six trains each way during winter months but this was doubled during the summer, and the construction of a passing loop at Wick St. Lawrence later became necessary for the heady practice of more than one engine in steam. The scheduled journey time became standardised at 45 minutes, the return fare being one shilling (5p). The new line was popular and, in order to accommodate all of the passengers, the WC&P found it necessary to double the length of its trains; from 22nd December, the trains consisted of two carriages instead of one. Authorisation for this was subject to the fitting of continuous brakes and the employment of a brakesman on all trains.

Despite the euphoria of having, at very long last, a working railway, the WC&P's hierarchy had not totally forgotten the proposed extension to Portishead. In 1899, the company was reconstituted, the status of a light railway officially replacing that of a tramway, and the appropriate powers for the extension were gained in the new corporate title of the Weston, Clevedon & Portishead Light Railway. The company's new status took advantage of the terms made available by the Light Railways Act

preparing itself for the grand moment of its opening to the public, the inspector's request to view the locomotive stock was met with blank looks. An 0-6-0T named *Clevedon*, which had been used for the engineering trips, was away for repair and, just weeks before the anticipated public opening, the WC&P did not have a replacement engine on order, let alone in stock. A hasty hiring had to be arranged.

WESTON-SUPER-MARE (W.C.&P.) STATION. 1936. The layout of Ashcombe Road station and yard can be clearly seen just four years before closure.

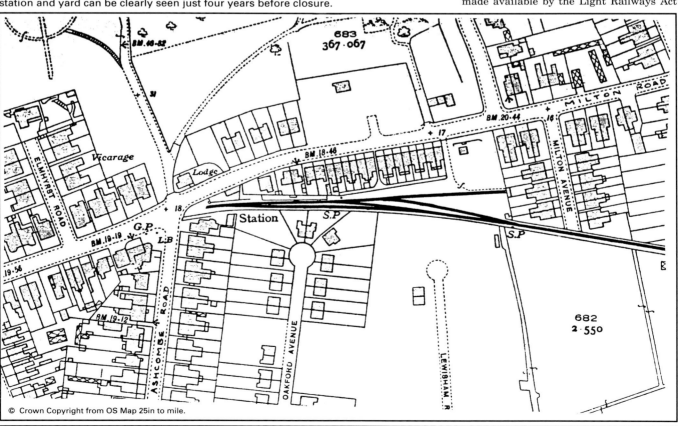

© Crown Copyright from OS Map 25in to mile.

of 1896. That Act was intended to encourage the promotion of rural rural railways, one significant aspect being that a line could be sanctioned by a Board of Trade Order rather than a fully-fledged (and very costly) Act of Parliament. Another major feature of the Act was that, for the first time in British Railway history, local authorities were permitted to subscribe to new schemes while, in some cases, Government grants or loans would be available to help out with construction costs. In the case of the WC&P, however, it seems that neither Somerset County Council nor the Treasury dug into their respective piggy banks to assist with the funding of the Portishead extension. Nevertheless, other aspects of the Light Railways Act proved financially beneficial to the WC&P, those including relaxation of the requirements for lineside fencing, gated level crossings and 'adequate' station facilities. In common with other railways authorised under the Act, the WC&P's part of the deal included observation of maximum speed limits and axle weights but, to be honest, the nature of the line hardly enabled fast running or the use of heavy locomotives.

The six mile line from Clevedon to the company's own station at Portishead was eventually opened on 7th August 1907, Manning Wardle 0-6-0ST No.2 *Portishead* (the second WC&P locomotive to carry that name) being in charge of the inaugural public train. Initially, eight trains were scheduled each way between Clevedon and Portishead with 30 minutes being allowed; the complete run from Portishead to Weston was scheduled for around one hour. The apparent glory was, however, superficial as the opening to Portishead crippled the WC&P financially. The cost of the extension turned out to be three times that

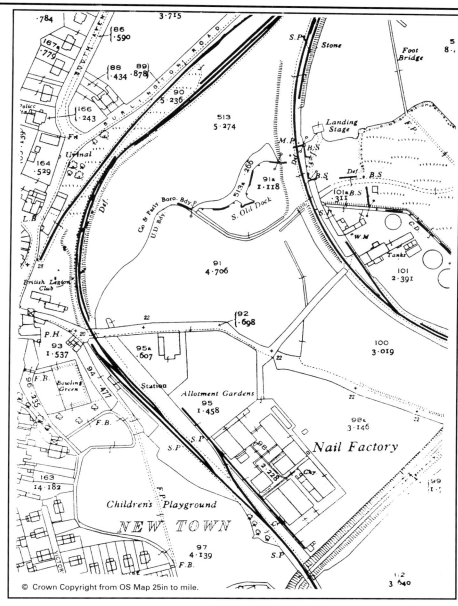

© Crown Copyright from OS Map 25in to mile.

Two more 25th June 1938 views of Clevedon. The main building was to the south of the line (the loco shed behind) but the platform itself was on the opposite side. (The late H. C. Casserley by courtesy of R. M. Casserley — 2)

projected and, although the company's revenue from the Weston-Clevedon section was just about adequate to cover its operating costs, it was nowhere near enough to provide surplus funds to subsidise the extension. Despite a financial restructuring in 1904 which had involved the formation of a holding company, the Weston, Clevedon & Portishead Docks Railway Co. Ltd., creditors became restless. On 30th July 1909, the WC&P went into receivership and, from that date, became the property of its major creditor, the Excess Insurance Company, the firm which had provided most of the finance for the extension.

II. Enter 'Colonel' Stephens

The creditor decided to keep the railway open in an attempt to recoup at least some of the monies due and, in 1911, appointed the doyen of light railway operators, Holman Frederick Stephens, as manager of the line. Stephens had been borne in 1868. He had been a pupil of J. J. Hanbury, the Superintendent of the Metropolitan Railway, at Neasden Works and had later worked in the Met's running department. His first administrative appointment had been as Resident Engineer of the Cranbrook & Paddock Wood Railway in

Kent and, by 1911, he had been involved with a number of light railways. Although he had become very familiar with under-privileged little lines, he didn't fancy the WC&P's chances one iota. Consequently, he willingly carried out instructions to negotiate with the Great Western with a view to a sale, but the GWR didn't want to play. The WC&P had previously considered a possible courtship with the Midland Railway. The light railway company's directors had toyed with the idea of extending southwards from Weston to join the Somerset & Dorset Railway near Highbridge and, had such an extension been financially viable, it could have encouraged the Midland, which had a joint lease on the S&D, to either lease or buy the WC&P in order to get a foothold in GWR territory. The WC&P, however, stood little hope of raising the money to construct such an extension.

Despite Stephens's expertise, the WC&P's uphill financial struggle continued and was later aggravated by the introduction of motor bus competition. One wasteful WC&P practice which Stephens did not tackle was that of light running. Even when the Portishead extension was opened, the company retained the midway point of Clevedon as its headquarters and, therefore, all rolling stock had to be returned there at the end of a day's duties. The WC&P's sparsely-filled coffers prevented any serious thoughts of relocating the locomotive department, let alone the addition of extra facilities.

Although primarily a passenger railway, the WC&P had its share of freight traffic. There were gasworks at Worle and Clevedon, and the railway undertook delivery and shunting duties for both. Quarry traffic originated at two points on the section north of Clevedon, one of these being Conygar Quarry, near Walton Park station. The quarry was laid with narrow gauge tracks which connected with standard gauge sidings and, in turn, the WC&P. The quarry company had, at varying stages of its existence, its own shunting locomotives for both of its gauges and the last engine, an Avonside 0-4-0ST, was used right up to when the quarry's own line was closed in 1935. Between Cadbury Road and Clapton Road stations, transfer sidings for the stone traffic from Black Rock Quarries were established in 1919. With a capacity of almost 100 wagons, the WC&P sidings took stone from trucks which used the 2ft gauge tramway from the quarries. The quarry company had its own narrow gauge locomotives, the first pair being Hudswell

Clarke 0-6-0WTs, but these were later replaced by petrol locomotives which, in turn, were ousted by diesels. Black Rock Quarries were eventually to provide over three-quarters of the WC&P's freight revenue, and the stone traffic continued almost until the light railway's demise.

The WC&P even had a grasp on the shipping business and, on paper, had its own sailing barges, *Lily* and *Sarah*, although their registrations were usually in the name of Holman Stephens. The barges operated from a wharf which was constructed in 1915 at Wick St. Lawrence, north of Weston, and linked to the WC&P by a short branch. It was hoped that passenger and freight traffic to and from South Wales would use the wharf but, as all three towns on the railway's route had well-established pleasure-steamer links with other Bristol Channel towns, passenger traffic failed to materialise. As for the wharf's freight traffic, the most charitable description of trade was 'steady', the main commodity being coal which was shipped from South Wales for Worle and Clevedon gasworks and, of course, for use by the railway itself.

After the Great War, the newly-formed Ministry of Transport started to formulate plans for the grouping of Britain's railways, and the WC&P's main creditor, the Excess Insurance Company, thought that it had been presented with a way of offloading its

questionable asset. The Great Western, however, knew the WC&P rather too well and the folks at Swindon fought tooth and nail not to be lumbered with such a liability. As a result, the WC&P came to be one of just thirteen light railways which eluded absorption by any of the 'big four'.

In the summer of 1922, four trains were scheduled from Portishead to Weston with three making the reverse journey. An additional train left Portishead at 8.45am but ran only as far as Clevedon. Five other services were advertised from Weston to Clevedon only, with four from Clevedon to Weston. Journey times over the whole line ranged from 60-70 minutes while the section between Clevedon and Weston took between 30 and 35 minutes. In Bradshaw's, the WC&P timetable listed only ten of the stations between Portishead and Weston although a footnote explained that trains would call at the other seven stations when required. To find the WC&P timetable in Bradshaw's, one had to look between the East Kent Light Railway (another 'Colonel Stephens' line) and the London-Norwich service of the Great Eastern!

The growth of road transport in the 1920s and 1930s was a hefty nail in the steadily-closing coffin of the WC&P, and it has been suggested that the main reason behind the railway's continuance of operations was the philanthropy of the Excess Insurance Company. One of the few steady sources of traffic was the stone from Black Rock Quarries but, of course, the WC&P could not keep its corporate head above water just from that one source. The company's future was not helped when, in

Clevedon loco shed c.1927 with Manning Wardle 0-6-0ST on left, tractor loco on right and *Hesperus*, the Sharp Stewart 2-4-0T behind. (Photomatic)

1931, the enigmatic Holman Stephens passed away at the comparatively young age of 63, a cruel series of strokes having left him paralysed. Although popularly referred to as 'Colonel Stephens', the rank which he attained with the Royal Engineers during World War I was, in fact, that of Lieutenant-Colonel. The task of overseeing all the little lines in the 'Colonel Stephens' empire fell to his former Chief Assistant, William Austen, who, although a very capable administrator, couldn't quite match Stephens' ability to keep even the most unlikely railway operational. During Stephens' reign, operating costs on the WC&P had been trimmed to the proverbial bone, but at least the line gave a faint impression of being a proper working railway. By the late 1930s, however, the weed-infested tracks, shabby station buildings and poorly maintained locomotives clearly confirmed that the WC&P was indeed on its last legs.

III. The Final Years

When the Government took control of the nation's railways at the start of World War II, the WC&P was, once again, excluded from the master plan. By this time, traffic had dwindled further and so the Bowler Hats could not justify the expense of maintaining the line. In the last full year before the war, the WC&P carried just over 86,000 passengers and, although a lower annual figure had been recorded on three occasions, the total had, prior to 1920, never dropped below 105,000. At its peak, the WC&P had carried over 200,000 passengers annually, but it wasn't just the totals which affected the company's revenue. In 1901, over five thousand of the tickets sold were first class but, in 1938, the number of passengers lashing out on first class fares was just four.

The issue of closure notices met with some token protests but, generally, realism prevailed and the inevitable was accepted gracefully. The last train left Weston for Clevedon at 6.15pm on Saturday 18th May 1940 and was hauled by ex-LB&SCR 'Terrier' No.4, but the tumultous send-off it was given did not fool the Ministry into reconsidering the line's future. Government statisticians were well aware that the number of passengers on that last train was more than usually used the line in two whole days. The deceptiveness of passenger figures for 'last trains' was to become a feature of the 1960s but, at the time of the WC&P's demise, the loss of a railway was rarely considered such a major event. By contrast with the scenes at Weston and Clevedon in 1940, the last train on the Basingstoke-Alton line in 1932 had carried just one passenger while, in 1933, the closure of the Lee on Solent branch in Hampshire had been witnessed, so the story goes, by just six men and a dog.

Although the Great Western had refused several opportunities to purchase the WC&P as an operational concern, the former readily bought the remnants after closure for £10,000. One of the uses which the GWR had in mind for the line was that of storage. The war had brought a sudden hiatus to the export of coal through the South Wales ports of Cardiff, Barry and Newport, and the coal trains were causing congestion at the ports. Despite the limited accommodation and lightweight construction of the WC&P line, it was viewed as potentially useful for storing trains loaded

Manning Wardle 0-6-0ST departs from Portishead for Clevedon on 19th April 1924 with a typical mixed train. The coaches (see Section VI) are ex-Metropolitan Railway stock. (LCGB)

with Welsh coal. It seems, however, that no such usage was ever made of the line, and the tracks were lifted in 1942-43. The GWR expressed its opinion of the WC&P's rolling stock by selling or scrapping everything except the two former LB&SCR 'Terrier' 0-6-0Ts.

In 1956, plans were mooted for a revival of the WC&P in the form of a narrow gauge line offering a combination of a local public transport system and a tourist attraction, but nothing came of the idea. Consequently, the WC&P became one representative of the relatively small number of railways which disappeared irreversibly from the maps before Nationalisation.

Today, comparatively little of the WC&P's route has been built over but, nevertheless, even the most enthusiastic railway historian has to have an exceptionally well-trained eye to spot any remnants of the line. Between Portishead and Clevedon, the trackbed is still just about discernible in places, and a brick wall from the old Black Rock exchange yard now provides shelter for a herd of Fresians, none of which, sadly, seems able to tell a light railway from a lavatory brush. South of Clevedon, it is possible to see some of the bridge lintels where the line crossed drainage ditches while, at Weston, the site of the station has, remarkably, not been redeveloped but, nevertheless, yields no real clues as to its former use.

Interestingly, though, as late as 1971, one-inch Ordnance Survey maps still showed 'course of old railway' for at least half of the distance between Weston and Clevedon.

IV. The Route

The impecunious little WC&P was spared any major expense on earthworks as virtually all of its route passed over very level land. The Weston-Clevedon section was so flat that any hummocks in the landscape were usually attributable to either buried sofas or the work of moles with gout. Between Clevedon and Portishead, the WC&P's route passed through the scenic Gordano Valley although, quite sensibly for the company's engineers and accountants, the line stuck firmly to the valley floor.

The rails used on the Weston-Clevedon section were flat-bottomed and 56lb/yd, the Clevedon-Portishead section being treated to 60lb/yd rails. Around 1919/20, a short section of track to the north of Clevedon station was experimentally relaid on concrete blocks instead of sleepers, every third pair of blocks being trussed with metal bars. The experiment must have been at least partially successful as the blocks were retained for the rest of the line's life but, perversely, it seems that no other section of track was similarly treated.

Little seems to be recorded about the signalling of the line although it is certain that the 'minimalist' school of thought

Portishead station in 1927 with ex-LBSC 'Terrier' 0-6-0T (WC&P No.2) in charge of the 'Triplet' set. (Photomatic)

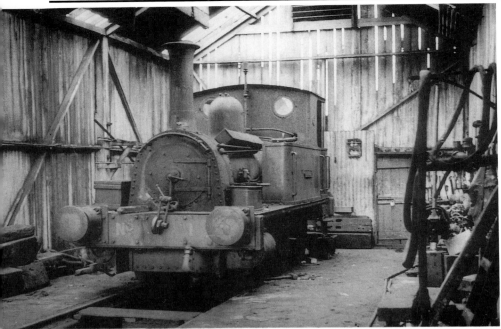

Dubs 2-4-0T No.1 *Clevedon* **at Clevedon shed, 25th June 1938.** (The late H. C. Casserley by courtesy of R. M. Casserley)

applied. It is, however, known that Lieutenant-Colonel Stephens purchased the Saxby & Farmer equipment from the Bideford, Westward Ho! & Appledore Railway when that company's assets were auctioned in 1921, four years after the line's closure, and that the intended recipient of the equipment was indeed the WC&P.

The route of the WC&P started at Ashcombe Road station in Weston which originally had a low wooden platform, a higher platform being erected in 1919. Passenger facilities comprised little more than the obligatory ticket office, waiting room and toilets, all of which were housed in a distinctive curved-roofed building to the rear of the platform; a small brick-built shelter on the platform was provided in later years. There was a run-round loop and a siding into a small goods yard.

The first stopping place along the line was Milton Road halt (1 mile), which had a short siding and a small shelter on its gravel-faced 'platform'. If that halt had minimal facilities, it was positively luxurious when compared to Bristol Road halt (1⅛ miles) which opened in 1912 as little more than a token request stop alongside a level crossing. Worle station (1¾ miles) was renamed Worle (Moor Lane) in 1913 and Worle Town in 1917; its original low wooden platform was removed completely circa 1917, a new timber-built waiting room-cum-ticket office being provided alongside the line at ground level. One of the two sidings at the station originally served the adjacent gas works, but the closure of the works in the early 1920s enabled a revision of the siding accommodation.

At Ebdon Lane halt (3 miles) and Wick St. Lawrence (3¾ miles), passenger facilities at both consisted of nothing more than a wooden shelter, although the one at the latter was at least large enough to justify a door and a couple of windows. Beyond Wick St. Lawrence station, the spur to the jetty on the River Yeo diverged; the jetty was some 270ft long and had concrete facing supported by timber and concrete piers. Four more stopping places, Ham Lane halt (5 miles), Broadstone halt (5¾ miles),

Kingston Road halt (6 miles) and Colehouse Lane (7 miles), comprised little more than small shelters alongside ungated level crossings. Any hints of raised passenger platforms were conspicuous by their absences, although a raised milk-churn platform was provided at Ham Lane. It is known that Broadstone halt was added some time after the line opened, but while the halt's opening date has often been quoted as 1927, its appearance in the 1922 Bradshaw's clearly contradicts that information.

The WC&P's nerve centre, if that is not too flattering a term, was at Clevedon (8¼ miles). The passenger facilities were similar to those at Weston and accommodated in a curved-roofed building, the original low station platform being replaced by one of more conventional height in 1919. The yard alongside Clevedon station contained a twin-road engine shed and a three-road carriage shed, behind which a line curved sharply to provide a link with the terminus of the GWR branch from Yatton. The connecting line was, however, rarely used and this was due, not only to a lack of interchange traffic, but also to the tightness of the curve. The sharp curve has often been cited as the reason why some of the WC&P's six-coupled locomotives sometimes ran with part of their coupling rods removed, the nominal conversion to 0-4-2 or 2-4-0 format enabling them to negotiate the curve should the need arise. In view of the GWR's insistence that any use of the curve would be, most definitely, at the WC&P's own risk, it is a plausible theory. The partial removal of coupling rods to ease a locomotive's passage over curving tracks was not unique, some other light railways adopting a similar practice until the Board of Trade recommended its cessation. To the north of the WC&P station at Clevedon, the line crossed a road junction in the town centre and, as a safety measure, it was stipulated that the maximum speed over the road was to be 4mph with all trains being led by a railway official carrying a red flag. That practice quite probably had a certain wry appeal for Holman Stephens.

Northwards from Clevedon, there was Clevedon East halt (9 miles), Clevedon (All Saints) halt (9 miles), Walton Park halt (9½ miles), Walton-in-Gordano halt (10s miles) and Cadbury Road halt (11¼ miles), all five of which were devoid of raised platforms and consisted instead of just small wooden shelters at roadside crossings. Of those five, All Saints halt was not opened until 1917 and was adjacent to one of the few gated level crossings on the entire line. Apparently, the crossing gates were lengthy enough to cause problems for an under-muscled crossing keeper when a strong wind was blowing. In those days, there was no Brian Clough to extol the virtues of Shredded Wheat.

The next stopping place along the line, Clapton Road halt (12¾ miles), was one of the sparsest of the lot, not even a shelter being provided; Portishead South (13k miles) at least had a shelter, if not a raised platform. The terminus at Portishead (14 miles from Weston) had, from 1919, the dignity of a platform, albeit a low one, and a decoratively-finished wooden building. There was a run-round loop at the terminus and a couple of sidings, one of which served Mustad's nail factory. Beyond the platform, a spur continued in order to connect with the GWR branch on the route to the pier.

V. Locomotives

As mentioned earlier, the workings on the WC&P's opening day were entrusted to a hired locomotive, Kitson 0-6-0ST *Harold*. For the first six months or so of the WC&P's operations, that locomotive shared the work with 0-6-0T *Clevedon*, which had been built by Walker Brothers of Wigan; it is, however, not altogether clear whether *Clevedon* was hired from contractors or purchased by the WC&P. The WC&P's acquisition of two locomotives in 1898 enabled the disposal of the two original steeds, *Harold* being returned to its owner and subsequently sold for the princely sum of £240, while *Clevedon* met an unknown fate.

The first locomotive which the WC&P could definitely call its own was Stephenson-built 0-6-0T *Portishead*. Built in 1887, it had seen service with the contractor, William Jackson, on the construction of the Freshwater, Yarmouth & Newport Railway in the Isle of Wight and also the Exeter to Heathfield branch in Devon. From here, however, records get a little hazy. Jackson had been the contractor engaged on the WC&P until lack of payment in 1897 resulted in his departure but, if records are to be believed, the aggrieved Jackson readily sold the locomotive the following year to the company which owned him money. Whatever the truth behind the story, the 0-6-0T was taken into WC&P stock, only to be sold to the Renishaw Iron Works in Sheffield in 1901 where it is believed to have survived until the late 1930s.

The WC&P's next two locomotives were purchased from the Furness Railway. Both were Sharp Stewart 2-2-2WTs, one having been built to 'B3' class specifications in 1866 (Furness No.35) and the other to 'B2' specifications in 1857 (latterly Furness No.12A). The WC&P named them *Weston* and *Clevedon* respectively. Before being delivered to the WC&P, *Clevedon* was overhauled by the Avonside Engine Co. in Bristol and fitted with a decent cab, the 'roll-over' style of cab roof nevertheless being retained by *Weston*. It appears that the two locomotives arrived in Somerset wearing their Furness Railway livery of red; considering that one of the hired locomotives, *Harold*, had worn a vaguely similar plumage, the WC&P undoubtedly looked on that colour as the nearest thing to a standard company livery. Neither of the 2-2-2WTs had long lives ahead of them, *Clevedon* being scrapped in 1904 and *Weston* in 1906. Those two locomotives have often been referred to as WC&P Nos.1 and 2, but the company did not instigate a numbering policy until around 1906 and, therefore, those numbers would not have been carried.

After the Stephenson 0-6-0T *Portishead* had been sold in 1901, a replacement was sought. It arrived in the form of a 2-4-0T which had been built by Dubs & Co. for the Jersey Railway in 1879. When the Jersey Railway had been converted to narrow gauge in 1884, the engine had been sold to a firm of contractors for work on the North Cornwall Railway and eventually arrived in Somerset with the name *General Don*. This was replaced by the name *Clevedon* in 1904 when the former-Furness 2-2-2WT which had carried that name was cut up. Prior to that, the 2-4-0T had the distinction of being the first WC&P engine to carry a number, that being, not altogether surprisingly, No.1.

Between 1903 and 1907, the WC&P saw a welcome boost in passenger traffic during the summer months, and locomotives were hired when necessary from C. D. Phillips of Newport, industrial-type Kitson 0-6-0STs being the usual machines. Nevertheless, the WC&P made one short-term acquisition during that period, the locomotive in question being a Sharp Stewart 2-4-0T which had started life in 1873 as No.53 on the London, Brighton & South Coast Railway. At its third renumbering in 1886 it became LB&SCR No.497, by which time it had been inscribed with the name *Bishopstone*, but it was sold to George Cohen & Co. for scrap in 1890 for the princely sum of £164. What happened afterwards is a little vague. The WC&P is known to have purchased the locomotive from Cohen's in 1903, but this miserable

A 1925 vintage view of 2-4-0T No.1 (originally built for the Jersey Railway), probably at Clevedon. (Photomatic)

scribe is unable to find any evidence that the machine had performed any work since having been sold for scrap in 1890. Would the WC&P really have bought an engine which had languished on a scrap siding for 13 years when, presumably, other more-usable machines were readily available elsewhere? Another grey area concerns the WC&P's naming of the engine, as some reports suggest that the name *Portishead* was carried, while other dispute this. One of the few firm facts is that the locomotive was withdrawn from service by the WC&P in 1906.

The WC&P's next locomotive is a little better documented. It was a Manning Wardle 'M' class 0-6-0ST, which had been built in 1881 for a contractor and, after passing to another contractor and then a colliery company, had been purchased in 1894 by the Burry Port & Gwendraeth Valley Railway where it had been named *Cwm Mawr*. It passed to the Avonside Engine Co. of Bristol in 1904 as part-payment for a new BP&GVR engine and, after overhaul, was resold in 1906 to the WC&P

where it became No.3 *Weston*. It was regarded as a useful machine although, in later years, it was hampered by a lack of maintenance. Nevertheless, it struggled on until the demise of the railway company, only to be sold for scrap by the GWR.

Another secondhand Manning Wardle 0-6-0ST was purchased by the WC&P in 1907. This locomotive had been built or contractors in 1890 and, after several changes of ownership, had finished up with the contractor engaged on the WC&P's Portishead extension. Under WC&P ownership, it became No.2 *Portishead* and had the distinction of hauling the inaugural train on the Portishead extension. It was sold in 1926 to the contractor engaged on the construction of Portishead power station and, after its work on that site was finished, was left to rust in peace before being cut up in the 1930s.

Despite the WC&P's precarious financial state, it purchased a brand new Hudswell Clarke 0-6-0ST in 1908. Given the name *Walton Park*, albeit with no number, the locomotive had only a short stay in Somerset as it was dispatched in 1912 to the Bere Alston & Calstock Light Railway (better known as the Callington branch of the Plymouth, Devonport & South Western Junction Railway), then to the Shropshire & Montgomeryshire Light Railway and, finally, to the East Kent Light Railway. The 'Colonel Stephens' connection was evident, the upgrading and relaying of the Callington branch having been supervised by Stephens, as was the management of the other two companies. *Walton Park* finished its 'Colonel Stephens' days in 1940 when it was sold by the East Kent to an industrial user. It was scrapped in 1947.

In 1911, the WC&P bought a Sharp Stewart 2-4-0T which had been built in 1876 for the Watlington & Princes Risborough Railway. When that company had been absorbed by the GWR in 1883, the locomotive had become GWR No.1384 and had subsequently performed on the Lambourn, Blagdon and Hemyock branches before being sold in 1911 to the Bute Works Supply Co., from where the WC&P acquired it. The WC&P christened it No.4 *Hesperus*, the choice of name no doubt being made by Holman Stephens who was a classical mythology buff. That interest had been inherited from his father who had

Manning Wardle 0-6-0ST (WC&P No.2 *Portishead*) **at Clevedon, 1925.** (Photomatic)

been an art critic for the *Athenaeum*, many 'Colonel Stephens' railways finishing up with ancient and well-used locomotives which sported deceptively grandiose classical names. As for the WC&P's *Hesperus*, its axle loading was only 8 tons 8 cwt, but the timber bridge at Wick St. Lawrence nevertheless collapsed under its weight in 1934 and the locomotive subsequently saw little action. It was broken up at Clevedon in 1937.

After World War I, the WC&P's financial plight was all too clear but, in 1919, the company seemed to thumb its corporate nose at the creditors by purchasing a brand new locomotive. This was another Manning Wardle 0-6-0ST which became No.5; unlike the WC&P's other two Manning Wardles, it had almost solid wheels. The locomotive lasted as long as the railway company but was scrapped shortly after the GWR took over in 1940.

Like all self-respecting 'Colonel Stephens' railways, the WC&P had its share of internal-combustion motive power. In 1921, a four-wheeled Drewry petrol railcar was purchased and, with its three gears, it could manage 25mph and return over 15mpg. The railcar weighed six tons and had 30 seats. It's nickname of 'The Flying Matchbox' was coined, not out of mirth, but of affection as it proved to be a very popular machine with the public and so, in 1923, a matching 24-seat trailer was purchased. It was too much to hope that the economy and popularity of the railcar would single-handedly reverse the decline in the WC&P's fortunes, but the machine at least slowed down some of the financial rot.

A further Stephens-inspired economy was the purchase in 1921 of a Muir-Hill rail tractor principally for shunting duties on the jetty at Wick St. Lawrence. The tractor had 40in diameter rear wheels, weighed in at some 46 cwt, and was capable of hauling 60 tons on the level but, unfortunately, was damaged beyond repair by a derailment shortly after its arrival. It was 1926 before a replacement was purchased, the new arrival being of a similar basic design but with all four wheels of 40in diameter, enclosed bodywork and a haulage capacity of 75 tons.

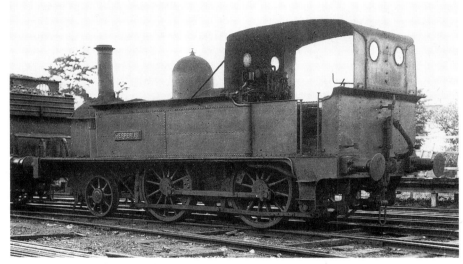

Opposite side views of Sharp Stewart 2-4-0T of 1876 as WC&P No.4 *Hesperus* **(ex-GWR No.1384) at Clevedon in 1925 and 1929 respectively.** (Photomatic; the late H. C. Casserley by courtesy of R. M. Casserley)

In 1926, one of the WC&P's Manning Wardle 0-6-0STs was deemed past its sell-by date and so a replacement was sought. By then, Lieutenant-Colonel Stephens had seen ample evidence of the usefulness of secondhand LB&SCR 'Terrier' 0-6-0Ts on some of his other lines, and so he had no hesitation in purchasing ex-LB&SCR No.643 *Gipsy Hill* for £785. That locomotive had started life in 1877 as LB&SCR No.43 and had been rebuilt to 'A1X' specifications in 1919; it is alleged to have been painted black by the Southern Railway before being sold to the WC&P where it became No.2 *Portishead*. It gave excellent service and was to outlive the WC&P itself.

After seeing the advantages of the Drewry railcar which had been purchased in 1921, Lieutenant-Colonel Stephens had no hesitation in snapping up the Southern Railway's 40hp Drewry car which was offered for sale in 1934 for only £272. The ex-SR car weighed in at 10 tons 17 cwt and could accommodate 22 passengers plus a small amount of goods. It had been delivered to the SR in 1928, its original 50hp engine having been replaced in 1930 following a major breakdown, and had worked the Andover-Romsey, Reading-

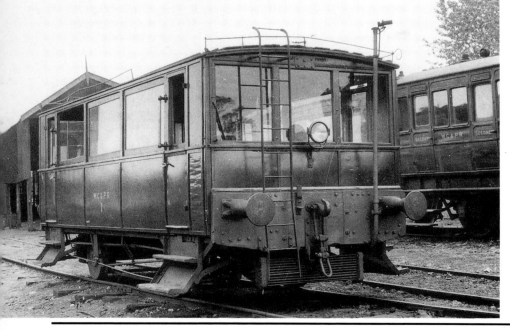

Drewry petrol driven 1921 railcar (WC&P No.1 — 'The Flying Matchbox'!) at Clevedon on 25th June 1938. Part of the centre coach of the ex-LSWR 'Triplet' is also seen. (The late H. C. Casserley by courtesy of R. M. Casserley)

Blackwater and New Romney-Dungeness services reasonably successfully. It performed well on the WC&P where it continued to sport its SR livery complete with the number 5, but after the line's demise it was not looked on with any enthusiasm by the GWR and was scrapped. It is believed that the coach body finished up as a sports

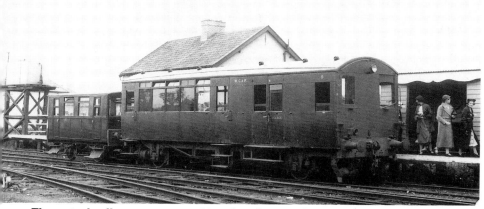

The petrol railcars were considered as locomotives on the WC&P. This is the ex-SR example (WC&P No.5) at Clevedon on 25th June 1938, in company with the 24 seat trailer purchased in 1923 to accompany the first railcar. (The late H. C. Casserley by courtesy of R. M. Casserley)

WC&P No.4, one of the two ex-LBSCR 'Terriers' acquired for the line, seen at Clevedon on 26th June 1938. (The late H. C. Casserley by courtesy of R. M. Casserley)

pavilion at a Swindon school.

The last locomotive to join the WC&P stock list was another ex-LB&SCR 'Terrier' 0-6-0T, purchased in 1937. Its price is variously quoted as £400 and £800, but even the lower sum would have been a considerable outlay considering that the WC&P was approaching its death throes. However, the company had, at the time, only three other active locomotives, one of which was in an abysmal state of repair, and the expenditure was viewed as a better alternative to hiring a locomotive from the unsympathetic GWR. The new 'Terrier' became WC&P No.4 and retained its SR livery, albeit with the lettering and numbers blacked out. It had been built in 1875 as No.53 *Ashtead* but had latterly carried No.2653, conversion to 'A1X' status having been undertaken in 1912; it had performed little work since being laid aside at Eastleigh in 1934 but was to have a share of fame in 18th May 1940 when it hauled the last train on the WC&P.

When the WC&P closed, only the two 'Terriers' escaped the torch. Both were taken into GWR stock, No.2 *Portishead* becoming GWR No.5 although the nameplates were retained, while WC&P No.4 became GWR No.6. The former was treated to a major overhaul in 1941 while the latter received only minor attention, and both were dispatched to St. Philip's Marsh shed in Bristol sporting new GWR liveries. Their duties included work on the harbour lines, usually the province of pannier tanks, but their intrusion did not last too long as, in 1943, No.6 was put in store and did not turn a wheel in anger until being condemned in 1948. Its still-active chum, No.5, was transferred to Taunton shed in 1948 although it spent much of its time outstationed at Bridgwater, then moved to Newton Abbot in 1950. However, it proved rather underpowered for its designated station pilot duties and was soon dispatched to Swindon and placed in store. It was finally withdrawn in 1954.

Mention has occasionally been made of the liveries applied to the WC&P's locomotives although, to be honest, a vaguely standard colour scheme was the best the company's coffers could justify. In the company's early days, the delivery of a locomotive in anything resembling dark crimson was gratefully accepted as a nice bonus although, by the mid 1920s, the official party line was that the official WC&P livery was green. However, the exact shade of green worn by the WC&P's locomotives and rolling stock tended to vary as paint was considered to be too expensive to be applied either evenly or regularly.

VI. Rolling Stock

At first, the WC&P owned six carriages which had been bought from the Lancaster Carriage Works at a bargain price after their intended purchasers in Argentina had pulled out of the deal. The carriages were a rather bizarre sight on an English country railway as they had, at each end, open observation platforms guarded by wrought iron railings. This feature was, however, well suited to the WC&P as the company's intermediate 'stations' were usually little more than roadside halts devoid of raised platforms, and so the steps from the coaches' observation areas proved essential. Each of the carriages accommodated ten

Two of the original WC&P 'South American' bogie coaches at Clevedon c.1926. A former Metropolitan four-wheeler is also seen. (Photomatic)

WC&P No.13 (ex-Metropolitan Railway) at Clevedon on 26th June 1938. Note the side steps for use at roadside halts. (The late H. C. Casserley by courtesy of R. M. Casserley)

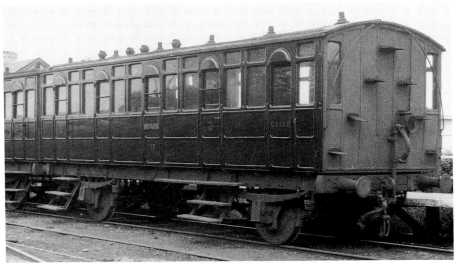

BASIC DIMENSIONS OF WC&P STEAM LOCOMOTIVES								
No.	Name	Type	Wheels (ft in)	Cylinders	Weight	Built	Bought	Wdn.
—	*Weston*	2-2-2WT	5 6¼	15 x 18 (i)	30t 10c	1866	1898	1906
—	*Clevedon*	2-2-2WT	5 6¼	14 x 20 (i)	30t 2c	1857	1899	1904
—	*Portishead*	0-6-0T	4 6	16 x 20 (i)	21t 0c	1880	1898	1900
1	*Clevedon**	2-4-0T	4 0	10 x 19 (o)		1879	1901	1940
	(*Portishead*)	2-4-0T	4 0	12 x 17 (i)		1872	1903	1906
3	*Weston*	0-6-0ST	3 0	13 x 18 (i)	19t 10c	1881	1906	1940
2	*Portishead*	0-6-0ST	3 0	12 x 17 (i)	18t 10c	1890	1907	1926
—	*Walton Park*	0-6-0ST	3 7	14 x 20 (o)	29t 10c	1908	new	1912
4	*Hesperus*	2-4-0T	4 2	12 x 17 (i)	24t 7c	1876	1911	1937
5	—	0-6-0ST	3 0	12 x 18 (i)	20t 0c	1919	new	1940
2	*Portishead*	0-6-0T	4 0	12 x 20 (i)	28t 5c	1877	1926	1954†
4	—	0-6-0T	4 0	12 x 20 (i)	28t 5c	1875	1937	1948†
*Originally retained former name of *General Don*. †Passed to GWR.								

WC&P No.15, one end of the well-used ex-LSWR 'Triplet' set of coaches, on 26th June 1938. (The late H. C. Casserley by courtesy of R. M. Casserley)

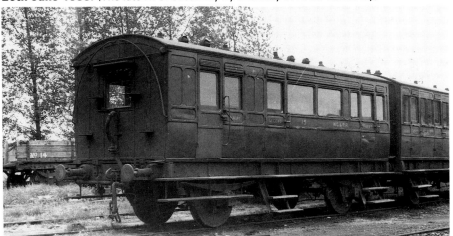

first class passengers but their additional second class capacities varied from 35 to 45. It may seem unlikely that such an impecunious company as the WC&P could be credited with a 'first' in British railway history, but those carriages were the first in the land to be illuminated by acetylene gas, that innovation being shown to the company's then Traffic Manager, Edward Wintour.

No additional coaching stock was required until the opening of the Portishead extension in 1907. Fortunately for the poverty-stricken WC&P, the Metropolitan Railway had a surfeit of coaches available at knock-down prices after its recent electrification, and so seven four-wheeled compartment coaches were purchased. Six of those operated as close-coupled pairs, and all had to be fitted with steps as the WC&P penchant for platform-less roadside halts persisted on the Portishead line.

In 1924, a close-coupled set of three ex-L&SWR four-wheeled carriages was purchased; known as 'The Triplet', they were the most extensively used WC&P carriages during the 1930s. A four-wheeled ex-Taff Vale compartment brake was purchased in the late 1920s but, it seems, was used only as a stand-by. Despite the obligatory fitment of vacuum brakes, hand braking remained the most commonly used method of stopping trains on the WC&P; accidents were not unknown, one at Worle in 1903 resulting in two fatalities, but the apparent disregard for braking regulations seems not to have drawn the attention of the Board of Trade.

The WC&P's freight stock comprised some 25 or so open trucks varying in capacity from six to ten tons, and one covered van. All appear to have been secondhand acquisitions from the Midland Railway. There was also a six-wheeled ex-Great Eastern brake coach which was used by the WC&P to carry milk churns and other goods by the WC&P and, it is believed, an ex-Great Central passenger coach used for similar purposes.

SECONDARY SOURCES
(and suggested further reading):

The Weston Clevedon & Portishead Railway, Peter Strange, Twelveheads Press 1989.

The Weston Clevedon & Portishead Railway, Colin Maggs, Oakwood 1964.

Railways of Bristol and Somerset, Martin Smith, Ian Allan 1992.

Locomotives of the GWR, RCTS.

Locomotives of the LB&SCR, D. L. Bradley, RCTS 1969.

Locomotives of the Southern Railway, D. L. Bradley, RCTS 1975.

BACKTRACK Vol.5 No.6, article by Peter Cooper.

Britain's Light Railways, Martin Smith (to be published by Ian Allan, Spring 1994).

For the most part, the first changes under new BR ownership were the varied liveries to be seen on the locomotives; but even then it took time to settle down and this pair of views, taken at Camden in May 1949 illustrate the point. Stanier 'Jubilee' Class 5XP 4-6-0 No.45555 *Quebec,* one of the very first to be built in 1934, still carries its LMS post-war livery (black lined in maroon and straw) and its cabside number and front numberplate are clearly applied in the LMS pattern not the new standard BR style. In due course, BR rationalisation saw to it that the Power Class 5XP became redesignated 6P, but not until some years after this picture was taken.

The second view shows rebuilt 'Patriot' Class 6P 4-6-0 No.45535 *Sir Herbert Walker K.C.B.* Entirely in the 'LMS' school of design, this particular example was not rebuilt until 1948 and emerged from shops before new BR standard liveries had been adopted. Like many principal ex-LMS types shopped at Crewe at this time (and maybe not altogether surprisingly!), it was given the LNWR lined black livery (subsequently adopted for 'secondary and mixed traffic' types) until a decision was made. The rebuilt 'Patriots' were rated equivalent to the 'Royal Scot' 4-6-0s and given the same LMS 6P classification, later changed to 7P after the above-mentioned BR changes. They were also to receive smoke deflectors during BR days. Note that two of the surrounding tenders still retain their LMS liveries.

ERIC BRUTON *AT LARGE*

THE YEARS OF CHANGE: 1948-52

Since its launch, one of the most popular features of MODELLERS' BACK-TRACK has been a regular series under the general title 'The Eric Bruton Album'. Eric is both a photographer and a modeller with a highly perceptive 'eye' for detail of a kind which escapes most folk but is invaluable to modelmakers and also adds much to our general understanding of the historic railway scene. Furthermore, the data which always accompanies his pictures is more than usually comprehensive. In this feature, advantage is taken of the larger book format to present a rather more extended contribution than usual. The main theme is that of the changing railway scene during the first few years after Nationalisation, mainly on the new London Midland Region (with a few exceptions), including a very interesting 'tailpiece' on the early duties of one of the first of the new BR Standard locomotive types to come into service — the relatively unknown 'Clan' 4-6-2s.

By 1950, the new liveries were decided and many of the more important express classes were quick to receive them, like rebuilt 'Royal Scot' No.46157 *The Royal Artilleryman,* seen passing Penrith yards with the up 9.30am Glasgow Central to Birmingham express on 5th June. But the carriage stock (as in our own time) took longer to become harmonious. Red and cream was by now the standard treatment and many in this train are thus finished; but at least three vehicles retain their LMS livery while the second coach in the formation is wearing 'Plum and Spilt Milk' colours, a remnant of one of the experimental 1948 schemes (a semi-revival of the old LNWR style) which did not find favour.

Only the locomotive livery on this 13th June 1950 view at Workington (Main) reveals the new order — all the carriage stock on view retains LMS colours. The train is the 11.00am Carlisle-Whitehaven local, comprised mostly of cascaded pre-group corridor stock of LNWR origin and headed by LMS Standard Class 2P 4-4-0 No.40695, itself a post-group development of a Midland design but with reduced height boiler mountings, slightly smaller wheels and sundry minor modifications. An interesting detail is the profusion of water butts, both on the main platform and in the adjoining sidings. The water was for carriage cleaning purposes not for fire prevention!

A week later, on 20th June 1950, a down Class H through freight heads for the far north round Rose Street curve, Inverness in charge of Stanier Class 5 4-6-0 No.45123, fitted with tablet exchange equipment on the cab side, almost certainly in unlined black livery and BRITISH RAILWAYS in full on the tender. The front numberplate is to the new BR style but the cab side number is rendered in LMS type characters and in the final 'high' LMS position. This apart, nothing has changed from LMS days and the signal box is pure Highland Railway in style.

A speedy way to establish changes (and rather important to the operating staff) was to alter the all-important running number of an engine at the earliest moment and leave the rest alone for the time being — and as this pair of views shows, the 'leaving alone' could often last a long time. In the first shot (11th June 1950) Class 4F 0-6-0 No.44459 has its new number with the original LMS markings on the tender, the general livery being obviously in quite good order. It was seen running tender first at Clifton, returning to Tebay yard with two brake vans after working a permanent way train earlier in the day. Both brake vans are to the final LMS design but the leading one has the deep weight box which reveals it as either 1944 vintage or even a post-1947 repeat, built under BR auspices.

In the second view, the same engine in the same condition (and still looking quite smart) makes an attractive picture almost two years later as it runs past the craggy heights of Grayrigg Common, overlooking Dillicar, on 28th May 1952. The train is the down 9.32am Lindal-Tebay (for Derwenthaugh) coke empties from Millom Ironworks. The working of these coke trains across the Pennines was once a familiar sight. East of Tebay they took the Stainmore route of the old LNER (ex-NER) and right to the end usually contained at least a few characteristic wooden-bodied NER coke hoppers. At least four can be distinguished in this train, the leading example still being lettered 'NE' on the side in large characters.

By 1952, it was rather less common to see the more important types showing little sign of standard livery but in this picture, taken on 4th June, Fowler Class 4P 2-6-4T still carries its BR identity in unlined black and with 'LMS' pattern markings (save for numberplate) when most had by now become lined black with the proper BR emblem. The location is near Kendal on the Windermere branch and the train is the 3.25pm Windermere-Liverpool Class B stopping passenger. The engine is Oxenholme based (11C) but might well be working through to Preston and the carriage formation is still typically LMS for intermediate distance service: a three coach 'Inter Corridor' set (two brake thirds plus composite) and a non-corridor third as 'strengthener'. The coaches are all to LMS design: composite and third from the pre-1930 fully panelled period, brake thirds from the immediate pre-war Stanier period with welded underframes. The leading coach still retained its LMS livery.

For the most part, pre-BR locomotive designs tended to remain associated with their 'region of origin', but in a few cases — before the BR standard designs had been settled — company designs were also built by what had once been rival concerns. This was especially true of the post-war Ivatt LMS types, the only 'modern' designs introduced by any of the 'Big Four' companies for secondary workings. Two examples are seen here at Penrith on 29th May 1952 in the shape of Class 2 2-6-0s Nos.46447 (left) and 46478. The latter was one of some 38 examples built at Darlington during 1951-2 for use in former LNER territory. Appropriately, it is waiting departure with a train for Darlington composed of Thompson LNER non-corridor stock, still in 'painted teak' livery. The other example seen is in charge of the Keswick branch train (hidden under the roof) and was built at Crewe — this being an LMS service, of course!

As with the LMS lines, so too on former LNER routes, the company tradition lasted well beyond 1947 which, on the East Coast, resulted in the appearance of a complete class of new express engines of pure Doncaster pedigree, none of which ever saw service in LNER ownership — the Peppercorn Class A1 4-6-2s. However, many of them entered service when new in LNER green livery with BR markings. One such is seen here, No.60136 (later to be named *Alcazar*) departing from King's Cross in charge of the down 11.30am 'Queen of Scots' Pullman on 2nd July 1949. It is worth mentioning that the Gill Sans locomotive insignia adopted by BR in the form seen in this shot, was very much influenced by the LNER which had adopted it as standard after the 1939-45 war in succession to its former shaded style.

Some of the pre-BR colour schemes, albeit with new ownership markings, lasted for quite a number of years and of them, Southern malachite green seemed to fare especially well if looked after properly. This example from the Isle of Wight is typical: beautifully finished ex-LSWR Class 02 0-4-2T No.32 *Bonchurch* seen at Freshwater on 18th May 1952 on the occasion of the RCTS tour of the island. This class of engine dated from 1899 and examples were moved by the Southern to the IOW soon after the 1923 grouping. As with both LMS and GWR locomotives, it was not uncommon to see the new ownership marked in 'company' style characters until the LNER-inspired Gill Sans took over. Here, the lettering is rendered in Southern 'sunshine' style and the numerals are also purely SR in shape.

Of the old 'Big Four', the GWR seemed less changed than the rest, probably for a variety of reasons. Firstly, the locomotives retained their numbers, having cast numberplates which were decreed expensive to change; secondly, colour photography was rare in railway circles at the time and the new red/cream carriage livery looked very like the old GWR two-tone scheme in a b/w picture. Thirdly, after a relatively short period of blue livery for the main express types, GWR green became the basis of the new BR standard green, adopted for all express types from 1951 onwards. However, just as elsewhere, until new insignia were agreed, ex-GW locomotives had their BR ownership rendered in company style markings, such as the tender lettering on No.6027 *King Richard I* as it skirts the sea wall near Shaldon Bridge on 10th June 1949 with the down 'Cornish Riviera'. The engine was blue at the time, the 'Kings' being the only GW class so painted and some of the coaches were red and cream, though these cannot be distinguished.

Undoubtedly the first really obvious change (colour schemes apart) was the introduction of new BR standard locomotive types from 1951 onwards, starting with the Class 7 'Britannia' Pacifics. The next year was to see the introduction of a lightweight Class 6 4-6-2 design of broadly equivalent power output to an LMS 'Jubilee' and rated accordingly. It was hard to see the real justification for such a design and although more were planned, in the event only ten were built, all named after Scottish Clans. Many of them were sent to Glasgow Polmadie (66A) when new and this and the next series of pictures shows some of them at work in the northern fells during the first months of their life: May and June 1952. In this picture, the first of them, No.72000 *Clan Buchanan,* has just taken water at Dillicar troughs in the beautiful Lune gorge with the 10.50am from Glasgow to Liverpool on 2nd June. The train, though all red and cream, is comprised wholly of former LMS stock.

The 'Clans' were regularly rostered to specific services during their first months in service and the remaining views show them working just two of these trains, each a balancing working for the other in terms of both engine and at least some of the carriages. The northbound train was the 2.00pm 'combined' Manchester and Liverpool to Glasgow and Edinburgh express and in this view, No.72003 *Clan Fraser* is seen heading north over Dillicar troughs on 27th May and seems not to be taking water — most trains did but a 'dry run' was not unknown.

These two pictures of the 'combined' down train were taken on two successive days, 5th and 6th June 1952 at Dillicar and just south of Shap Summit respectively. The engines are Nos.72001 *Clan Cameron* and 72002 *Clan Campbell* and the similarity of viewing angle allows easy comparisons to be made between the train formations. In both cases a brake composite leads but the types are quite different. In the first train, the carriage is a Stanier rebuild of an earlier wooden panelled design (the rainstrips on the roof indicate its origins) but in the second case, the carriage is an older unrebuilt fully panelled type which, incidentally, has not been given a red band above the windows. In both cases the second coach is a newly built full composite of LMS design but not built until after 1947 — note the slightly more 'clipper' shaped cross-profile. There then follows the dining section. On 5th June it was a twelve-wheel composite but on 6th June it was an older car (in shadow) with a corridor third separating it from the composite. These sets also feature in the balancing 'up' working — see next set of views.

This pair of pictures shows the outward half of this balanced out and home 'Clan' working, the 1.45pm Glasgow-Liverpool service on 26th/30th May respectively. In the first view (taken just south of Shap Summit) No.72003 *Clan Fraser* drifts down the bank while in the second pic- ture, No.72001 *Clan Cameron* is seen approaching Grayrigg. In both cases the engines are hauling the same set of coaches which worked alternate days each way: none of the currently fashion- able intensive rostering in those days! The first five coaches are brake third/third/composite diner/composite/brake composite — all LMS design stock, the composite being again of the post-1947 type. *Clan Fraser* was photographed next day with the same set heading north over Dillicar troughs — see earlier view.

In this final pair of pictures, the 'other' set of coaches is featured on 5th and 7th June with *Clan Campbell* and *Clan Fraser* respectively. The locations are the Lune gorge and between Shap Summit and Shap Station. In both cases, the dining car seen in the shadows in the previous view of the northbound train near Shap summit is now revealed as an early standard LMS composite car of LNWR styling and still painted in LMS colours. The five coach formation at the head of the train is still present but formed up differently, the corridor third being now beyond the diner.

Ivatt 4-2-2 No.264 on a down express made up of East Coast Joint Stock. The train has just crossed the Midland Nottingham to Lincoln main line on the level to the north of Newark. The photograph shows the Midland line just short of Milepost 121 with the River Trent in evidence on the right. The date of the photograph, as in most of those in this series, is thought to be between June 1901 and June 1902, the main pointer being the fact that the GNR standard locomotive headlamp code is still in use. This was due to be changed to the Railway Clearing House standard from January 1902, but there is some evidence to support the theory that in practice the change did not happen immediately; the locomotive carries the original GNR Express Passenger code.

No.264, a King's Cross engine, was built at Doncaster in June 1901 as Class A5 and is therefore less than a year old, probably with Driver Harry Tappenden, its regular driver, at the controls. The train is composed of East Coast Joint Stock twelve-wheelers, the first being a Doncaster-built four compartment brake third, and the second and third being saloon type vehicles built to the more bulbous York outline.

*Regular BACKTRACK contributor **Paul Strong** recently unearthed this fascinating set of early GNR images and sent them on "just in case you are interested"! They had little by way of supporting information and nothing at all is known of the photographer, not even his name. We therefore asked **Nick Campling** if he would be willing to do some detective work and his efforts revealed that all but one were taken within a very short period of time. His results are presented here: a fascinating 'time capsule' of a long-gone age.*

TURN OF THE CENTURY GREAT NORTHERN

Ivatt 4-4-0 No.1331 is shown on an up express at Milepost 119. This location is about ¼ mile south of the junction where the GN/LNWR Joint Nottingham line joins the East Coast main line south of Newark. The locomotive is GN Class D1 (also known as the '1321s') built in November 1898 and allocated to Doncaster. The train is comprised of a mixture of GN Howlden-designed stock, the first vehicle being a standard six-wheel five-compartment third, followed by a five-compartment rigid eight-wheel brake. The next vehicle, partly obscured by the signal post, is a corridor clerestory 45ft full brake. The remaining vehicles appear to be six-wheelers including a TPO vehicle. The locomotive has a small indicator shelter on the offside footplate, possibly so that a riding engineer could monitor temperature and pressure, or simply observe the inside valve gear in motion. The signal post is typical of the GN period with a split somersault and spectacle.

Stirling Single No.664 on a down express at Barnby Crossing. The crossing was near Milepost 118½. There was no station and the actual village of Barnby in the Willows is about two miles to the north east. The locomotive is an 8ft single built in June 1881 and here shown in original condition except for a replacement Ivatt tender which tends to dwarf the locomotive. No.664, a Doncaster engine, was the first Stirling Single to be built with a plain splasher, and was exhibited at the Stephenson Centenary Exhibition at Newcastle on Tyne in 1881. The train comprises two 45ft Howlden vehicles (see MBT Vol.1 No.4) followed by a number of six-wheelers. Despite the busy traffic on this line, the crossing keepers appear to have cultivated a fairly good crop of brassica!

Stirling Single No.1007 on the up 'Scotchman' at Grantham station, probably just after a locomotive change. Built in March 1895 and allocated to King's Cross, No.1007 was the penultimate Stirling Single and is shown here coupled to the largest of the Stirling tenders. It subsequently became the only locomotive in the '1003' batch to be rebuilt by Ivatt with a domed boiler. Its regular driver was quoted as stating that No.1007 was the best uphill performer that he had driven on the King's Cross-Grantham route. Note the side chains hooked up into the fashionable 'double Albert' position — ie like a watch chain. In the down platform there rests a train of typical GN four-plank opens with a rather grubby looking road van with the unmistakably typical 'GN 4' endposts.

Ivatt D1 4-4-0 No.1376 at Grantham with a down express at the same period. No.1376 was built in December 1900 and allocated to York. It is therefore likely to have just taken over a York train at Grantham. The photograph which is similar to, but not the same as that credited to the Rev. Parley in *British Trains of Yesteryear* by Hamilton Ellis (LPC 1960), was taken at the north end of Grantham station. Of particular note are the shallow platform, which could not have been much more than eighteen inches above rail level, and the track ballasted with a very fine material to just above the sleeper level. Of the train, very little is apparent except that it appears to comprise Howlden six-wheel coaches.

Remaining at Grantham, this view shows Class C1 Ivatt small Atlantic No.983 on a down express at the south end of the station. The original print is dated 17th June 1902, although No.983 still carries the old GN headcode for an express. No.983 was built in May 1900 and allocated to Doncaster. It is shown in original condition, but it was later superheated by the LNER and lasted until April 1936. On the left, standing in the locomotive spur in front of the maltings, is Stirling 2-2-2 No.877 as rebuilt by Ivatt with domed boiler in November 1901. No.877, Class B4, was originally

built in May 1884 and was allocated to King's Cross from which shed it regularly performed on the tightly-scheduled Sheffield Diners. On the right are two Howlden six-wheel vehicles, one a six-wheel 32ft full brake, and the nearer possibly a family

saloon since it is fitted for both vacuum and Westinghouse brake, and would therefore travel outside the GN area. Note also the ground signals of the period each bearing a number corresponding to the signal lever, in this case Nos.32, 44 and 45.

At Grantham again on the same day, but in this case further south near Ransome's factory. A double-headed down express, with two Class D1 4-4-0s, No.1338 leading. No.1338 was built in October 1899 and was a Grantham-based locomotive. It is likely to have been assisting a failed D1 since it was unusual to find double-heading on this main line at that time. The train comprises twelve wheel clerestory East Coast Joint Stock. Note again the common GN four-plank wagons on the left.

Stirling Class B4 2-2-2 No.877 on a down East Coast express on Muskham troughs. The train is the same as that in the photograph of 4-2-2 No.264, but in this case the difference in outline between the Doncaster and York built coaches is far more noticeable. The troughs were near Milepost 122, and over 2,000ft in length. Even with manpower as inexpensive as it was at the turn of the century, it is doubtful that the GN would employ a man merely to sweep the footpath by the trackside, so one imagines that the duty of the man with the broom was to clear the wooden water trough of fine ballast which must have been thrown up by the passage of each train taking water.

Rebuilt Stirling Single No.95 on an up Sheffield to King's Cross dining train on 21st May 1902 passing Trent Lane signals, Nottingham. The locomotive, allocated to Grantham, was built in 1889, and was rebuilt by Ivatt in August 1897 with a domed boiler and Ivatt-style cab. The train comprises a 32ft six-wheel full-brake, a 45ft brake composite and third, and two early GN twelve-wheel clerestory diners. Particularly noticeable is the splendid gantry of GN somersault signals with lower level repeaters, some of which are obscured by steam.

Finally, by way of contrast and a few years later, a down East Coast Express is now hauled by Class C2 4-4-2 No.301 passing Milepost 133, near to what is now the village of East Markham, north of Tuxford. No.301 was built in May 1905 and allocated to King's Cross. This factor together with the RCH standard locomotive headcode and the lack of lining on the front bufferbeam suggest that the photograph was taken c.1906. The milepost and fencing are both typical of the Great Northern.

The classic outside-cylindered 'mixed traffic' locomotive (Walschaerts valve gear, valves on top) in an early and seminal form: R. W. Urie's Class H15 4-6-0 of 1914. No.485 was one of the very first to be built and is seen here in Southern Railway condition (Maunsell superheater fitted c.1927) at Woking on 30th July 1938 with a Bournemouth train. (F. E. Box Collection — NRM)

The British six-coupled mixed traffic (or 'general utility') engine had a somewhat complicated origin; in its final form (the LMS and BR Class 5 4-6-0s and their associated 2-6-0s) one could see the fusion of several lines of thought. Happily, most important developments along the way were still at work during the final BR steam period (many still survive, of course) and collectively, allowed a valuable 'history lesson' to be appreciated. This article offers a broad outline of the evolutionary process which created this state of affairs.

Somewhat off its normal 'beat', but rendered more interesting in consequence, GWR '43xx' 2-6-0 No.6369 was photographed at Warrington at an unknown date in the 1930s. Important though these engines were, they did not typify the common strand of later evolution, for the GWR continued to use inside Stephenson gear for 'mixed traffic' locomotives when all the others had gone to the Walschaerts arrangement.

The story goes back to the earlier days of the twentieth century when attitudes to locomotive design slowly began to change. The reason for this is that the philosophical basis on which the 'mixed traffic' engine depended was by no means fully accepted in the early days of steam. There was a strong feeling of 'horses for courses' as far as locomotive design was concerned during most of the nineteenth century and the idea that one could have a sort of 'do anything' locomotive would have been anathema to most of the more famous engineers.

There were many good reasons for this. To start with, traffic readily sorted itself into passenger (the express engines were

ED TRAFFIC LOCOMOTIVE

By David Jenkinson

The SE&CR Class N 2-6-0s of 1917 were strongly influenced by, but not a copy of, Swindon practice. Nicely symbolic of the relationship is this view of Southern No.A853 (later SR No.1853) at Barnstaple Junction with a GWR train c.1927. This was one of a batch of 50 Class Ns built for the SR in 1925. Construction started at Woolwich Arsenal but was completed at Ashford. (Hall Collection — NRM)

usually cascaded to local work when replaced by later and generally larger designs) and unbraked freight and mineral traffic for which speed was less important than sheer pulling — and stopping — power; express freight was, as yet, a relatively minor need. Secondly, poor front end design with restricted steam and exhaust passages made it impracticable to achieve high rotational and piston speeds; the pistons would have 'run away' from the steam. Express engines needed large coupled wheels for speeds in the 70s; freight engines had small coupled wheels to give them high drawbar pull (see also 'Big Wheels' BACKTRACK Vol.6 No.1). Contemporary wisdom was that never the twain would meet in one engine.

By the turn of the century, there was a growing nucleus of freight or passenger-rated traffic, largely of a perishable nature, which could move in train-load quantities and demanded fast transits in continuously braked wagons. There were some tentative moves to cater for these needs; Robinson on the Great Central was perhaps first in the field with his 6ft 4-6-0 'Fish' engines of 1902/4 for the Grimsby traffic, though within a few years he had also built 5ft 4-6-0s which seem to have been more for general freight than for mixed traffic roles. On the LNWR, the 19in 'Goods' 4-6-0s of 1906 saw much excursion traffic as well as freight. But it took the advent of superheating, from about 1910, and the consequent more widespread adoption of piston valves, to initiate the front end improvements which would make the mixed traffic

locomotive a realistic concept. Perhaps the eight hour day and the breakdown of 'one driver, one engine' after World War I also contributed.

In Britain, two lines of evolution developed more or less in parallel, along with two wheel arrangements, the 2-6-0 and 4-6-0, and it may be helpful, before going much further, to devote a few words to these fundamentals. In mechanical terms, the differences largely centred round the valve gear. The GWR (and others) favoured the inside Stephenson link motion for two-cylinder engines whereas the alternative form made use of the more accessible outside Walschaerts gear which absorbs less energy in its drive mechanism, having fewer frictional surfaces to overcome. It is also less subject to wear and more precise in its action, but these aspects had only partially been employed at Swindon — in the four-cylinder 4-6-0s such as the 'Stars', (and, later, the 'Castles' and 'Kings'). The origin of the outside Walschaerts gear two-cylinder locomotive must be sought elsewhere.

The classic arrangement as it developed in Britain (and inspired in large measure by contemporary American practice) was with the valves on top and early examples of the idea were to be seen in the 2-6-0s designed by Gresley for the GNR in 1912 and (in the 4-6-0 field) with R. W. Urie's mixed traffic Class H15 and N15 engines for the LSWR. In time, these spawned the immortal 'King Arthurs', but their philosophy lay at the root of the LMS and BR Class 5 4-6-0s, wherein Swindon ideas were fused with these other developments.

Turning to the two principal wheel arrangements, although 4-6-0 and 2-6-0 mixed traffic engines tended to evolve simultaneously, the latter were slightly earlier in the field in terms of sheer numbers and we need to start with these. In this context, for the avoidance of misunderstanding, it should be mentioned that at

Gresley's three-cylinder alternative was the K3 2-6-0, introduced on the GNR in 1920 and built in considerable numbers by the LNER until 1937. This is No.3822 (later LNER 1982/BR 61982) of the final 1936-7 Darlington-built series at an unrecorded location. A more detailed account of this class, including drawings, was published in MODELLERS' BACKTRACK Vol.1 No.2.

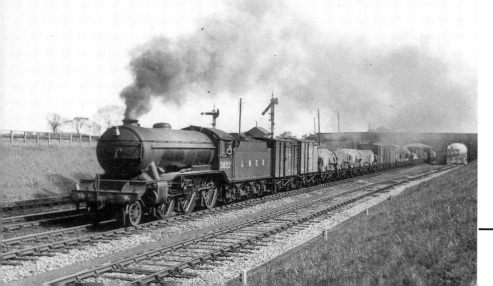

'Horwich Mogul' No.42785 (one of the original 100 examples built by the LMS in 1926-7) emerges through an overbridge near Clifton on the West Coast Main Line with an up Class H 'through' freight from Carlisle on 14th June 1950. This class of locomotive was hardly altered in design detail or utilisation for the whole of its working life. (Eric Bruton)

There is little doubt that the Stanier 2-6-0 came into being in 1933 because of the new CME's wish to introduce his new ideas and that he used the existence of a management wish for yet more Horwich Moguls as a convenient opportunity to try them out. This view shows No.42983, the penultimate member of the class, in charge of a down Class H freight climbing Shap on 26th May 1952. (Eric Bruton)

much the same time as the genuine mixed traffic 2-6-0 began to appear in England, the same wheel arrangement was also being introduced in modest numbers in Scotland: on the CR with the McIntosh '34 Class' of 1912 and on the G&SWR with the Drummond '51 Class' of 1915. These, however, as their small coupled wheels indicated, had no pretensions to mixed traffic status; the leading truck was little more than a means of spreading the weight of the massively-built 0-6-0s from which they were developed. The CR in particular was wedded to the inside cylinder 4-6-0 for handling express freight, notably its '908 Class' of 1906 with 5ft 9in wheels.

In essence, therefore, and although there were some exceptions which will be considered later, the classic British mixed traffic locomotive embodied two outside cylinders and intermediate-sized coupled wheels — and the undoubted forerunner was Churchward on the GWR with his '43xx' 2-6-0s of 1911. Hard on his heels was Nigel Gresley with his GNR Class H2 2-6-0s of 1912 (LNER Class K1, later Class K2 after reboilering). Both used 5ft 8in coupled wheels. But as noted above, these two engineers chose different forms of valve gear. The original 4ft 8in diameter boiler on Gresley's 2-6-0 was a little inadequate to supply hard working cylinders and was quickly replaced by a 5ft 6in version. In this form they came fully into their own as true mixed traffic locomotives, handling both fast freight and some passenger trains at times of pressure.

The only other pre-grouping railway to adopt the 2-6-0 in mixed traffic form was the SE&CR, with the 'N' Class produced at Ashford from 1917. There were strong Swindon influences embodied in them but

Technically 'mixed traffic' but in reality 'special purpose': Gresley's three-cylinder K4 2-6-0 design for the West Highland Line, dating from 1937. This is the last of them, No.3446 (later LNER 1998/BR 61998) *MacLeod of MacLeod*. A sister engine (first LNER No.3445, later 1997/61997) was rebuilt with two cylinders in 1945, becoming in effect the prototype for the Peppercorn K1 class of 1949, a far more universal mixed traffic type. (BR ScR)

a long lap outside Walschaerts valve gear was used. By the end of 1922 the first of the three-cylinder version (Class N1) had also been built; both used 5ft 6in coupled wheels. Also by this time, Gresley on the GNR had, in 1920, built the first of his celebrated three-cylinder 2-6-0s (LNER Class K3), carrying a very large 6ft diameter boiler. Both the GNR and SE&CR three-cylinder designs used a similar conjugated valve gear to drive the middle piston valve from the outside gear, originated by H. Holcroft at Ashford. The K3s must have been leading contenders for the title of the roughest-riding engines of modern times!

In the first post-grouping decade, the 2-6-0 mixed traffic engine came into its own. The newly-formed LMS saw a need for true mixed traffic engines on a considerable scale and Hughes catered for it (after a lengthy evolutionary period and some anguished redesign to make it acceptable to the Derby lobby) with the Horwich Moguls of 1926, more familiarly nicknamed 'Crabs'. This proved a very successful and highly economical design, running to 245 engines, and retained a higher profile than the subsequent batch of 40 Stanier 2-6-0s with taper boilers, produced in 1933.

The LNER multiplied its K3s, only fitting improved cabs and larger tenders by way of change, but the six smaller K4 2-6-0s of 1937 could only be classed as mixed traffic in a technical sense, since they were special purpose engines for the West Highland line. On the GWR, the '43xx' 2-6-0s were built until 1932, again with

Mixed traffic in every sense except for its nickname: Highland Railway 'Jones Goods' 4-6-0 No.106 at an unrecorded date and location c.1920.

Urie's Class S15 4-6-0s were a 1920 version (with 5ft 7in driving wheels) of the H15 type (6ft wheels) and eventually some twice as numerous. Like the H15s, they were also built in SR days under Maunsell's supervision and this picture shows No.30837 of the 1927 series on a Class H freight at Reading East Junction heading for Tonbridge in 1958. (M. W. Earley Collection — NRM)

detailed improvements, while Maunsell on the Southern continued to build two-cylinder Ns and small numbers of the three-cylinder N1s. After the Sevenoaks disaster of 1927, they were augmented by two-cylinder rebuilds of the 'K Class' 2-6-4Ts and a solitary three-cylinder rebuild of the 'K1 Class' tank, both having 6ft coupled wheels. A few further engines of both 6ft designs were subsequently built new. These 'U' and 'U1' engines were in practice more in the nature of passenger than mixed traffic locomotives.

But by the mid-1930s, enthusiasm for the 2-6-0 had waned. Just as it had proved its superiority over the 0-6-0 in riding and was capable of being built to a size and power capacity equal to a medium-sized 4-6-0, it was not perceived as having as much basic stability at the higher speeds now being demanded as a front bogie could provide. There were, of course, those who had held this view much earlier and went straight to the 4-6-0 layout for mixed traffic engines. But one should not overlook the man who actually started it in Britain, David Jones on the Highland; his 'Big Goods' engines pioneered the British 4-6-0. 'Goods' they might be dubbed but on the heavily-graded Highland lines, their 5ft 3in wheels made them suitable for passenger and freight alike.

Urie on the LSWR shunned the 2-6-0 completely, preferring the 6ft 'H15' of 1914 and the 5ft 7in 'S15' of 1920 (both of them 4-6-0s) for the fast West of England freight trains. Massive machines in the classic mould of two outside cylinders with Walschaerts valve gear, they were not out of place on Southampton boat expresses either. Robinson on the GCR, having had to accept Baldwin 2-6-0s from the USA during the locomotive famine of 1900, continued to

The LNER (ex-NER Class S3) B16 4-6-0s, three-cylinder engines first introduced in 1919 and designed by Raven, were eminently suited for mixed traffic work, though not (as built) in the Walschaerts gear 'family'. The example illustrated (LNER 2364, later LNER 1435/BR 61435) was extensively rebuilt by Gresley in June 1937 to the form shown here in order to bring these already excellent engines more in line with modern practice. The rebuild was highly successful and six more were converted in 1939-40 becoming Class B16/2 (the originals now being B16/1) with a typical Gresley arrangement of two outside sets of Walschaerts valve gear with conjugated motion for the middle cylinder. The war then caused a pause but more rebuilds were justified (1944 onwards) and came out during the Thompson period with three independent sets of Walschaerts gear. (LNER Official)

The GWR 'Manors' were lightweight mixed traffic 4-6-0s designed particularly for use on the Cambrian section. This is No.7820 (formerly *Ditcheat Manor*) coming to a stand near Oakengates, late in its working life, with an up Class C freight on 18th September 1965.

One of the versatile GWR 'Hall' Class 4-6-0s, No.4940 *Ludford Hall* at speed in Sonning Cutting on 10th October 1953. (T. E. Williams Collection — NRM)

Typical Stanier Class 5 work: The 7.30am Class E (partially fitted) Edge Hill to Carlisle express freight en route to Shap Summit (banked by a 2-6-4T) on 6th June 1952. The engine (No.45388) was one of the many examples built by Armstrong Whitworth during 1936-8. (Eric Bruton)

build 4-6-0s for mixed traffic work, notably the 'Glenalmonds' (LNER Class B8) and later, the four-cylinder 'Black Pigs' (LNER Class B7) until 1924, always with Stephenson link motion. And on the North Eastern, following Wilson Worsdell's pioneering two-cylinder 4-6-0s of 1899 with 6ft 1½in wheels (originally used for express passenger work but later drafted onto fast main line freight and excursion duties), an enlarged version appeared in 1911 to be followed by Raven's three-cylinder 5ft 8in design in 1919 (LNER Class B16). On the LNWR, the 6ft 3in 'Prince of Wales' design, essentially a passenger 4-6-0, was found sufficiently versatile to perform many of the express freight duties.

So when, at the end of 1924, Collett at Swindon took one of Churchward's 6ft 8in 'Saint' 4-6-0s and rebuilt it on 6ft coupled wheels as a mixed traffic locomotive, larger and with greater power and speed than a '43xx' 2-6-0, he was setting off along an already well-trodden road. The resultant 'Hall' class went into production in 1928

and proved a highly versatile design, at home on almost any sort of work save at the extreme ends of the operating spectrum, the latter usually being interpreted as high-speed long-distance express passenger or heavy slogging freight and mineral work. In due course, the 'Halls' were supplemented on the GWR by smaller-wheeled versions of the same theme, in some cases using recovered parts from the '43xx' 2-6-0s which were now being withdrawn. The 5ft 8in 'Manors' were lightweight engines designed specifically for work on the Cambrian section, but the only justification for the 5ft 8in 'Granges' was to use recovered 2-6-0 wheels under an otherwise standard 'Hall' chassis and boiler.

It took the move of William Stanier from

Doyen of the Gresley V2 Class and the only one preserved: LNER 2-6-2 No.4771 *Green Arrow*, **from the National Railway Museum Collection, stands at York station while undergoing a steam test c.1978.**

Swindon to the CME's chair of the LMS in 1932 to bring the modern 4-6-0 mixed traffic engine into Euston thinking; in fact, Beames (the former LNWR CME but now in charge at Crewe) had actually offered an up-dated, but less than sophisticated, version of the 'Prince of Wales' to LMS management as a possible contender. But there was little point in modifying any previous type and Stanier's new Class 5 4-6-0s, when they emerged in 1934, were seen to be a thoroughly modern fusion of ideas, most of which, as we have seen, had been developing in many different parts of the country over the best part of the previous generation.Though based in some measure on the 'Hall', the Class 5s were built with outside Walschaerts valve gear (with more than a hint of Horwich to it at first) and (after less than a year) progressively higher superheat than had ever been used at Swindon.

The Class 5s were built in enormous numbers from 1934 onwards — Armstrong Whitworth alone at Newcastle built no less than 327 in the space of 31 months — to meet the insatiable appetite of the operators for a machine which could run the accelerated Midland Division expresses (regularly achieving 85-90mph), work the through freight service over Shap while being available at weekends for the Blackpool and Llandudno holiday traffic and all but monopolise the tough Highland line with its long 1 in 60 and 1 in 70 gradients. Successive improvements to the design in the form of roller-bearing axle-boxes and Caprotti valve gear, together with modifications to increase their repair mileages, demonstrated how correct had been the basic concept. Even the BR Class 5s were not much more than 'dressed up' versions of the Stanier type, built largely to avoid offending the other regions had the LMS design been perpetuated!

The LNER was the last of the 'Big Four' to embrace the two-cylinder mixed traffic 4-6-0 concept in any quantity in the form of Edward Thompson's very fine B1 Class — a near-equivalent of the LMS Class 5 and built to the tune of over 400 examples from 1943 onwards. But there were interesting reasons for this delay. Nigel Gresley was

Thompson's LNER answer to the LMS Class 5 was the B1 4-6-0 of 1942-3. This is No.61050 waiting to depart from Liverpool Street with 'The Broadsman' train in the early 1950s. Like the Class 5s, the B1s continued building well into BR days, but this example was one of the mid-1946 batch for the LNER built by the North British Loco. Co. The first series, after the initial 41 named examples, was not to be thus distinguished.

LNER 'might have been'? In 1945, the LNER (under Thompson) rebuilt K3 2-6-0 No.206 (later LNER 1863/BR 61863) into two cylinder configuration as Class K5. It was a far more handsome engine than many of Thompson's efforts with Gresley's designs and by all accounts it was very successful too: more economic, easier to repair and better riding than a K3, though more expensive and time-consuming to rebuild compared with simply repairing one of the latter. In the event, although more conversions were planned, No.206 remained the only one of its kind, though it is interesting to speculate whether the B1 4-6-0 class would have been built in quite the same numbers had the K5 prototype led to more extended development. The engine is shown here ex-works in 1945 with lined black livery and utility 'NE' on the tender — one of relatively few LNER engines to be treated after the war in what had been a very familiar pre-war style. (BR ER)

happy with his K3s and so far as is known, did not consider a mixed traffic 4-6-0 — though there was a preliminary scheme for a three-cylinder passenger 4-6-0 which would have taken over some K3 work. When something bigger was required by the LNER for higher speed mixed traffic work, Gresley went instead for the 2-6-2 form in the shape of the classic V2 of 1936. These superb locomotives, arguably amongst the most efficient machines ever built in Britain, were really almost too sophisticated for the general 'run of the mill' mixed traffic trade. For one thing, their high axle loading limited their route availability and secondly, the complications of the conjugated gear caused maintenance problems, especially during the 'hurly burly' conditions of the Second World War. But 'on song', they were magnificent and

A 'Penrith Lizzie' leaving Penrith on 29th May 1952. No.46456 was built at Crewe in 1950 and the train is the 4.55pm ordinary passenger to Workington Main via Keswick and Cockermouth. This was one of many workings where the lightweight Ivatt 2-6-0s took over responsibility from elderly pre-group types with great success and considerable economy — exactly as intended. (Eric Bruton)

Attractively proportioned but arguably not really necessary: BR Standard Class 4 4-6-0 No.75038 climbs Camden bank with the 6.06pm Euston-Northampton 'local' on 22nd July 1962. This design was not much more than a tender version of the ubiquitous Class 4 2-6-4T and it is a fair bet that the latter could happily have performed most of the work just as easily! (T. W. Williams Collection — NRM)

made a massive contribution on the East Coast system.

It is generally assumed that Gresley's final design, the somewhat smaller V4 Class 2-6-2s of 1941, of which only two examples were to be built before he died, would have been his 'Class 5' equivalent had he lived; but this was not to be. With Gresley's sudden death in 1941, new influences came to bear in the shape of Edward Thompson, who had a hearty dislike of much of Gresley's cherished practice, particularly the use of three cylinders where

two would suffice and the conjugated valve gear for the inside piston valve. Thompson's mixed traffic offering was the two-cylinder B1 4-6-0 of 1943 (the first of them actually came out at the end of 1942), very much in the Class 5 philosophy but nevertheless a distinctly Doncaster/Darlington product. Mechanical weaknesses it certainly had but in train working and economy it could hold its head high with any other form of mixed traffic 4-6-0.

So the three-cylinder mixed traffic engine died with the work of Gresley and Maunsell and thereafter the two-cylinder alternative reigned supreme. It was a clear-cut trend which R. A. Riddles could not ignore when he came to produce his BR standard engines from 1951 onwards.

But the 2-6-0 was not dead; it was merely dormant. On the LMS, six years of war ended with a large backlog of scrapping elderly engines which had been keeping some fairly important branch lines running — the Cockermouth, Keswick and Penrith and the Kettering-Cambridge lines spring immediately to mind — from which the larger mixed traffic engines were barred by weight. Ivatt sold the operators the idea of new, lightweight 2-6-0s, fitted with all the 'mod. cons' provided on larger engines and giving the enginemen the shelter and comfort to which they were entitled. The result was the little Class 2MT 2-6-0s of 1946 which quickly established their worth — and also brought envious looks from the

British mixed traffic steam at its very best. This superb study of Stanier Class 5 No.45150 on Bushey troughs epitomises the very essence of the latter-day mixed traffic concept as far as steam was concerned. The train was the up 6.40am Wolverhampton to Euston on 28th April 1951 and this finely composed and exposed picture seems a wholly appropriate way to conclude this particular account — or this book as a whole for that matter! (Eric Bruton)

LNER which was in a similar position: 'Penrith Lizzies' the LMS men called them! The GWR typically looked down its nose at these 2-6-0s, set about proving that a Dean 0-6-0 goods was better and ended up having what it was forced to take.

The same philosophy produced the Ivatt Class 4MT 2-6-0 in 1947. After a shaky start until the draughting was put right, they too became popular, taking over the M&GN Joint workings (amongst others) with great success. Both these and the lightweight 2-6-0s formed the basis for the eventual BR standard designs (76xxx and 78xxx series respectively), as had the Class 5s in the 4-6-0 field (73xxx series), the latter design being supervised by Swindon. But apart from bringing a bit of extra fun to locomotive spotters, it is hard to see most of the BR types as being as truly fundamental as had been some of their prede-

cessors. But it is at least interesting to note that except for the Class 9 2-10-0s, a genuinely new concept, virtually all of the final main line steam locomotives built in the country embodied the classic mixed traffic philosophy.

The story of the British mixed traffic engine was essentially a tale of a 'coming together out of complexity' and even though I have ranged quite widely in order to review this variety, the purist will note that I have not included any of the 6ft 2in 4-6-2s, either company or BR-designed, despite the fact that their coupled wheel size qualified them (theoretically) for such status. But in the British context, even the smallest wheeled 4-6-2 was never seen as a mixed traffic engine in the sense which most would define the term.

Author's Footnote: It is only proper that I should express my great indebtedness to John Powell for agreeing to read the first draft of this article. He was kind enough to make many valuable comments and contributions which I have been very happy to incorporate in this final version. Sadly, as we went to press, I was told of his recent death. He will be sorely missed and I would like to dedicate this article to the memory of this very fine man *DJ*